I0822987

# Drained

# Drained

## REDUCE YOUR MENTAL LOAD TO DO LESS AND BE MORE

LEAH RUPPANNER, PHD

**AVERY**
an imprint of Penguin Random House
New York

AVERY
an imprint of Penguin Random House LLC
1745 Broadway, New York, NY 10019
penguinrandomhouse.com



BOOK DESIGN BY ANGIE BOUTIN

Library of Congress Cataloging-in-Publication Data

Names: Ruppanner, Leah, author.
Title: Drained: reduce your mental load to do less and be more / Leah Ruppanner, PhD.
Description: New York: Avery, [2026] | Includes index. |
Identifiers: LCCN 2025027356 (print) | LCCN 2025027357 (ebook) |
ISBN 9780593850909 hardcover | ISBN 9780593850923 ebook
Subjects: LCSH: Mental fatigue | Burn out (Psychology)—Prevention | Self-realization. | Women—Psychology
Classification: LCC BF482 .R87 2026 (print) | LCC BF482 (ebook)
LC record available at https://lccn.loc.gov/2025027356
LC ebook record available at https://lccn.loc.gov/2025027357

Printed in the United States of America
1st Printing

The authorized representative in the EU for product safety and compliance is Penguin Random House Ireland, Morrison Chambers, 32 Nassau Street, Dublin D02 YH68, Ireland, https://eu-contact.penguin.ie.

The stories in this book are based on real people whose data have been drawn from decades of research. Names and identifying details have been changed to protect the privacy of individuals.

*This book is dedicated to all the women out there who are trying to make this world a little brighter, lighter, and better for us all. I see you. I appreciate you. I love you.*

# Contents

## Part I
## Meet the Mental Load


Chapter 1 Making the Invisible Visible 3

Chapter 2 The Eight Types of Mental Loads 25

Chapter 3 The Seven Stages of the Mental Load 57

Chapter 4 Silencing Wasteful *Shoulds*, *Musts*, and *What-Ifs* 83


## Part II
## The Unload


Chapter 5 Identify What Is Draining Your Mental Load 107

Chapter 6 Clarify Your Goals and Values 133

Chapter 7 Align Your Mental Load Spending 151


## Part III
## The Reload


Chapter 8 Create a Mental Load with Purpose 169

Chapter 9 Delegate Some of Your Mental Load 189

Chapter 10 Money Changes Everything 207

Chapter 11 How to Talk with Our Spouses and Get Results 237

**Conclusion: What We Owe Our Daughters** *253*

**Appendix: The Mental Load Audit Worksheets** *261*

**Acknowledgments** *275*

**Works Cited** *277*

**Index** *283*

# Part 1
# Meet the Mental Load

## Chapter 1

# Making the Invisible Visible

THIS IS A BOOK ABOUT UNPAID LABOR, FULFILLMENT, AND HOW women can make space in their lives to create more meaning, love, and joy.

But first, let's start with a story about a school play.

My friend Kristen's sixth-grade daughter was in a performance of *Matilda* one Saturday afternoon. It was a busy day for Kristen after what had been a busy week at work. In the weeks prior, she had made sure the grandparents were invited, and then answered their million questions about how to download the tickets, where to park, and whether they'd be able to hear anything if they sat in the back, because those were the only seats still available.

She picked up flowers so her daughter would feel special after the show, made cookies for the potluck cast party that would follow, and showed up an hour before curtain to volunteer, as parents were expected to.

Prior to arriving at the theater, Kristen did a quick clean of the house, since the grandparents were all coming over after the show, while trying not to worry about whether her daughter's sudden resurgence of stage fright that morning would mean a setback in her overall confidence, which Kristen had been hoping would be bolstered by her featured role in the play.

Then her phone dinged because her other daughter was at a birthday party but had forgotten the gift and Sophia's mom couldn't pick them up from the party after all, so how was she supposed to get home? Kristen wanted to hand the whole communication thread over to her husband but had found that when he got involved in text threads with other moms, they wrote back to Kristen anyway. For similar reasons, he wasn't the go-to host for the grandparents: His response to their queries—if he answered at all—was a cheery "Just follow the directions on the website. See you there!"

By the time Kristen took her seat, she was tired, resentful, and flooded with other people's needs. She felt sad, too, because she just wanted to enjoy all her family being near to celebrate her child's star turn.

"I kept asking myself this thing I've been asking since they were babies," she told me. "Which is, like, *Am I doing this whole thing wrong?* This is supposed to be the fun part, right?"

Kristen tried to express her feelings of stress to her husband, but he told her she worried too much. "Relax," he urged. "Just be where your feet are." While he meant this response to be freeing, Kristen found it dismissive. He didn't *get it*—and comments like these seemed to confirm that the problem was with her.

When Kristen was telling me all of this, I understood exactly how she felt, and why her husband's reaction rubbed her the wrong way.

A lot of advice for women who feel stretched thin assumes that women are doing the stretching themselves: that we spend energy in places that don't matter and worry about silly things that don't deserve our attention. It presumes women are piling on self-inflicted stress for no reason.

But my decades of research show that women aren't being irrational here. Instead, we are anticipating a penalty for forgotten birthday gifts, lack of postshow flowers, and grandparents who don't feel appreciated—not because we are perfectionists but because experience has taught us that we will be held accountable for those things. We know that if we drop a ball, we're likely to find it thrown back in our faces.

It turns out there's a lot of data to back up those experiences—if we look in the right places. Finding those places is a big part of what I do as a sociologist researching the mental load. I have found that it is not just mothers at school plays who are carrying heavy mental loads, but it is women looking after aunties, nieces, siblings, pets, parents, partners, and more. We all carry a mental load, and yet somehow women have been saddled with the greatest weight.

## MEN AREN'T DIRT BLIND—THEY *CAN* SEE THE MESS

Let me give you an example from a research project I conducted with colleagues Sabino Kornrich at NYU and Sarah Thébaud at the University of California at Santa Barbara. We set out to test an idea that kept popping up when I presented on gender inequality in household chores—an idea that blamed women for letting themselves get stuck doing an unequal share of the work that keeps homes running smoothly.

I've long been interested in housework (as a concept, not an activity, thank you very much) and have spent over twenty years publishing articles quantifying that labor and investigating why, even in the most equal countries in the world, women still do more housework than men.

These papers helped build a robust body of interdisciplinary research on which factors made the biggest impact on the domestic labor gender gap—working hours, income level, paid family leave, etc.—and resulted in tons of data from decades of research showing that the inequality is structural, not individual.

But even as I got invited to talk about my findings all over the world, again and again I kept hearing the same argument—from both men and women—that women were doing more house cleaning because they were more likely to "see the mess" in a house. According to this theory, women's standards are just too high.

I heard similar things when I wrote or presented on research showing that couples are more likely to fight and divorce when women do a disproportionate share of the housework. Among the responses, invariably, would be a this-is-more-of-a-comment-than-a-question about how perhaps the real problem was that women are just "controlling" or "neat freaks."

It wasn't just lay readers either. Even scholars in related fields told me, based on zero evidence, that domestic inequality was due to these women being overly invested in a high standard of cleanliness. If that was true, the solution was obvious: Women, individually, should decide to care less about whether their homes are messy. If women didn't care so much, then they could spend less time cleaning and less energy resenting their partners' lesser contribution to cleanliness, men would feel less nagged, and the divorce rate would plummet. Win-win-win, right?

Now, I *do* think that women should care less about the cleanliness of their homes. In fact, I think everyone should: Our lives are busier now than ever before, and if something has to give, I'm in favor of its being housekeeping rather than socializing, parenting, career building, or (heaven forbid) sleeping. But the idea that women are, en masse, neat freaks who are making themselves miserable for no reason at all? That just didn't add up.

A big part of my work is noticing patterns in behavior that seem to defy logic and reexamining the whole equation to figure out what variables we're missing.

Sociology is a fantastically effective tool for this, so I designed a study that would expose these unseen factors that drive our behavior, like throwing a black light on a crime scene. After all, it *would* seem like a win-win for women to simply let go of the mental load of tracking and performing more domestic tasks. So why were so many parents choosing to spend time and mental energy this way, against their own stated preference? And why would so many of these couples have mismatched expectations around domestic tidiness that broke along gender lines? Are women really more invested in keeping a clean home because they can "see mess" that men don't, or because they derive gratification from controlling the domestic sphere?

The study idea was simple. First we would test whether women could, in fact, see mess better than men. It seemed unlikely that women's eyes were physically distinct in ways that make them better than men's at spotting piles of clothes on the couch, but it was possible that women had been in some way socially conditioned to notice mess more immediately or intensely. We could design a way to test both.

Next we would measure the consequences of being perceived as messy for men and for women. If the consequences were the same for both groups, it would suggest that internal pressures—standards women put on themselves—were a major factor. But if the study showed that consequences differed, we'd have evidence the pressures were external: The black light would reveal that women's generally higher investment in housekeeping was a way to avoid being punished for messiness in ways that messy men are not.

To gather the data, we first showed participants a photo of an open-plan living room and kitchen. Half of our research participants got a photo in which the room was messy and half got one in which the room was clean. Then we asked them to rate the room as messy or clean and to rate the personal traits of the person who owned the room. Here is the twist: Some were told that the room was owned by "John" and others by "Jennifer."

Right away, men and women study participants rated the messy room equally messy, and the clean room just as clean. The idea that men are "dirt blind," or that women more reliably notice mess? That's garbage—go ahead and neatly chuck it in the bin, no matter what gender you are.

Men and women notice mess equally, perceive the same level of messiness when looking at the same scene, and are equally aware of what constitutes a clean room.

Then we asked some harder questions related to participants' opinions of Jennifer's or John's housekeeping. Again, a clear pattern emerged: People judged the room more harshly if they believed it belonged to a woman. In fact, even when presented with a photo of a clean room, our research participants rated it as needing more urgent cleaning if they were told it belonged to Jennifer rather than John.

So women are held to higher standards of cleanliness than men even when their rooms are objectively "clean"—good enough is perceived as not good enough if it's women's work.

Then we asked our research participants to rate Jennifer's and John's moral character based on the state of their room—whether they were responsible, hardworking, considerate, likable, or neglectful. Here's where things got interesting: Participants thought Jennifer was a less moral person than John, even if their rooms were relatively clean.

We also asked them what would happen if someone dropped in unexpectedly, like a boss, relative, or friend. We asked this because people often think others will judge them for things they themselves may not really care about, like the pile of shoes by the door. Would the visitors' opinions of Jennifer change? And would Jennifer feel uncomfortable based on the state of the room if these people showed up unannounced?

The answer was a resounding yes—Jennifer would be seen as a less capable and competent person. And yes, Jennifer would feel uncomfortable hosting company even in that clean room.

This is why women worry about the standards. This is why they anxiously clean before guests come over. This is why mothers apologize for the state of their mess to unannounced guests and offer lengthy explanations for why backpacks and toys and sports equipment are strewn across the hallway.

They believe others will see cleanliness as evidence they are competent, trustworthy, valuable people, and messiness as evidence of the opposite—*and they are correct.*

Men are not held to the same standards and do not face equivalent penalties.

So even if a heterosexual couple shares the cleaning of the home, it will be the woman who is held accountable for the planning and execution of homemaking, and even if she is not consciously thinking about it, she knows it. When women talk about the sky-high standards of having homes that are always in an Instagrammable state, these standards are not in their heads. These pressures are real, the consequences for women are significant, and we have the data to back it up.

This is one of the many research studies I conducted through my lab to understand how women experience the world. I have spent decades studying these types of questions: Why do women do more at home? How do we help men step into the family? Why do housework and childcare create so much conflict between partners? What is the impact of all the invisible labor, or the mental load?

I've looked at thousands of studies on these topics. I have personally combed through hundreds of thousands of data points. I have published over seventy-five academic articles and a book on the insights I discovered. I have shared my research findings with millions of people around the world.

This has been my passion and life's work for decades. I use sociology as my superpower to help us all better understand our worlds.

## UNLOCKING SOCIOLOGY AS YOUR SUPERPOWER

Sociology is the study of why people do what people do. Sociologists aren't focused on you as an individual per se. Rather, we think about the structures that surround you and the ways those structures, and the norms attached to them, make you, me, and your neighbor down the road act a certain way.

We ask questions like "What kinds of decisions would mothers make about their jobs and families if they lived in a country with free, high-quality childcare?" Or "Do women fight more with their husbands if they are surrounded by other women who make more money, work full time, and are divorced themselves?" And "When fathers take paid leave to care for their children, do they step into new roles at home long term as a result?"

And when we study what's going on with a group that's collectively struggling, we move the conversation away from blaming and shaming individuals for their decisions and work to reveal the invisible topography of the world they live in, the opportunities and barriers shaping their lives without their even knowing it.

Sociology provides the lens through which we can look at our actions, our thinking, and our behavior to parse when we are following scripts that were handed to us from birth and when it is time to write a new story. Sociologists coined the term *role model* because we know that people follow the behaviors of others, in ways that are sometimes optimal and sometimes not. Sociology gives you the satellite view of what is happening in your life to see the power of everything around us that impacts how we all move through the world.

Unlocking sociology as your superpower helps you start to tear up the scripts that no longer work for you, and to move through the world with less nonsense and more confidence.

That's why sociology is an exceptionally good tool to better understand mental load—a concept I've been studying for years. *Mental load* has become a more familiar term in the last few years, but popular coverage of the concept often reduces it to its smallest parts, treating it as shorthand for making lists or a synonym for household management. It's true that mothers' mental load includes a lot of that work, like keeping track of permission slips and ensuring that fridges are stocked with milk and children are coiffed for Crazy Hair Day. But when we look more closely, we discover that mothers' mental loads are bigger and more complex, a heavy alloy of emotional and mental elements that drags down every aspect of their lives.

That's why I describe the mental load as "emotional thinking." It's the difference between managing a calendar at work, which might be logistically demanding but often holds some emotional distance, and managing the family calendar, which is often stressful *and* emotional, because it involves anticipating things going wrong and dealing with the consequences of letting down the people we love the most.

It's also the difference between keeping a home tidy enough to find what you need and keeping it tidy enough for you to avoid the social and professional consequences of others' judgments—which, as we have shown in our research, equate messiness with lower worth for women but not for men.

It sounds like sweating the small stuff, but a lot of it is the stuff that sustains family life.

Did you remember to sign the permission slip for the excursion to the zoo—and if not, will your kid be left out of a major school event? Are your kids doing too few extracurriculars—and now they have too much screen time and not enough skill building around hobbies that can help on their college applications? Did you remember to schedule a date night—and if not, what does that say about your relationship? This work is not just thinking. It's *emotional thinking*.

It is invisible, boundaryless, and enduring.

All people carry a mental load: mothers and fathers, child-free adults, and even children. But the average composition of our mental loads looks different across those groups.

My research shows that fathers carry a significant mental load related to their family responsibilities. But the differences in cultural roles for men and women mean that fathers' family responsibilities are much more aligned with the daily grind of work and the big-picture project of career building. It's not only that the consequences of relaxing standards for domestic labor and child-rearing are lower for dads, though that's true too (and we'll talk more about it in this book). For dads, the mental load of bringing more money home from work feels like it's in service to their family responsibilities, rather than in conflict with them.

Millennial dads, in particular, are excited about the fact that they are spending more time with their children than previous generations did. Signaling at work that they are good fathers is a key way to humanize themselves—fathers are seen as more endearing, approachable, and likable because they care for their children.

This doesn't create mental load conflict for fathers—they feel good making contributions to their workplaces, and they feel good spending more time with their children.

Their mental load investment in work can be stressful but often makes their lives feel richer—working hard to help fund a mortgage on a new house, save for kids' college tuition, or take a long-desired family trip to Cancún.

These are mental loads well spent.

But for mothers who also have a job that provides a paycheck, the mental load they carry for work feels in constant conflict with expectations of them at home—investment in one area at the *expense of* the other. Mothers worry one or both is always getting short shrift and end up feeling guilty about whatever choices they make, like they are failing at work *and* at home.

In a way, they are—because our cultural narrative around what makes a good worker and what makes a good mother each demand constant availability and sustained commitment. With their energies siphoned on two fronts, they end up fragmented, overwhelmed, and exhausted. This creates two different experiences in the world of parenting: fathers feeling excited by their mental load investments while mothers feel drained. It means that mothers always feel like they need to give more—good enough is never enough. They are striving toward some unattainable level of perfection and feeling bad when they inevitably fall short.

As I will tell you throughout this book: It's not just you. And it is not just parents. The mental load is a weight we all carry, but, as I will outline in this book, women are sold a handful of lies that make their mental load heavier and more toxic.

The good news is that people are talking about the problem of mental load a lot more often than when I first started studying it. The bad news is that all this conversation has not created meaningful change for many mothers, who are still just as overwhelmed and frustrated as they were when I published my first paper on housework in 2008. Why are we still seeing women saddled by the work at home and feeling exhausted by it all?

The missing ingredient was the mental load. And until recently, we haven't understood what exactly the mental load is, and why it's so heavy for mothers.

People are still unaware that this is not something women are doing to themselves, and that the solution isn't just to care less. Because we don't understand the mental load, conversations around parenting, gender equality, and labor keep bumping up against this *thing* we can't accurately see or measure. And it's so much bigger than keeping the house clean.

We wonder why birth rates are down even in countries with robust social supports and pronatalist policies; we wonder why women are still underrepresented at the top levels of business despite having record-high college graduation rates; we wonder why the pay gap persists despite corporations pouring money into campaigns around confidence and power poses.

As someone who has studied all these things, I've come to a startling conclusion: The mental load is at the heart of the problem.

Mental load burnout is the thing that makes women feel like they're running at top speed but barely moving forward. It's what makes even markers of success—new babies, new jobs, new homes, career advancement—feel exhausting. Mental load is the invisible cognitive-emotional work that drains women and makes them feel like they are living on a kind of paycheck-to-paycheck energy.

The demands of an unwieldy mental load are draining even the most successful women and holding back countless other women from feeling successful at all.

I had spent years measuring what all the work women do at home does to their careers—limiting their ability to get promoted, reducing their chances of making more money, and increasing their risk of dropping out of work altogether. I looked at how doing it all at home impacts women's marriages by increasing conflict and the risk of divorce. I documented its impact on parenting—how it leads to intensifying feelings of guilt, time pressure and poor mental health, and less sleep.

But I started to grasp the shape and magnitude of the problem only when I went hunting for what keeps women staggering under this load, the forces that keep them from saving energy for themselves.

I found a host of expectations, myths, and explicit and implicit threats to them and their families for violating those expectations, just as Kristen experienced the day of her daughter's school play. I kept finding again and again, across study upon study, the ways that we have set women up for failure.

We keep asking women to do more and more, holding them to incredibly high standards, and then punishing them when things inevitably go wrong.

As soon as people heard about my research, they started sharing their own school play stories. I will share some of these conversations throughout the book along with stories gathered from my formal research.

I hear about childcare challenges, arguments with spouses who just don't *get it*, and a feeling of constant, unrelenting pressure to be perfect. I hear stories about failed outsourcing that cycles right back to Mom's lap, of overwhelm bubbling out through yelling at everyone, and of scattered brains trying to keep track of it all. (Later, I'll tell you more about the myth that women are better multitaskers, whether through nature or nurture. Spoiler alert: We're not. We're just expected to do more work.)

The deluge of all these personal stories convinced me there was something big here, and I designed studies that would let me collect more data and sift through it to find patterns. Through a coordinated set of formal interviews, surveys, and focus groups, I heard a consistent theme of women trying to stay afloat in a life with porous boundaries, answering work emails when they're supposed to be watching kids' soccer games and fielding calls from school nurses about sick children in the middle of important meetings.

I identified that across all the tracking permission slips, finding lost socks, and making sure holidays feel special, there were eight distinct categories of mental load work:

1. Life organization
2. Emotional support
3. Relationship hygiene
4. Magic making
5. Dream building
6. Individual upkeep
7. Safety
8. Meta-care

I measured the way women were holding mental loads not only for ourselves but also for our children, our partners, our workplaces, our extended families, our friends, our community, our environment, our political systems, and more. I started to recognize the ways women were describing taking on this unpaid work not because they wanted to but because they were operating under a kind of duress that they weren't even always consciously aware of—saying yes because the alternative was worse and blaming themselves either way.

I am a working parent myself, and studying these struggles and conflicts from ten thousand feet as an academic gave me a perspective that not only led to breakthrough research at my lab but also transformed my life personally. I found myself using the data from my lab to recognize patterns in how my own time and attention were being spent, and the research from all the amazing academics around the world to make more informed decisions about where my precious time and attention went.

Once I saw the data on how women's energies are siphoned away from them and started to recognize the carrots and sticks that keep us in this pattern, it was impossible to unsee. It's a form of reverse gaslighting that allows you to think, *Wow, I'm not delusional, and I'm not alone; this isn't about* me *at all.*

I saw how myths about gender and labor had infested my thinking and piled tasks onto my mental load, even as someone who studies gender and labor. With this new understanding, it was impossible to feel like a failure. I saw more clearly the ways in which I had *been* failed.

I was fired up and energized; with the capacity I'd regained by being more intentional about what deserved my precious energy and, importantly, what did not, I was assembling an ever-larger dossier of proof that we'd fundamentally misunderstood what mental load is and how it functions in real women's lives.

And then came March 2020.

## THE MOTHER OF ALL MENTAL LOADS

For someone who studies mothers' unpaid work, seeing the first months of the COVID-19 pandemic was like watching a tsunami roll in. Women at the top—CEOs, politicians, and world leaders—left their careers because it was all too much. Mothers with less money, resources, and support lost their homes, jobs, and loved ones. Article after article emerged with heart-wrenching quotes from mothers at the breaking point—and they sounded a lot like the women I'd been talking to.

My lab at the University of Melbourne, along with wonderful colleagues Caity Collins, Liana Landivar, and William Scarborough at leading universities across the world, kicked into overdrive to track the scope of the problem.

We measured how mothers' employment dropped during the pandemic, especially in states where schools were operating remotely. We revealed that telecommuting kept some mothers employed but didn't help those in jobs that couldn't be done at home, nor moms with the littlest kids in the home. We found that even breadwinning mothers had to reduce their employment, unable to overcome the added pressures of keeping everyone safe and tending to the heightened demands of work, family, and life during the pandemic. We showed that when heterosexual couples had competing responsibilities, mothers picked up most of the added childcare and housework, at the expense of their sleep and sense of calm.

Other researchers had similar findings. Over the first year of the pandemic, with many schools closed, Brookings found that mothers of kids under age twelve were spending eight hours per day on childcare and six hours on their jobs, while dads were spending five hours on childcare and eight hours on work. The Institute for Women's Policy Research found that four out of ten women reduced their hours or stopped working during the pandemic, and the Center for American Progress found that the average college-educated woman who temporarily left paid work during the height of the pandemic stood to lose between $346,000 and $785,000 of income over her lifetime as a result. A study at Oregon State University reported that 68 percent of working moms (and 42 percent of working dads) were experiencing parental burnout, defined as "when chronic stress and exhaustion occur that overwhelm a parent's ability to cope and function." In real time, my colleagues and I were documenting the deterioration of twenty years of gains in women's employment over a few short months—a titanic loss to women's professional and personal lives that didn't disappear with the introduction of a vaccine.

In a culture that asks women, especially mothers, to be everything to everyone without any of the social supports available in other countries—affordable childcare, paid parental leave, mandated access to flexible work, vacation time, or sick leave—the experience of feeling scattered, distracted, and an inch away from complete breakdown is near universal. But even as I interviewed women about what they were going through, I realized how many of them thought that the problem was specific to them.

They didn't just feel stressed out; they felt guilty and ashamed.

Under the weight of a crushing mental load, many seemed to be concluding that they just weren't strong enough to hold it up. Along the way, I heard them wrestling with questions that my lab had found answers to: questions like whether dropping down to part-time work would solve the problem of being overextended (*We studied that, and it turns out that working part time* increases *work-family conflict!* I wanted to shout). I saw them throwing themselves at huge problems, trying to absorb all the shock, stress, and anxiety so their children and partners didn't have to.

That's when I realized my mission had changed.

I couldn't just measure what was happening. Women all over the world urgently needed help understanding what they were dragging around, why it was so heavy, why it wasn't their fault, and how to lighten it.

From that goal, this book was born. I sought to replicate my own experience of unlearning myths about how I "should" be balancing things and started to think systematically about what was worth the investment of my attention and emotion. I began considering what systems, policies, and workplaces would help mothers thrive and started planning a new kind of research focused not just on observing but on intervening: a coordinated series of case studies, focus groups, and concrete solutions that would test whether the combination of myth busting and strategic thinking that had realigned my life was replicable.

The answer was a resounding yes.

For decades, we have told women that they are responsible for solving this mess. And we have told them that the solutions to all their problems at home are to: (1) gain more power; (2) have men *and* women do more; (3) engage in self-care; (4) outsource to others; and (5) wake up earlier.

While the real solutions that could ameliorate our mental loads—including bold policies that cap work hours or give parents fully paid leave after childbirth or that audit pay to ensure mothers aren't being punished—seem too distant or difficult, we have instead told mothers to work harder and meditate. We have pushed the burden of fixing broken systems onto the backs of individual women, which is pernicious and unfair.

What we need now is a range of policy changes that reflect the fact that most families are those where both parents work, *but* we also need some old-school consciousness raising and concrete tools to help lighten the load.

Without these, is it any wonder mothers are holding on by a thread and burnout is at an all-time high? We put mothers into an impossible situation, offer pseudosolutions that rely on women's *additional* emotional-thinking work, and then blame women when things go wrong.

Of course women feel like something is wrong with them!

We have diagnosed women as the problem when they are, for many, the lifeline.

I started to imagine: What would life look like if we saw these external pressures for what they are—if we admitted that, yes, you're not making this stuff up, you *are* still treated differently from your husband or your brother in a host of insidious ways? What if, instead of either expecting women to submit to gendered expectations or telling them to stop worrying about them, we started from different assumptions? That our attention and energy are precious. That the social pressures responsible for keeping women in line are very real—but also a lot less threatening in the light of day. That any real help would stop dismissing women's fears and anxieties as being "too controlling" in favor of helping women to prioritize their energy.

It was by asking these questions that I started to shift my gaze from who was doing what in the home to focus on the invisible work that underpins it all—the mental load. This work required me to get clear on what the mental load actually *is*—because until we make that invisible work visible, we can never have honest conversations about its impact. We can never make informed choices about which loads we might deliberately take on and which we might refuse.

I started to think about how to make us all aware of how valuable our mental load energy is and the urgency of protecting it. I identified the small changes that I have made in my life as a result of being a sociologist—caring less about mess, wearing mismatched socks, and reducing my expectations of what constitutes a "good" job at home—that are my keys to carrying a light mental load and investing my precious energy into my loftiest goals and wildest dreams. I started to test whether these solutions would help others and found that seeing and valuing this work is critical to reaching true equality—which is why this book will bring my discoveries out of the laboratory and into daily conversation.

Once we are aware of where our energies are going, we suddenly have a whole new set of choices about our precious mental resources. It's like discovering that the bucket holding your time and energy—your capacity for the emotional-thinking work that holds all our lives together and makes them more meaningful—has had a hole in it for years, slowly draining it away drip by drip. But with care, insight, and hard work, we can patch and repair it to keep our energy whole.

The tactics in this book will do just that, helping to reduce our waste of resources and our worry about whether store-bought cookies are as good as homemade, whether we offended our colleagues in a meeting when we expressed a different opinion, and whether our parenting is "good enough" benchmarked against a different time or different people.

Our mental load energy is not infinite, so spending it impulsively and letting outdated social norms or unexamined assumptions siphon it away leaves us with less to spend on things we care about.

That's where this book comes in.

## THE MENTAL LOAD AUDIT IS BORN

This book is a tool kit built from my lab's research, designed to help you identify and plug up drains to free up capacity to live the life you truly want.

The first part uses the most up-to-date findings from my lab to explain what the mental load is and why it is so crushing for women. It helps us understand why despite being "mental," it's not all in our heads. It draws upon decades of research I personally conducted alongside the expertise of hundreds of sociologists, psychologists, anthropologists, political scientists, and gender studies professors studying related issues. It uses my training as a sociologist—understanding the ways in which our actions are based on expectations or norms that are telegraphed to us from birth—to help me figure out what's going on. And it combines expertise with real-life stories from interviewees to help us all understand why the mental load is so heavy.

After giving the big picture on how we ended up here in the first place, this book will then provide resources to complete a Mental Load Audit to identify where your mental load energy is going and whether it is worth it. This section will help detect whether the magic making of hosting a home-cooked Thanksgiving meal is work we want versus feel required to do—and the tools to assess whether the price of skipping that obligation is worth it. It will introduce you to research participants who have done this work already and share their stories of challenges and successes.

Finally, this book will help provide ways to check whether doing this work is bringing us closer to our goals, and to think about what kind of world we *could* live in if parents, especially mothers, had mental loads that are full of capacity to respond to opportunities and fulfill their wildest dreams.

I have witnessed firsthand the power of this work—seen it create real-time aha moments for mothers and fathers alike.

It makes the invisible visible. It provides us all with the language to, for the first time ever, talk about the multiple mental loads we are all carrying and why some are so costly.

I have witnessed fathers, finally, see the breadth of the invisible work their wives have been doing to keep their lives and families running. And I have seen mothers take charge of their mental load spending to create lives that are more fully aligned with their goals and dreams.

I have had people come back to me, years after participating in the research, to tell me how transformative this process is. It saved their marriages. It taught them to spend less of their mental load on nonsense. It helped them align their energy to nourish their souls.

You don't have to be bitten by a radioactive sociologist for this way of seeing the world to become your superpower too—you just have to read this book and act on what you learn. It gives you not only information but also tools to do something with those insights to lighten your mental load.

Through my research, I have reduced my own mental load by rejecting the notion that a clean house makes me a good woman, engaging my child in time-consuming daily creative activities makes me a good mother, and being constantly available to colleagues makes me a good worker. They don't, and asking women to perpetually do this work sets them up for failure.

I won't participate in my own destruction—and you don't have to either.

This book will serve as an alarm system to make sure we don't, and a beacon to remind us where we *want* to go—toward a life with more meaning, love, and joy.

Let's go!

## Chapter 2

# The Eight Types of Mental Loads

JULIE IS A RESEARCH PARTICIPANT IN ONE OF MY FIRST STUDIES ON the mental load. She was enthusiastic about signing up for my study because, as she tells me in the interview, she loves learning tricks to make her life better and hopes my research will help her lighten her heavy mental load. We meet at a local coffee shop on a winter day punctuated by dark clouds and harsh rain. Quick with a joke and serious about her work, Julie is a child psychologist raising two teenagers with her husband, Paul, who is a marketing manager. She is absolutely delightful to talk to and I am immediately convinced that she is the heart of her family.

Julie reads a lot about parenting and feels she is up to date on the latest trends. She keeps seeing the term *mental load* mentioned, but it seems like this nebulous thing that she can't quite understand the limits of. She thinks it's likely that she does a lot of her family's mental load but isn't sure if calling to check in on her mother-in-law counts—isn't that just being a good person? She keeps an eye on her son's diet to make sure he is getting enough non–junk food calories, but isn't this just part of being a good mom? She spends part of each day listening to and strategizing with her husband about his challenges at work, but isn't this just part of being a good partner?

For Julie, this is the work we do for one another as humans—it makes her feel good. She mostly enjoys being the person her friends and family come to with their problems and loves the connection that comes from helping people she loves. But sometimes it can feel like this work looms over her life in a way that feels exhausting, like she is a tap that has been left on.

She turns to me to ask, "What exactly is happening with this mental load thing, anyway?"

I tell Julie what our lab recently discovered: Everything Julie described above is a type of mental load, and each one uses some drops of her energy. Julie, like many mothers, is carrying not one but eight different types of mental load, with each taking a bite out of her mental load capacity and pushing her into burnout.

"Why haven't I heard about this before?" Julie asks me.

I'm not surprised she hasn't. These are new insights emerging from the research in my own lab. At the center of our research is studying parents like her, and from these conversations, we've discovered the mental load is much more complex than previously thought. These ideas haven't been out in the wild, so of course Julie hasn't heard of them yet. The challenge for a parent like Julie is that she doesn't yet have the language to describe the complexity of the mental load.

She doesn't know how to describe its weight.

Julie looks at me in a way that seems equally shocked and, for the first time, seen.

"I knew I was carrying a lot, and I ended each day feeling exhausted," Julie tells me.

But she also knows that if she describes what she's doing, it all sounds pretty normal. Julie is just doing what many of us do on a given day—getting ready for work, doing her job, and spending time with her family.

"I often felt confused about why it all continued to feel so heavy. I have a good job that I like, and my kids are so independent now. I mean, I am no longer changing diapers and chasing toddlers. But I still feel so stressed," Julie tells me.

Her children have grown, but somehow her mental load hasn't eased.

And even though her husband Paul's life looks similar—he also gets up, goes to work, and spends time with their children—Paul seems to wear it all more lightly. He somehow has the time and brain space to hit the gym and tinker with home improvement projects, while Julie spends most weekends catching up on the paperwork she can't cram in during the week. It all feels so much heavier for Julie, and she can't articulate why.

I tell Julie that this isn't her fault and, if we are being honest, it isn't Paul's either. Without an understanding of *why* the mental load is so different from how it comes across in article-length mentions we read in the news or see on social media, and the *language* to describe each of the eight drains, Julie and Paul have never been able to have an open and honest conversation about who is doing what and why it is such a drain.

I take a deep breath and prepare to give her the orientation I offer all study participants who want to get clear on their mental loads.

## THE MENTAL LOAD AS EMOTIONAL-THINKING WORK

The first tool I give Julie is an understanding of how the mental load is different from other types of cognitive work we do to keep our lives moving. This is based on a research project I did with colleagues at the University of Melbourne—Dr. Liz Dean and Associate Professor Brendan Churchill—where we showed that the mental load is *thinking work with emotional weight.*

When Julie reads about the mental load on parenting blogs or in news articles, she hears it described as something akin to an extended to-do list. People on her TikTok page and Instagram reels talk about the mental load as the invisible work done to keep the family running. These descriptions of the mental load are close, but they miss a critical component: The mental load is tied to the people we love and the lives we want to live.

The stakes feel high—the stakes *are* high—which is why the mental load is so taxing on our mental health and difficult to delegate to others.

Let's look at an example of an almost-empty tube of toothpaste. If the mental load were just life-thinking work and list making, it would look something like this: *I see the toothpaste is running out. I need to put toothpaste on the shopping list.* Once the toothpaste ends up on a shopping list and is purchased at the store, the task would be completed. Mental load done.

But the mental load is *emotional-thinking work*, which means when the toothpaste looks low, our running thoughts can look something like this:

*I see the toothpaste is running out. I need to put the toothpaste on the shopping list so my family's teeth don't get cavities, rot, and fall out. What if I can't get to the store in time? Can we brush for a day or two with just water? I wish I were a dentist—wait, didn't the dentist give us toothpaste at our last visit? Where is that travel toothpaste? I think my youngest took it. Actually, I don't think I've seen the youngest brush his teeth all week. And the kids are eating so much candy and sticky carbs from the holidays. Do they already have cavities? I can't believe I let us run out of toothpaste. Ugh, I am doing a terrible job at all of this! How do the other mothers do it? I better google how much plaque can be re-*

*moved with just water and a toothbrush, in case I can't get to the store today, and also how long you can go without brushing before you get cavities. Who will go to the store to buy the toothpaste? I have so much to do today; maybe my husband can do it. But he'll probably just buy the first tube he sees, and the youngest wants the toothpaste with the Minions on it. The older kids prefer the toothpaste with the whitening. Wait, can a ten-year-old use a whitening toothpaste, or will this strip their enamel for life? Do they just want this because some influencer told them to buy it? Shoot, I was going to limit their screen time, but I haven't checked in a while. Are they watching too much bad content on their phones? I'll need to check this after I add Minions and whitening toothpaste to the shopping list and check the shared calendar to see who's doing what today.*

Phew!

The first example is straightforward cognitive work: Remember to purchase toothpaste. Sometimes our mental load energy does operate this simply: Buying toothpaste is just buying toothpaste, functioning like another item on the to-do list. But often we experience the second type of mental load: thinking work that is deeply emotional, tied to the health and well-being of our family. Then buying toothpaste is about being a good parent, setting children up for prosperous and healthy futures, and making sure they feel loved. It is the result of years of monitoring children's likes and dislikes, tracking the status of all the happenings in the home, and making sure everyone is thriving, or at least okay.

Sometimes our tracking can tick over into anxiety and overzealousness, as in the example above. What starts as a single thought about toothpaste running low turns into an existential crisis about whether we are good parents.

We can train ourselves to recognize where this can veer into unhealthy territory—rumination that doesn't increase the likelihood of better outcomes. But it's not always clear: Sometimes the consequences of getting a choice wrong can be serious—children's teeth rotting or their developing poor dental hygiene habits *for life.* Something as simple as toothpaste is about ensuring that the people we love the most (including ourselves!) are healthy and cared for.

I tell Julie that the goal is not to eradicate our mental loads—we need some of this work to live better, more organized, and more productive lives. Rather, our goal is to figure out when mental load spending is wasteful and how to stop these snowballs from turning into avalanches. I need Julie to think about whether she is spending too much mental load energy in ways that are making her exhausted—is she operating in mental load burnout?

## THE MENTAL LOAD BURNOUT SCALE

The next tool I give Julie is our mental load burnout scale to help her figure out whether she is spending her mental load too quickly. I ask Julie, "Are you carrying a bunch of Minions toothpaste mental loads? And are they worth the investment?"

A lot of mothers' mental load capacity, I discovered, is spent *anticipating and preemptively addressing problems that are unlikely.* They are constantly scanning everything happening in the family life, like a radar constantly tracking every move. It can be catastrophic thinking about all the possible things that can go wrong, from forgotten jackets to nuclear apocalypse. This can create incessant rumination that tips over into feeling overwhelmed.

If we treat every toothpaste-level decision as the potential first domino in a short and direct line toward toothlessness and other disasters, our mental load gets pushed daily toward exhaustion. As a baseline, before making any changes, I ask her to assess whether she is spending her mental load strategically and holding some energy for big dreams.

To help her do this work, I give her the following survey that we developed through my lab.

The quiz, along with her answers, is below.

| | **YES/NO and why?** |
|---|---|
| 1. Do you end many days feeling like you have spent more mental load energy than you started with (i.e., spending more than saving)? | Yes. Most days feel I drop into bed feeling exhausted, like I ran a marathon that day. |
| 2. Do you often feel exhausted by your mental load (e.g., quick-tempered, overwhelmed, loss of focus, anxious, difficulty sleeping)? | YES! I feel like a ticking time bomb, and anything is going to set me off. Most days, I don't feel like my real self. |
| 3. Do you often find it difficult to enjoy life's moments because of the constant thinking about what needs to be done next? | Ugh, yes . . . Last week I was so distracted at my son's basketball game because it ran overtime and I had to run my daughter to a friend's house. I was so angry on the car ride over that I think I scared everyone, including myself. |
| 4. Do you lack sufficient mental load energy to respond to an *opportunity* in your work, family, or other areas of your life? | Yes. There is so much I want to do at work, but I just can't find the energy to do it. |
| 5. Do you lack sufficient mental load energy to respond to an *emergency* in your work, family, or other areas of your life? | No. When things go wrong at home or at work, I usually find the energy somewhere. |
| 6. Do you find it difficult to find enough mental load energy to plan for the future? | Yes and no. I feel like I am running from one emergency to the next, so that is a yes. But then I am trying to make sure the kids are set up for their futures, so that is a no. |
| **Total number of YES responses** | 4 (or 4.5 maybe?) |

Julie is like most of the mothers I encountered in my research—they are constantly running close to empty. Most mothers responded "yes" to almost all of these questions; they were living with high levels of burnout but were holding a little precious mental load energy for the next inevitable emergency or to build up others' dreams.

It makes them feel exhausted, fragmented, and unwell.

It means mothers often put themselves at the bottom of the list to make sure everyone else is doing okay.

The difference Julie felt between her and Paul wasn't all in her head. Broadly, fathers' stress around mental load doesn't look the same; they aren't running themselves into mental load burnout in the same ways mothers are. When Julie asked Paul to fill out the same survey, they discovered he had much more energy left in his reserves. Paul, like most of the fathers in my research project, had a mental load capacity that was in surplus.

Paul, unlike Julie, didn't spend his son's basketball game ruminating about whether the meat loaf would keep if the game went into overtime. Paul, like many fathers I interviewed, didn't see this as his job or a productive use of his energy. Rather, Paul was laser focused on saving enough mental load energy to respond to opportunities at work, to step into complex projects, and to work toward a promotion. Paul was laying big and bold plans for his future and making sure he had enough gas in the tank to get there.

This was a stark difference from mothers, like Julie, who by and large is spending through her mental load daily by giving to others.

Julie couldn't figure out why she often felt so unhappy when their partnership was, on the face of it, pretty equal. Paul took the kids to practice, showed up to their award ceremonies, and often picked them up sick from school. Paul did the dishes, cooked meals, and was present for his children when they needed him. Theirs was a partnership that many would dream of—and yet Julie still felt constantly on the edge of overwhelmed.

The problem, I told Julie, was that they had never tackled the mental load.

Julie wasn't ungrateful for all Paul did, and Paul wasn't a jerk for not doing more. Rather, without the right language, they hadn't yet had an honest conversation about who was doing which mental load pieces. This meant that each was spending it in ways that made the scales imbalanced without their even being aware.

Where are you on the mental load burnout scale? Are you running in deficit? Or is your mental load in surplus? If you have a partner, what does your partner's mental load look like? Are your scales in balance? Most of the pen-and-paper work in this book will come in later chapters, but please take a moment to get an objective sense of where you are right now. (For your convenience, all of these materials are collected in an appendix at the back of the book.)

We need to understand where you are first, before we step through what is draining your energy. The more *yeses* you have in this table, the closer you are to mental load burnout. The more *nos*, the more mental load energy is in your reserves for life's big opportunities and challenges.

| | **YES/NO and why?** |
|---|---|
| 1. Do you end many days feeling like you have spent more mental load energy than you started with (i.e., spending more than saving)? | |
| 2. Do you often feel exhausted by your mental load (e.g., quick-tempered, overwhelmed, loss of focus, anxious, difficulty sleeping)? | |

| | YES/NO and why? |
|---|---|
| 3. Do you often find it difficult to enjoy life's moments because of the constant thinking about what needs to be done next? | |
| 4. Do you lack sufficient mental load energy to respond to an *opportunity* in your work, family, or other areas of your life? | |
| 5. Do you lack sufficient mental load energy to respond to an *emergency* in your work, family, or other areas of your life? | |
| 6. Do you find it difficult to find enough mental load energy to plan for the future? | |
| **Total number of YES responses** | |

Start thinking about these questions regularly as a reminder of the status of your mental load health. You can pin this to a wall or put it on your desk to come back to regularly as a check-in on how your mental load is tracking. Life will be full of ups and downs, and so will your mental load. Sometimes you will need to draw down your mental load energy into burnout to achieve great things. But like all things in life, our mental load capacity can't constantly be overdrawn.

These questions serve as a pulse check to help you identify whether you are running through too much mental load energy too quickly, inching toward burnout—or whether you are spending in ways that position you to achieve your wildest dreams.

This is the first step in taming the mental load: to take an honest look at spending.

As you walk through the rest of the book, this assessment will serve as the foundation for figuring out when you are veering off course and need to get yourself back on track.

## THE EIGHT TYPES OF MENTAL LOADS

Now that Julie has figured out that she is in mental load burnout, I next ask her to start thinking about the eight different types of mental load. I share the most recent findings from my research. After years of looking at parents' mental loads in Australia and the United States, I learned that the mental load wasn't one singular task but rather eight different types of work. As an American raising a family in Australia, I am constantly learning about the differences between these two countries—but counter to what I expected, these eight mental load types were more or less the same for people on opposite sides of the world:

1. Life organization
2. Emotional support
3. Relationship hygiene
4. Magic making
5. Dream building
6. Individual upkeep
7. Safety
8. Meta-care

Let's dig into each one in turn.

## Type 1: Life Organization

*Life organization* is a mental load category most people understand. It's also the way the mental load is described in popular culture. It is the invisible work everyone does to ensure that home, work, and life are all running smoothly. Life organization is like a game of Whac-A-Mole where one task disappears and another emerges, or even worse, two or three pop up at the same time and you have to decide which one you are going to whack. They are the "treadmill tasks" because they are constant and never-ending.

When I talk Julie through this mental load category, she easily recognizes how her mental load is being spent on these tasks. Julie carries a lot of the family's life organization, including coordinating the care of her children, pets, and aging parents.

When her kids were little, Julie was the one to make sure they had clean socks, packed lunches, and someone to pick them up and drop them off at school. As her children entered their teen years, this work morphed into checking homework, making sure sports uniforms were clean, and organizing driving lessons.

On the professional front, Julie spends mental load energy making sure her work is done well, deadlines are hit, and emails are responded to in a timely fashion. Julie feels this life organization work as the work she is constantly doing to ensure that everything is happening as it should and everyone is where they need to be.

Paul shares a lot of this life organization work. He spends his mental load organizing the mornings so he can drop the kids off at school before he heads into work. Paul spends part of his days thinking about how to get his work done early so he can attend the school's award assemblies or the kids' sports games. Paul is also in charge of monitoring the fridge to make sure it is stocked for dinner.

Together, Julie and Paul love the feeling of crossing things off their list, reaping the rewards of well-planned holidays, meals, and vacations. Completing the life organization work fosters a deep sense of accomplishment. This creates incredible joy for them as parents when their efforts help their children to thrive. This is energy often well spent.

But sometimes this work can be crushing, distracting, and exhausting because it is never-ending. It feels imbalanced in the marriage. Julie feels like she is doing more than Paul and is ultimately responsible for picking up the pieces if things go wrong. She has stepped into the role of manager of the home—the "mom-ager" trap many mothers fall into that will be discussed in the next chapter—which means that it is Julie who makes sure everything is happening as it should and everyone is happy.

This is not uncommon. In fact, it happens in the *majority* of families we studied. This dynamic sets moms up for more stress, strain, and feelings of being overwhelmed and can make mothers' life organization mental loads heavy.

## Type 2: Emotional Support

Julie talks a lot about being the heartbeat of the family. When I probe her a bit more about what this looks like in practice, she tells me a story about when her daughter was entering her preteen years.

Julie tells me, "I know from my training that the preteen age is hard. At that time, there was just so much conflict in my daughter's friend group. One day friends would become enemies. Then, just as quickly, they were all best friends again. All of this created a huge amount of anguish and big feelings. What this meant in practice was that I had to be constantly on, and I often didn't know what emotions were coming my way."

The minute Julie would walk through the door after work, it would feel like—bam!—she was in the whirlwind of deep and long conversations about who had done what to whom that day. She'd listen to her daughter offload about the latest dramas with her friends or teachers or whoever was important to Julie's daugther.

When I ask Julie what this meant for her own emotional state, she tells me, "I know it was good that my daughter was talking to me about all of it. I wouldn't want her to keep it all in and then punish herself with shame and anger in all the ways I did as a child. I mean, I think this was the age when I started to develop my own demons, you know? But sometimes I'm like, *I don't have the energy for this.*"

Julie never would have thought about this as a form of a mental load. It is so obviously different from the work of making sure everyone has the school supplies they need. Figuring out how to be present and appropriately supportive for a family member seeking comfort is indeed another form of mental load labor that many parents, especially mothers, carry.

Whereas before, she felt guilty that those conversations with her daughter left her feeling drained rather than closer and more connected, especially given her career choice as a therapist, simply acknowledging that this was emotional-thinking work rather than just quality time is a relief.

This is the mental load work of *emotional support*, and it involves noticing moods, checking in after particularly stressful events, and providing help through life's inevitable big and small moments. It's also the work of actively listening, workshopping solutions, and offering a sympathetic ear through friendship challenges, budding romantic relationships, and interpersonal squabbles.

Emotional support isn't work we do for ourselves. Rather, it is work we do for others: our children, spouses, extended family members, neighbors, and friends. This kind of work is often impossible to delegate to someone else. This is mental load energy that Julie was giving each and every day to her daughter during those critical years.

Once I give Julie the definition of this type of mental load work, she realizes she is also doing emotional support at work. In her job as a therapist, she provides emotional support to her clients. She signed up for this—but it doesn't seem to stop there.

When Julie leaves the treatment room, it feels like she is providing this emotional support work to her colleagues too. It is Julie they turn to when their marriages are on the rocks, their parents are ill, or they are navigating difficult bosses and office politics. My research was super clear: Emotional support work doesn't just happen at home.

Rather, parents are carrying emotional support at work when they try to decipher subtle facial expressions on Zoom to determine "Is my team unhappy or just distracted?" or do more obvious things like checking in with colleagues after babies are born, parents fall sick, or other big life events happen. It is important work. It tethers us to one another, lubricates relationships, and ensures that people feel good in their day-to-day lives. Job descriptions don't mention it, and performance assessments rarely account for it, but teams and companies directly benefit from the cohesion and productivity made possible by this kind of work.

It is also complex and often exhausting work because it changes, shifts, ebbs, and flows.

In our research, parents discussed the content of the emotional support work at home getting more serious as children age. Julie describes what she sees in her practice. When children are little, their emotional hurts are important but feel less consequential. But as children grow older, the emotional support work becomes intense and high stakes, tied to big experiences like exploring their sexuality, bouts of depression, and all the pressures that come from social media.

It means parents burn through more mental load energy to do this emotional support work, weighing each word internally before uttering it. The stakes of this work can be high, and it feels like getting it right is important. In this way, providing emotional support can be fulfilling, a way to support the people we love. But this can be a particularly big drain.

Here is the catch: I found mothers are doing way more of this work than fathers, both at the office and in the home.

Providing this energy to everyone is running through mothers' mental load capacity and burning them out. Fathers aren't doing the same work. They aren't investing in emotional support in the ways that mothers are, and dads have more energy as a result.

Are mothers wrong in all of this—should they be giving less and saving more? Do women just care too much? The answer is *sometimes* yes—but not always. My work getting to the bottom of which kinds of mental load expenditures are investments and which are drains helps clarify.

Julie tells me, "I assume the mental load for things I shouldn't or don't even need to. I spend hours brainstorming solutions for problems faced by colleagues, friends, and family going through hard times. And it eats up a lot of my energy thinking about how I can help them, which is draining. There is a whole chorus of people in my life, including Paul, who tell me these are not my problems, and I shouldn't care so much. But how can I turn my back on people in need?"

It makes Julie feel like a bad person to not emotionally support everyone—and she is getting something back from that investment. But it's still a net negative, draining her energy and pushing her into burnout. Our goal is to use the Mental Load Audit later in this book to help Julie and you to clarify when that heavy emotional support work is worth doing.

## Type 3: Relationship Hygiene

Julie tells me that after she and Paul became parents, their intimacy frequency changed. "We used to do what we wanted when we wanted. But once we became parents, it was like the kids were our whole world. Our marriage got sidelined."

I know exactly what she is talking about, because I, too, found that my marriage changed with the birth of my daughter. And I'm not just talking about having less sex when there's a newborn around—I mean the opportunities for all kinds of intimacy, the things that make us feel loved by and connected with our partners. At the start, my husband, Casey, and I tried to go on dates or sneak out together. But honestly, we were just so tired and so smitten with our daughter that we would make excuses to come home early. Our duo had become a trio, and that meant we had to make a conscious effort to have the kind of one-on-one time that had built up our marriage to begin with. That effort is *relationship hygiene*, or the mental work of taking care of relationships for oneself, as well as one's children, partner, and extended family. It's the work of making sure everyone feels connected and loved, ranging from small acts of kindness like scheduling time for daily check-ins (me) to more grand gestures like planning vacations and special meals to celebrate each other (him).

When her children were little, Julie would do the mental load work of reaching out to parents of new school friends to set up playdates. It is also Julie who keeps track of favors to make sure they are repaid to friends and family who helped out in times of need. Julie is the one to remember to periodically call friends and her parents and in-laws to see how they are doing or send a thank-you note for a kind gesture or gift received.

When I ask about how this work is allocated in their marriage, Julie tells me she is largely in charge of it. Paul will sometimes reach out to his brother or friends to wish them a happy birthday. Paul did try to organize a monthly visit with his parents. But it is Julie who is making sure everyone follows through on well-laid plans to get together.

It is Julie who remembers, reminds, and nudges others to connect.

Does Julie like doing this work? When I ask her this question, Julie seems to agree that she has the best skills in the family to keep their social connections going. She often feels better after reaching out to friends and family to see how they are doing. But there are some moments where she finds this relationship hygiene work to be particularly draining.

I ask her for an example, and she gives me one name—Elaine.

Who is Elaine, you ask? Well, Elaine is the mother of her daughter's best school friend. Elaine means well and she cares a lot about the kids. Unfortunately, this care can often come off as judgy, critical, and undermining.

Julie tells me, "Nothing is ever good enough for Elaine. Not the way the other parents work the snack bar at the baseball games. Not the way some mothers don't watch their children closely enough. And not the way 'kids these days' wear makeup and pants." Elaine is a difficult person, which makes Julie keep her distance.

Why not drop Elaine altogether? Well, as difficult as Elaine is, Julie has to remain connected for her daughter. She has to sometimes talk to Elaine to make plans, keep tabs on the kids, and check in on the girls. But Julie loathes it, and even though the contact can be brief, the amount of mental load energy absorbed by preparing for the contact and debriefing afterward is huge.

"Why don't you reduce contact?" I ask. "Or care less? Or, better yet, hand all this correspondence off to Paul?"

Julie pauses and ponders.

"I could try," she tells me.

I know for many women this type of pruning work can be hard. Women are afraid of the social consequences. They are afraid they will hurt someone's feelings or be judged for being mean and ostracized because of it. They are anxious about the fallout of reducing contact for their kids, and continuing to tolerate someone unpleasant can feel like the better option.

But holding boundaries around our precious mental load energy is not a personality defect. It doesn't make us jerks. It doesn't mean we are bad people. It makes us smart. It makes us strategic.

We need to get clear on who deserves our energy and who doesn't.

As I walk you through the Mental Load Audit in chapter 5, one area we will focus on is creating worlds with less relationship hygiene energy going to our own respective Elaines.

## Type 4: Magic Making

My body instantly begins to tense when Julie starts to talk about her Christmas celebration. Of all the work that goes into building and balancing a full life, this is the work I most loathe. I was once quoted on Christmas Day in a major Australian newspaper stating, "I don't do magic making at Christmas." This headline was coupled with an article written by the incredible Wendy Tuohy and a photo of me at home, sunglasses on, book in hand, pool in the background, with a pop-out quote: "Sometimes we eat lasagna in the pool."

None of this is a lie—I don't do magic making at Christmas, and we literally do eat lasagna in the pool on Christmas Day (don't panic—December is summertime in Australia!). The fact that I was featured in a highly respected newspaper shunning the labor of magic making during the holidays was a career high. Even more impressive was the fact that my photo was right next to Santa's.

I shared with the world that my family had cracked the holiday puzzle—do nothing but eat lasagna while floating in a pool.

It felt like a true revelation that we all need to hear.

For Julie's family, unlike mine, tradition during the holidays is quite important. "Paul's family loves the holidays, but there are so many expectations."

When I ask her to give me an example, she starts to talk about napkins. "The table must be set a certain way, including these linen napkins that were his grandmother's. It is like these napkins are some sort of family heirloom." Keep in mind that it is a holiday meal, so there are kids spilling food and cranberry sauce everywhere, she tells me.

These napkins become equal parts deeply problematic and symbolic. They have to stay clean, and they have to be pressed, and they have to wipe faces.

"Why can't we just move to paper?" she asks.

With effort, I refrain from telling her that eating lasagna in the pool on Christmas Day guarantees no cleanup. Julie's napkin experience is my literal nightmare. Maybe they should stop the madness?

Welcome to the mental load of *magic making*, of making sure people and events feel special and the weighing of obligations and expectations against our own personal choices and preferences.

Magic making can be wonderful when it goes well and people are happy. Some of us love to do magic making for our families—for many people, this is work well invested.

For Julie, magic making is most special when it is just her immediate family.

Since the kids were little, Paul has organized trips to the beach, where the family spends the whole day searching for seashells, challenging one another to foot races in the sand, and wave jumping. Some of my best memories center on the joy of magic making for my daughter, Ava—like when I took her to her first movie, where we ate popcorn and laughed with a gaggle of children and she danced and sang in front of the big screen during the closing credits.

These moments are pure magic and mental loads well spent.

But often magic making intertwines with the worst parts of life organization or relationship hygiene—making a bunch of difficult people, whom sometimes we don't *really* care about and sometimes we love deeply, happy. I am talking about remembering gifts for extended family or planning meals for picky and judgmental relatives. I am talking about scrolling Instagram posts hashtagged #CoreMemories and feeling crappy that you didn't cart your kids off to a pumpkin patch in coordinated outfits for an adorable outing.

Again, why don't women just hand it off to their husbands or not do it at all?

Well, because women know they are the ones who will be held accountable for magic making across families and generations.

If the napkins aren't on the table, or Grandma's famous creamed onions that no one eats aren't made, and if as a result family cohesion suffers or the next generation feels a rupture with tradition rather than a sense of fond belonging, it is the women who will be held to account and not the men.

Mothers feel an incredible sense of pressure around re-creating magic from their own childhoods, even if it doesn't make sense in modern times. They prioritize homemade cranberry sauce even when store-bought will suffice. They personalize paper holiday cards even though everyone knows everything about one another's lives from social media. They buy or make thank-you cards even when emails or texts are well received.

It is work that feels weighty because it is work that often doesn't make sense anymore. We have less time and more convenience, but we still take the hardest path. All of this magic making requires effort that is greater than the appreciation it receives.

Often it is work that was drilled into us as young children, important ways to show love, thanks, gratitude, and class (in every sense). But if we are honest, this work is often done by default, based on traditions that have been long lost on purpose. It is often work that others—especially fathers—don't see as particularly valuable and thus don't do. It is work that women carry alone—and this work often ultimately lands in the trash.

If these types of traditions are important to you, then you should keep them.

But if you are doing them by default, they should be dropped. We need to figure out which *magic making* is truly magical and which is a total drain.

## Type 5: Dream Building

The next category that I tell Julie about is one that instantly resonates with her. Julie and Paul spend a lot of their mental load energy thinking about how to give their children opportunities to create lifelong passions and inspire big ambitions. Julie knows her daughter loves soccer, so she's always on the hunt for any skills sessions running within fifty miles of their city. Paul loves that his son is interested in French history and so has joined a Facebook group of Francophiles (his son wouldn't be caught dead on Facebook!) who share events, music, and interesting facts about all things France. These are mental loads spent engaged in *dream building* for the children, and parents invest heavily in them—they see them as critical to ensuring that their children are succeeding and their dreams are coming true.

We don't do this work just for our children. Rather, we do this work for everyone in our lives, including ourselves. Julie reflects on her own life and identifies that she spends some of her dream-building mental load focused on supporting Paul's dreams, which are often centered on success at work. This is work that Paul also invests in—making sure he is working toward his own career advancement. And they are having some good success—Paul is doing well at work, which makes them both feel accomplished.

"What about your dreams, Julie? How are your and Paul's mental loads being spent to advance your dreams?" I ask.

This gives Julie pause.

As for many of the mothers I interviewed, the urgent daily hustle and bustle of family life has absorbed attention that might otherwise go toward dream building for herself. As I will show you later in the Mental Load Audit, reigniting your own dreams is a critical investment of your mental load.

## Type 6: Individual Upkeep

When I tell Julie about the mental load of *individual upkeep*, she rolls her eyes at me and says, "Is this just about self-care?" I tell her that self-care is one part, but the mental load of individual upkeep is much bigger. It is the work required to achieve, maintain, or promote optimal physical and mental health and well-being and to present this image to the world.

"Oh," Julie responds. "So this is about Oprah."

Every day when Julie came home from school as a child, her mother would watch *Oprah*. The rules were firm: No one was to interrupt her mother from 4:00 to 5:00 p.m., not to ask what was for dinner, not to talk about their day, and definitely not to be driven to the mall. For one hour, Oprah's voice transfixed Julie's mother and thus was transmitted throughout the house.

"In the nineties and maybe into the two thousands, Oprah was telling women they *deserved* to have it all. You can work, you can be an amazing mother, you can be a sexy wife, you can look hot, you can prioritize taking care of your skin and hair, you deserve to lose that weight, and on and on," Julie tells me.

Julie could see all the ways these messages got channeled into her mother's psyche, from the self-help books she read to the meals they ate to the way she dressed. The message was clear: We can solve all our problems with an investment in ourselves.

Let's be clear: Oprah isn't to blame for any of this.

Gayle is. (Just kidding!)

Rather, it is what these Oprah-like messages symbolize—the idea that if we can just fix ourselves a bit more, we will be happy. It could be Oprah or a women's magazine or Instagram or TikTok or Pinterest. There is always something more to do or try—to get rid of wrinkles, tone waists, get rid of hair, or grow hair.

It is never-ending self-improvement. And it corrupts our mental loads because we find ourselves stuck on the treadmill of the mental load related to individual upkeep.

Sometimes engaging in this individual upkeep can feel satisfying, making us feel beautiful, cared for, and relaxed. Other times it can cause rumination, a doom spiral about all that we should do to look, feel, and be better—or a toxic internal argument about whether dyeing your hair is self-care to look and feel your empowered best or is evidence you've caved to the pressures of the patriarchy.

In my research, I've found that this mental load type is trickiest for women—few can find the sweet spot of individual upkeep that leads to improved health and well-being rather than a constant feeling of failure for not living up to social expectations.

I tell Julie about a main finding from my research: Mothers often wasted a lot of mental load energy on individual upkeep that was undone. They felt guilty when they didn't do the workout or iron the clothes. They were constantly feeling like they were trying hard but coming up short.

One mother even created a to-do list of all the individual upkeep she was supposed to do and then had to hide the list because she felt so guilty about how much of it was left undone.

The consequence is that mothers spend inordinate amounts of

mental energy and time thinking about ways to improve themselves at the expense of more impactful and meaningful endeavors.

It drains their energy, often without a clear benefit.

For me, it led to a huge amount of time spent thinking about food, diet, and health—a lifetime of mental load energy wasted on the size of my pants and the number on the scale. I had deeply internalized the message that there are good foods and bad foods and that any weight you gain is a signal of personal failure. A lot of my mental load was being chewed up by this thinking. I bought, hook, line, and sinker, the idea that I could personally achieve greatness if I just ate less sugar, no carbs, or whatever the current trend was in the diet industry. But the result of all this social pressure to eat "right" and "take care of myself" was to restrict my diet.

But as my diet got narrower, my mood grew more irritable and my thinking less clear. I realized that my "healthy habit" was nothing but a drain. The time and energy spent calculating Weight Watchers points, macros, or calories are resources you could choose to use elsewhere. It wasn't until I really looked at what was happening and made the conscious decision to quiet that voice in my head telling me food was "bad" and I was only a success if I fit into pants from my twenties that I was finally able to quell that mental load drain.

I had to disconnect from the idea that the size of my pants was an important measure of my success or value.

Setting down a heavy piece of that mental load helped me open up my diet to a wider range of foods and reclaim the brain space that had been devoted to an impossible, restrictive task. I started to feel like a human again.

I started to eat with great pleasure. I started to think less about the fit of my pants and more about the quality of my soul. And I could do my work with a brain functioning with the glorious energy of carbohydrates. I took the advice given by Anne Lamott in her book *Plan B: Further Thoughts on Faith*: "[R]efuse to wear uncomfortable pants, even if they make you look really thin. Promise me you'll never wear pants that bind or tug or hurt, pants that have an opinion about how much you've just eaten. The pants may be lying! There is way too much lying and scolding going on politically right now without having your pants get in on the act, too."

Individual upkeep should be spent on things that make us feel good and allow us to step into the world with confidence. It should not be spent in a battle with our pants.

## Type 7: Safety

I remember the day we were told there might be an active shooter on the University of California's Irvine campus. I was a PhD student working in the graduate student offices. It was early afternoon when we got a text telling us that someone had been spotted in tactical gear and we should shelter in place and lock our doors. I texted friends and professors I knew to see if they had gotten the message too and if they had any additional information. Everyone had and no one did.

We waited to see our fate.

It turned out to be a false alarm, but it was a scary moment. It took every bit of my mental load capacity in the moment and continued to weigh on my mental load every subsequent time I stepped on campus. Should I walk down the main open pathway or take a diversion with more cover? Did I know where the exits were in the large lecture halls, in case someone came in with a gun? Should I mince my words with upset students to avoid a misunderstanding that could lead to violence? It was a constant drain on my mental load capacity. As I have learned through my research, avoiding getting shot moving through their daily lives is a unique mental load drain that Americans carry.

This is one example of the mental load of *safety*, or energy spent ensuring the safety of yourself, loved ones, friends, family, and community.

Many American parents told me about their fear of being gunned down anywhere and anytime.

Julie worries about sending her children into the world only to have them randomly shot at schools, malls, movie theaters, grocery stores, and so on. She tells me about mental energies spent building contingency plans of barricading doors, telling the children to play dead, or hopping out of windows if faced with an active shooter. Julie often worries about whether teachers or security guards at her children's schools are adequately prepared for a catastrophe.

"I mean, we have seen it all—police and teachers who have frozen from fear and others who have acted heroically. It feels like once I finally quell this little voice running through plans in my head, another shooting happens, and it reignites. I mean, it could happen to anyone at any time, right? I have all these plans in my head about how to escape a shooter—sit on the aisle at the movies, know where the exit is at the grocery store, keep an eye out for suspicious people. It is unrelenting," she tells me.

No one is immune from being the target of a bullet, even presidents surrounded by Secret Service agents. What is the hope for the rest of us?

These experiences are unique to U.S. parents and not mental loads carried by others. As an American who has lived in Australia for over ten years, I am often asked, "Why don't you all take the guns away in the U.S., like we did after our first and last mass shooting?" It is hard to explain to others that Americans' relationship to firearms and the contentiousness around gun reform polarize our political system. It also absorbs American parents' mental loads, both in worrying about what violence awaits around the corner and in trying to figure out whether they themselves need a gun to combat it. Many of the American parents in our interviews are intimately connected to the effects of gun violence.

This makes the U.S. exceptional, but in the worst kind of way.

Gun violence isn't the only way parents' mental load energies are spent on safety. In interviews for my research, parents talked about constantly monitoring a locked doggy door to make sure toddlers couldn't escape, thinking about whether children were wearing bike helmets on their rides home from school, and tracking teenagers to ensure they were safe driving on roads at night. As I tell Julie, my research shows that the safety portion of the mental load is focused on ensuring that others are physically, emotionally, and mentally safe both inside and outside the home.

Certain groups of parents carried heavier safety mental loads than others—women, people of color, LGBTIQ+ parents, and people with nonbinary identities, to name just a few. Their mental loads are taxed by constant worry about their own and their families' safety as they move through the world, which can be unpredictable and dangerous. Because the consequences can be dire—sometimes fatal—it is nearly impossible to delegate or simply drop these mental loads.

We live in unequal social worlds, which drains some of our safety mental loads more than others'.

## Type 8: Meta-Care

Before having their first baby, Julie and Paul talked a lot about the kind of parents they were going to be. Paul wanted to be a more engaged father than his own, connected to his children's emotional worlds. He didn't just want to "do things" with his children. He wanted to "know things" about his children—their loves, their passions, and their challenges. Oh, and he wanted them to love the arts, learn a musical instrument, visit museums, and maybe even take a drama class.

Julie also wanted to be an engaged parent and hoped her children would come to her in times of need. But she also wanted them to learn to be compassionate people. She kept thinking about how to do this—should they get a dog so the kids could build empathy? Or maybe they should start volunteering so the children could learn the value of helping others? And shouldn't they get rid of all the plastics in the kitchen so they could model a commitment to environmentalism?

This is the world of *meta-care*, or the mental load work that captures the big-picture thinking, emotional work, and physical work around parenting. It is the work of making sure we are doing our mental loads and living our lives in ways that align with our values as parents and, more broadly, as people. It is the work of making sure we are parenting the way we want to parent and living the way we want to live. It is the work of tracking whether we are behaving in the ways that are aligned with the type of people we want to be.

Meta-care can be tangible—like monitoring the way we talk about diet, exercise, and the shape of our bodies in order to model good behavior for our children. Or it can be more existential, like thinking about whether we are getting this parenting thing right when everything is constantly in flux.

For Julie and Paul, meta-care is a conceptual cloud hovering over all their decision-making. Sometimes it shows up as a mental filter for their daily decisions, to see if their actions align with their values, goals, and parenting styles.

It is a thought about whether using a single-use water bottle is worth the environmental cost in a moment when it is so very convenient. Or whether raising our voice when our child brought home a bad grade was warranted or a softer approach should have been taken. Other times it shows up as a social comparison.

For Julie, meta-care means benchmarking against what she sees other mothers doing or what the most recent psychological research identifies as effective parenting practices. Do children need constant boundaries, or should these be more porous? What are the experts saying about discipline, and does this advice align with her views on being a good mom? Should she give her kids a cell phone with social media, like the other parents, or is this counter to her and Paul's desire to build more empathetic children?

For Paul, it is weighing his parenting choices against those of his father or grandfather. He wants to be a different dad from his own, so he is constantly playing through how to respond to his children. Paul is like many fathers in my research studies who wanted to break old approaches to fatherhood that they saw in their own fathers and grandfathers that were characterized by being aloof, distant, and disengaged.

What this means is that he can't parent by default, but rather has to carry a heavier level of consciousness. He is constantly running his parenting through a filter in his brain to help him figure out when he has it right, when he is slipping into old patterns, and when he needs to do something totally different. This forms a mental load drain, as Paul is constantly weighing his actions against his parenting values.

Julie hears a lot about these mental load drains in her practice. Many of her clients are families with neurodivergent teenagers who need a little more help to move through the world. "The parents are always having to sense-check next steps," she tells me, "because what may make sense for one child may not be effective for another. This requires a lot of patience and careful thinking." These parents talk a lot about making a range of parenting decisions that ultimately lead to better outcomes but are a drain. They have to pause before reacting. They have to think through contingency plans in case their children get overloaded. They have to be eternally patient in moments when their children are finding it difficult to self-regulate emotions.

Julie shares, "One client told me that even though they don't know who their kid will be on a given day, they have to be the same patient, calm, and loving parent regardless. Being this type of parent is important to their values. But it is hard work that takes a toll."

This is why meta-care can be so depleting—it often surrounds the other seven categories of the mental load and functions like a prompt that asks, "Is this the way I want to show up in the world? Am I living within my values? Do I want to do things differently from the model I learned from my parents or what I see in society writ large?" Meta-care is a category that sits over all the rest and involves a constant internal conversation about who we are and what kind of world we want. It is hard to know when we get this work right, as it is nebulous and its goals are often in some distant future—like, will my child be kind, empathetic, and a hard worker? Sometimes we see glimmers, and then other times our kids are jerks, and we wonder what we did wrong.

This work requires us to be flexible and nimble as our world changes. It requires patience, which can be difficult when we are burned out from a constant deluge of . . . everything. It requires additional energy when we are often running on mental load empty—tired, quick to anger, and exhausted by the many demands of our lives.

But it is mental load energy that is well spent, because it is invested in creating the world we want to live in. It is change making, so even though it takes a toll, it is incredibly valuable.

## LEARNING TO SEE THE MENTAL LOADS

The heaviness of these loads ebbs and flows across the year and across our lifetimes, intensifying when something is added (the birth of a child or a new job), something goes wrong (an illness in the family), or a deadline is looming (a major work presentation). At times, it crowds out other thinking, which leaves us with little room left in our brains for doing the stuff that matters—deep thinking work, or big, lofty dreaming, or even just recharging.

The mental load never stops—it is a constant tick, tick, tick, tick, tick, tick, tick about what needs to be done.

It has no end.

My research found that mothers hold two-thirds or more of the mental load work for all eight of the mental load categories. Even when they dislike the work, they still do the majority of it for the family.

I also found that until we make this work visible and explicit, mothers and fathers alike have no idea how much they're doing, or what their partner's load looks like.

Fathers are, for the most part, not actively trying to offload this work onto their spouses. Rather, they are investing their mental load energy in ways aligned with their cultural roles around breadwinning and being dads, and often are unaware that the work from the other categories is being done for them. In my interviews, it isn't until I tell them about all eight categories and ask them about their contributions to each that they realize they aren't carrying their fair share. Seeing the mental load in its entirety is critical to ensuring we can invest it in the things and people we love.

## Chapter 3

# The Seven Stages of the Mental Load

NORA IS A MOTHER OF TWINS WHO LIVES IN KANSAS CITY, KANSAS, where she works for a major grocery store chain. She and her partner, Ben, both work full time and so try to make sure they each do their fair share, which can, at times, be challenging with two preschool-age children. When I interview Nora for my research, I ask her to describe her mental load during a typical day. She tells me it starts with wake-up, which for the parents is at six thirty, but sometimes the kids are up earlier. When this happens, Nora and Ben start to go into problem-solving mode. Why are the kids not sleeping through the night? Are they sick? Is one waking the other up? Are they going through a sleep regression? Should they contact the pediatrician or give it some time?

Then the day starts with a bang—her daughter may be allergic to wheat, so they are trying to eliminate that from her diet, but it requires a constant scanning of ingredients. Pancakes are out. But what about the ketchup for the eggs? Does that have a trace of wheat in it? If so, will her skin allergy flare up?

Their son is able to eat anything, but lately his preference is peanut butter on everything, so Nora monitors the jars for any indication they are nearing empty. After breakfast, it is a mad dash to make sure everyone has everything they need for day care. One child was sent home with dirty clothes the day before, and they need to restock the extras in case of an emergency. This week is show-and-tell, and each child gets to bring in something special, so Nora and Ben have been keeping track of each's favorite toy, which somehow ends up wedged between beds, left in a closet, or forgotten in a car, shopping cart, or tangled bedsheets.

The kids are only one piece in the morning, as Nora and Ben both have to mentally prepare for the day's work. Sometimes Nora has a big client meeting and so has to ensure that her clothes are neatly pressed and stain-free, no small task in the house, given that the children are always covered in some combination of snot, juice, and Play-Doh. Ben is trying to raise his visibility with his boss and coworkers, so he is wondering if he should invite them out for a drink or to the home for a meal. But this would require a total restructuring of the evening routine—which could be okay, but who would do the day care pickup, clean the floors, and cook the dinner?

By the time Nora or Ben (they rotate!) drops the kids off at day care, both parents feel absolutely exhausted. It feels like a marathon in the morning to get the children into someone else's care. This is an experience that many parents across my interviews shared: The morning feels like an entire day, and it takes a superhuman amount of mental load energy to get everyone ready and out the door. This time is important, as getting the morning started right sets the tone for the rest of the day.

It was the loss of this mad rush that many parents cherished during the start of the COVID-19 pandemic. Slowing down in the morning was a silver lining I heard about across hours of interviews with parents. As terrible as those first few months of the virus were for all of us, the one thing that parents kept telling me was that they appreciated getting a little more time in the morning to cuddle children in bed and eat breakfast together without the scramble of getting everyone everywhere all at once. They were doing fewer steps in the mental load process when things were shuttered.

Herein lies the next tool we need to tame our mental loads: We need to understand how we "do" the mental load. It has multiple steps—seven, in fact—and each requires energy to complete. Getting everyone out the door in the morning is the perfect example of the stress and strain of each of these different steps. Nora and Ben are doing the mental load work of anticipating problems and needs of each member of the family, remembering everything for the day, delegating who needs to do what, executing well-laid plans, and monitoring it all.

Here is the problem with well-laid plans: Things always go wrong.

Despite all the prep work we do to make sure everything is well organized and running smoothly, life can be unpredictable. Just as you are about to step out the door, the dog dies (true story that happened to me), the kids have strep throat, or the dishwasher breaks, and everything is thrown into chaos. We have to spend more of our mental load building out contingency plans, and fast, to help make it all work, keep it all going, and make sure everything is happening as needed.

A key finding from my research is that we rarely see the mental load because it is done internally, in our minds. It is only when something is forgotten, like a child left at school without being picked up (another true story that happened to me), that we realize a step in the mental load process has been skipped. Typically, we move smoothly through the world because someone (usually a mother!) has spent their mental load energy to clear the path and pave the way.

The next step in our journey to truly understand why the mental load is so draining is to see its seven stages.

## THIS IS HOW WE DO IT: THE MENTAL LOAD PROCESS

The research is clear: Mothers are carrying heavier mental loads than fathers. Many mothers step into this work without even being aware of it. I ask them, "How did you end up doing the mental load in the family? Did you discuss it with your partner or children?" Mothers and fathers alike look at me with blank stares.

They had discussed who would do the cooking and cleaning. They had talked about who would stay home when babies were young. They had even negotiated who would drop toddlers at day care and children at school and who would take time off work to be with the kids during breaks or to get them to after-school activities.

But the mental load?

No, that seemed to have just seeped into their minds.

This, of course, is not true. Using sociology as our superpower, we know that women are socialized from birth to be helpful, caring, and kind. As I will tell you later in this chapter, culture sets the stage for mothers to be the mom-agers of the family. But it also means that fathers aren't carrying as heavy mental loads as mothers, in part because they aren't doing all the pieces.

In addition to doing more of the eight types of mental load, mothers are also doing more of all seven parts of the mental load process. They are shouldering it all while fathers are only dipping into some of its parts.

As I heard over and over again across my research projects, fathers *wanted* to share this work, but many couldn't see all the work that was being done around them and had no idea that their wives were carrying so much.

Here we go—no more excuses.

It's time to shine a light on the seven stages of the mental load. By seeing the mental load process for what it is—a range of different tasks that drain our mental load capacity—we can start to have honest conversations about how to share the load.

## The Seven Stages of the Mental Load

The mental load process has seven clear and discrete steps:

1. Identifying problems
2. Remembering
3. Strategizing
4. Decision-making
5. Delegating
6. Executing
7. Monitoring

And all of these are made more difficult by life's unpredictability.

Let's get an idea of each in turn.

First, parents *identify* the problems and needs of the family, the "who needs what" work that can be big or small. Next, parents have to *remember* what has to be done for everyone—it's the "here is what we need to do" work. Then comes the planning work. This can be broken down into three stages. First, parents have to *strategize* about the best course of action—the "let's weigh the options" work. Next comes *decision-making* work of deciding the best course of action—it is the "here is what we are going to do" work. After that, the *delegating* work emerges: determining "who is doing what." Then there is *executing* the work: doing the task and performing whatever was planned. Finally comes the *monitoring* work of making sure the entire plan is going well and troubleshooting anything that comes up. This entire process is shrouded by a singular, unnerving fact about life: It is *unpredictable*—which means the mental load also includes between one and three million contingency plans.

When the mental load goes to plan, it can operate like a cycle, moving through each step linearly and resulting in a positive outcome. These are mental loads that feel good and well spent.

Let me give you an example.

Say you want your child to try a new instrument, so you engage your mental load to move linearly from stage to stage—*identifying* your child's love of the tuba, *remembering* to put said tuba on a shopping list, *strategizing* about when tubas are on sale, *deciding* when to buy a tuba, *delegating* who should go to the store with your child to try the tuba, and *executing* the purchase. The end of this mental load process is *monitoring* whether your smiling child is happy while holding a new tuba at the end. She is? Success!

Often the mental load doesn't work linearly. It works in fits and starts.

We get stuck on one stage and can never move to the next. We burn through mental load energy anticipating problems that never emerge or remembering things that are unimportant. It can often feel like we are hitting all the keys on a keyboard at once—a lot of information that gums up our system. How do we do these mental loads? What do they look like and how do they work?

Let's turn to the research.

The first stage of the mental load work, figuring out what needs to be done, requires a huge amount of energy. Take the "my child wants to learn the tuba" example. In this stage, parents are looking at their child's likes, wants, and interests to determine whether music may be in their future. Sometimes we do this determining work casually, by listening intently to our children to see what is piquing their interest. Other times this can be more encompassing, functioning like an internal antenna constantly pinged by the subtleties of who needs what and when.

It is like a spidey sense that can't be turned off and is constantly focused on monitoring others in our lives. At its worst, when we are most concerned about our loved ones—worried that things are going wrong or their safety is at risk—it feels like full-blown surveillance. It can feel like constantly "being on," scanning for real or hypothetical needs or problems. It can feel like a continual ping-ponging thinking about things—like whether my child is out of shampoo, the family cat's sudden limp is a sign of lymphoma, my weird mole is getting worse, and I remembered to pay the water bill.

The constant stream of things that need to be tracked can be paralyzing, making it difficult to figure out which of these tasks should be tackled first. They are all important, but which ones are urgent and needing to be done now?

Mothers are much more likely to be perpetually tuned in to this identifying-problems work than fathers are, and it's made more costly by the *unpredictability* of life, which leads parents (usually mothers) to develop a million contingency plans for problems that often never arise. Also, mothers tend to put their own needs on the back burner, ignoring the weird mole or scratchy throat or other signs of their needs, to make sure everyone else's needs and problems get priority. All of this contributes to a feeling of burnout and exhaustion that mothers feel is difficult to tackle.

Susanna, a research study participant who is a real estate broker from Dallas, feels this part of the mental load process deeply. As summer vacation starts to creep up, so does her mental load. She has two adolescent kids, one a son who is thirteen and develops social anxiety from the inevitable social isolation that summers, which are punctuated by long stretches of time alone at home, inevitably bring. In previous summers, Susanna found she carried a constant mental load related to her son, worrying about whether he was spending too much time playing video games or whether the texts with his friends were playful or bullying.

Susanna would make sure to check in with her son at the end of the day, in case he wanted to share any of his feelings. Sometimes they had great chats, but other times it felt like he was holding back and said very little. She talked to other mothers of teenage boys, who reassured her that this was normal, but Susanna couldn't shake the feeling that something was going wrong with her son and he needed a little more support. She was spending a lot of her mental load energy surveilling his life, moods, and actions for any signs of a slide.

What all of this meant was that Susanna found it difficult to concentrate on other things, especially her job. During summertime, her work suffered, as she was often distracted by the mental load of what was going on at home. This constant rumination of trying to identify problems drew down her mental load capacity and left her exhausted.

After a particularly stressful summer, Susanna decided to take action and was determined to make this time better for everyone.

She started to hatch a plan.

This moved her into a new phase of the mental load. She began to *strategize* about the best course of action by doing the "let's weigh the options" work of trying to identify a way forward. This then triggered the *decision-making* work of deciding what should be done next, or the "here is what we are going to do" work.

Her solution? She decided to keep her son active and engaged in activities with friends, family, and neighbors. She weighed the options—they had tried summer camps in the past, but her children loathed them, which just made Susanna's mental load heavier. They were too old to go to their grandmother's house, and she also required a bit more care than in years past. Susanna decided that organizing a range of daily activities seemed the best option to give her son enough autonomy to goof around and enough structure to keep him engaged.

It wasn't the easiest option, but it was the ideal one for her son's unique needs and personality.

While creating a solution that worked for everyone else, Susanna absorbed the huge amount of mental load work, researching the options, weighing those options against her son's personality and preferences, and making the decisions about what should be done next.

She was also the one who ultimately did the next step of the mental load process, *delegating* the work of who was going to do what. But the weird thing was that even when the work was decided and the tasks were delegated, Susanna didn't feel like her mental load abated.

How could this be?

In deciding how to tackle summers, she had shared her feelings with her husband, Frank, and he was sympathetic and agreed summers were a real problem. He even volunteered to be a part of the solution by taking Fridays off to take their son on outings, which would help keep him active but would also increase his own stress, as the work would need to be made up.

In this way, Frank had stepped into the *executing* stage of the mental load process to lighten this piece for Susanna. But, as Susanna recounts, she was the one who had to *remember* each morning what was on the calendar for the day. Susanna remained responsible for the "here is what we need to do" work of keeping everyone on track. It was Susanna who was *monitoring* it all to make sure everything was operating smoothly and troubleshooting when problems inevitably arose.

Susanna didn't feel that Frank's mental load about summer was as heavy as hers. He wasn't haunted by constant surveillance of their son's mood, and he wasn't tracking what was happening now and wasn't as worried about their son's future.

I tell her that she is right.

Frank doesn't get it because he is carrying a lighter load than Susanna. He was stepping into pieces of the mental load, helping with the decision-making and executing work, but little else. For Frank, Fridays off meant the problem was solved, or, rather, that he was doing his part to solve it. Susanna, meanwhile, was doing all the rest—the remembering of who needed to be where, the delegating of who needed to do what, the identifying of when things inevitably went wrong and the strategizing about solutions, the monitoring to make sure planned events were on track, and the surveilling to look for any small or big changes in her son's moods.

This is a lot of work on its own, but then add in the emotional element, that the stakes of getting it right are high, and we can see why Susanna felt so exhausted by it all.

She carried this shroud of anxiety because if she got this wrong, her son's health would suffer, and she would feel like a bad mother. It was Susanna who was carrying the bulk of this. Frank, like many of the fathers I interviewed, was holding only a piece. The scales feel so imbalanced because they are.

## THREE MYTHS CONTRIBUTING TO MENTAL OVERLOAD

Mothers do the mental load the majority of the time. Even when the mental load is done linearly and has a clear and successful outcome, it is usually the mother who holds most of the steps. A linear process would look like this: You identify that your child will need to bring something to sell at the school's bake sale, so you track the school's website and email correspondence, remember that Thursday is bake sale day, strategize about which cupcakes will hold up best on a hot day, decide to make funfetti because it is obviously the best cupcake in the world (fight me!), delegate who will buy the ingredients at the store (Dad) and who will make the cupcakes at home (Mom and child), execute the baking of the cupcakes the night before, and monitor that your child doesn't forget them in the morning. In this example, the mental load moves step by step with a clear start and end. Sometimes our mental loads function in this way and completing the cycle feels great—a success! Well-laid plans were properly executed and people feel loved from the work.

But even in these well-laid plans, it is often the mother who is driving the ship. She is running through the mental load cycle for the cupcakes while simultaneously working through others—tracking the health of her aging mother, remembering to call her third cousin on his birthday, ensuring that the leftovers in the fridge are eaten, and making sure soccer registration is paid. It is the stacking of mental load cycle on top of mental load cycle that can be so burying, and mothers often carry all these demands simultaneously. Whereas fathers are thinking about the tasks at hand, mothers are like time travelers, trying to make sure everyone's past, present, and future are bright.

Why did mothers get burdened with the bulk of this labor? Why hasn't the mental load been more equally shared, so that when we get things wrong or things are forgotten, it feels more like a team error and less like a personal failure? Why is it that women carry around this extra burden of holding it all together?

Well, here again we can use sociology as our superpower to understand how gender myths, grounded in outdated social norms, make our mental loads so much heavier.

## Myth 1: Women Are Better Multitaskers

The first myth that women got sold that weighs down their mental loads is that they are better multitaskers than men. This means we expect women to be better equipped to carry the different components of the mental load process all at once. Of course a mother can remember to bring the forgotten lunch to school and the laptop to work and to remind her husband that taxes are due and to wish the babysitter a happy birthday, we are told. She can do multiple things at once because women are super-duper multitaskers! And this isn't a stereotype; it's a *compliment.*

Actually, it is a lie. The research is crystal clear—none of us are good multitaskers. Our brains can't do two things at once. Of course, sometimes we can walk and chew gum or drive and listen to music. Yes, this is technically doing two things at the same time. But these are tasks that aren't cognitively difficult—they are rote, so we can combine them without much conscious thought or effort.

Most of the time, attempting to do multiple tasks that are different from one another strains our brains—like trying to monitor whether our ten-year-old has made it home safely while simultaneously engaged in a work meeting. In these moments, our brains cannot do these two tasks simultaneously.

Let me give you an example. Imagine you're engaged in a conversation with friends out for dinner or at the family dinner table. You're supposed to be with other people, paying attention, listening to their lives, and caring. Just for one split second you decide to look at your phone. You get a text or an email or a ping about something happening in the world. That person continues to talk, and you think, *It's okay—I've got this. I can hear what they're saying and do something else at the same time. I can briefly check my phone and still be engaged in the conversation.*

Then they turn to you and ask some question about what you

thought or how you felt about what they had just said. You have no idea what just happened.

It feels like you are in a time warp, aliens have taken you, and you just woke up not knowing who you are or where you are.

What is going on here?

The answer is that your brain cannot do two things at once—listen to your loved ones talk *and* read a text message—without something getting lost. We are all terrible multitaskers because our brains are not designed to do this work.

What our brains are good at is moving quickly across tasks, or task switching, and that makes us *feel* like we're multitasking. You can move quickly from listening to a friend to reading that text message. The fact that you do this so quickly makes you *feel* like you're multitasking, but you aren't.

You can't do two things in your brain at once—you're just switching tasks.

Critically, this task switching takes a mental toll, and there is a lag as our brain makes the change from one task to another. When our brain is toggling among a range of tasks that need to be done, it spends energy on each jump, pausing to refocus on the matter at hand. Remembering to bring the streamers to the work party while also trying to reply to an email isn't multitasking; it's introducing mental strain and inefficiency.

When the brain gets a lot of different information, it has to process it all and decide what it should do first and what it should ignore. It is a bit like a traffic jam, with your brain deciding which car will go through.

Because we have only a limited amount of mental energy, this process tires our brains. It is difficult for our brains to switch between tasks that sit in different parts of the brain. It slows us down, increases our mistakes, and drains our brain's battery. Each change takes a piece of our energy even before we dig into the task we're switching to. We need more rest after doing constant task-switching.

What this means is that parents who are constantly switching among mental tasks—noticing whether the pet hamster has enough food, monitoring children's moods, remembering homework due dates, building contingency plans for aging parents, paying attention at work, and so on—are drawing down their mental load capacity.

I may be at work flipping through my to-do list of tasks that need to be done at home—scan the pantry for tomato sauce, check the dogs for ticks, remember to move the laundry into the dryer—but I can't physically complete these tasks *unless I am at home*, and thus they ping-pong around my brain all day long. We are often focused on tasks that we can't remove from our mental to-do list, which means we need extra mental energy to remember them for a later time (when we are home!). They cause a drain twice and can feel like never-ending rumination.

We think we are holding it all together, but we are increasing the chance that we'll make mistakes and everything will fall apart. This is made worse when the stakes are tied to the emotions, ambitions, and dreams of those we love. When the stakes are high but we have no ability to execute the task, our brains exhaust themselves switching from one thought to another.

Let me give you an example from my own life. Seven years ago, my husband, Casey, opened a small microbrewery called Westside Ale Works in Melbourne, Australia. His ambition was to bring California-style beer and pizza to a city where craft beer was just starting to take off. Casey hadn't worked in a brewery or pizza joint before starting this business, but he had spent a decade home brewing and he is an excellent cook. This was a *big* dream that required our entire family to rally around him. Our daughter, Ava, who was seven at the time, helped paint the floors and dressed like a 1950s waitress for his grand opening. I would come on weekends and evenings to pour beer and make pizzas (sometimes for confused students who couldn't quite place me—I am your professor!), and we all cheered on Casey to support this big and bold ambition. Let me tell you that I never imagined we would move to Australia, let alone open a brewery there! But achieving these great dreams required a lot of faith and bravery and, in our case, our entire life savings.

It was also a huge draw on my mental load. I had to manage the demands of co-owning a small business on top of raising a thoughtful, badass child, excelling in my own job, and building toward my own career advancement. This juggling act looked different depending on the day—sometimes I was the one who came to the brewery when people called in sick, or the one who called the plumber when the pipes inevitably got clogged. Other times we needed to strategize about next steps—whether to grow the business or scale back, when to hire new staff, or how to navigate Australia's confusing and immense bureaucracy.

I monitored the business's success and Casey's energy level: Were there enough good online reviews to bring people in? Did Casey need a break to recharge? Should he take a day off to help with the administrative side of things and spend one-on-one time with our daughter? Then, just when we thought we had it all together, we would be hit by a global pandemic, or an unexpected bill, or a war in Ukraine that led to a grain shortage, and on and on. These were things we could never have anticipated, and they drained our mental loads and our personal finances. From experience, I know running a small business is not for the faint of heart.

The mental load I had attached to making this dream a continuing success rarely functioned linearly and often dipped into one and then another component of the mental load process. And a lot of it had to do with things beyond my control—both because owning a small business exposes us to greater risk from global events and because, even though I'm a co-owner, this was really Casey's dream, and I was in it on his behalf.

Sometimes my brewery-related mental load was more heavily tilted toward remembering what needed to be done, and other times toward strategizing about next steps. But I mostly spent a lot of energy identifying problems, monitoring, and surveilling it all. I was constantly scanning for small changes in Casey's and my daughter's moods to then provide some emotional support and help identify solutions.

It is this scanning work that can be so exhausting—like keeping our eyes on the horizon for the emergence of some threat. But in addition to watching for lions, we are scanning our loved ones' emotional well-being, dreams, ambitions, and relationships—plus the volume of toilet paper in each bathroom.

This is what can make the mental load so tiring for all of us. But for women specifically, who are sold the big, fat, stinking lie that they are inherently better multitaskers, this work can be particularly damaging.

The reason?

Instead of taking on one thing at a time, like doing all the remembering for the household, we get spread across the seven steps of the mental load—switching from one task to another on a moment's notice and operating as the safety net for anything our spouse, kids, or colleagues drop. These are loads on top of loads, and because our mental loads are scattered across a range of activities, stages, and people, it can feel like an overload.

As fathers told me across interview after interview, they weren't worried about mental loads being forgotten because they knew their wives would remember and pick up the slack. They didn't need to be the multitasker of the family because they knew their wife had it all under control.

Expecting women to operate at full capacity while carrying a fragmented mental load sets them up for a toxic combination of failure and self-blame (because regardless of whether they are consciously aware of the stereotype that women are better multitaskers, they tend to believe they *should* be able to track every piece at once). We feel like failures when we can't do it all at once, even though, again, the research is clear that none of us can multitask!

In my research interviews, mothers often did understand that they were doing mental loads that were wasteful. They knew that keeping track of it all was often unnecessary but couldn't figure out how to stop themselves.

When I asked people what it is about mothers that allows them to "do it all," many parrot back the nonsense myth: "Women are just better multitaskers!" I could tell many mothers held this as a badge of honor even though they were so very close to burnout. When I'd tell them the science doesn't support this claim, many would go quiet, reflecting on the hold this nonsense had had on their lives for years.

It is no wonder that women need more sleep—they have brains that need to recover from the constant mental demands of multitasking. Research shows that women, across all ages, report sleeping longer than men do. In one study I conducted, which took data from 137,000 Americans, I found that married women slept, on average, sixteen minutes more per day than married men. Now, this may not sound like a lot, but when we look across a year, it means that married women are spending close to one hundred more hours in sleep each year than married men. Single women sleep even longer and, even without the distraction of a snoring spouse, sleep longer than single men. Women biologically need more sleep. I would posit that the drain of trying to multitask everything all day long likely contributes to their need for more time in bed.

Where do we go from here?

Well, we need to stop saying that women are better at remembering the birthdays and the work deadlines because their brains are built for multitasking. We need to stop telling women they are better at remembering the shin guards at home and the finance reports at work because they are better multitaskers. We need everyone—fathers, employers, and children alike!—to understand the drain of multitasking on mothers' energy.

Women aren't better multitaskers—we are just asking them to do more work.

## Myth 2: Women Are Better Household Managers

The next myth that sets moms up to do more of the mental load process is the notion that women are better household managers, based on the false belief that women are inherently better at identifying their family's needs and demands. This myth is based on an outdated stereotype of women as nurturing, caring, and maternal with the counternarrative that men are bumbling, detached, and incompetent. Men are good at being managers at work but incompetent at home. And mothers are perfectly designed to track everything at home, which means they are distracted at work.

These are lies that set women up to step into this role of momager based on two flawed assumptions—that women are inherently better at doing the work and that fathers are bumbling idiots when it comes to children.

These big, fat lies are bad for dads too, as they deny fathers the joys of the ups and downs of parenthood. It means that fathers often feel less confident stepping into these roles—believing that mothers can just do them better, so they should let them do it. Add the lie that women are better multitaskers, and we can see how easily Mom's role as the boss of it all can stick.

This idea that mothers are naturally better managers at home is also bad for their mental load. They step into the mental load without any negotiation or discussion. They just do it all because they are told they are better at it all.

What this looks like across my interviews is that mothers often find themselves teeing up information for fathers to be the ultimate decision-makers or providing detailed plans for fathers to execute. Mothers are absorbing more of the mental load process than fathers because they are the ones in charge. One father in my interviews told me, "My wife usually gives me a list of things to do on the weekend—lists of what we need from the store, birthday parties to attend, or sports games to take the children to and places we can visit for a short day trip. She hands me the list and I execute."

This is typical of many dads who are overseeing the executing work, but with their wives doing all the rest: identifying, remembering, strategizing, deciding, coordinating, and monitoring what went into those lists. In my research I saw that this resulted in fathers feeling in charge despite the scale being tipped in their favor—their wives were still carrying the bulk of the weight. They were oblivious to all the behind-the-scenes work done to set them up for success.

The result of all this hard work is that fathers get to have experiences with children that go well, build connection, and are fun. Mothers' invisible work often goes unnoticed and unappreciated.

When men come to realize all the planning work that went into their well-executed days, they feel bad. But some describe mothers who find it difficult to step out of the mom-ager role to hand the entire task to their husbands. This means mothers need to figure out whether they *want* to remain in the role or let someone else take a turn.

Here again we need to use sociology as our superpower to help identify when outdated lies invade our thinking—that women are better at multitasking or at being the bosses of our families. These outdated social norms don't make sense anymore and they don't serve us well. They imbalance the scales and mean that fathers do only a part of the seven mental load stages, while mothers are staggering under the weight of the rest.

At best, men get off the hook for the work, and at worst, these myths exclude them from the joys of parenting. Mothers can, at times, be gatekeepers when they should be gate openers. Instead of inviting fathers into the process of juggling the many demands of modern family life, mothers sometimes cling to their "I can do it all, thankyouverymuch" mentality and other times feel it's easier to simply do everything themselves than to ask their partner to do it. Sometimes they hold on to too much because they are worried about the consequences of letting go.

Once mothers open the gates, we can see all the value of fathers' parenting: Fathers report better emotional well-being and connection to their children, share the housework and childcare more equally and for a longer time, and have children who are more likely to come to them when hurt or needing something.

Engaging fathers is good for fathers, their marriages, their children, their workplaces, and our communities. My interviews showed that when fathers became the primary caregivers of their children for one reason or another, it opened them up to the incredible mental load drain that parenting has on mothers and empathy for us holding it all together. Fathers told me about losing jobs or having a partner who got sick, which required them to step into family life as never before. This experience of being the go-to for their children shifted them in ways they could have never imagined, allowing them to experience the deeply rewarding role of loving, caring for, and nurturing another human. Through these experiences, they gained so much empathy for their children, themselves, and mothers everywhere who were doing this work day in and day out. It changed fathers for the better and allowed them to build out skills that otherwise would have lain dormant. Engaging fathers in the deep care of children underscores that mothers and fathers are equally valuable at this work, and anything telling us otherwise is pure nonsense that *must* be dropped.

## Myth 3: Your Relationship Is Equal— and Equality Means Everyone Does the Dishes

I am sorry to be the bearer of bad news, but . . . if you think your relationship is equal, you are probably wrong. I have been studying housework for over twenty years, and across the data I have looked at, studies I have read, studies I have designed, and people I have talked to, one thing is clear: Men still aren't doing as much as women.

When I tell people—especially men—this fact, they often tell me I am wrong.

They are different from their fathers. They are spending more time with their children, doing more dishes, and picking up around the house. They rattle off all the things they're responsible for, and it's a long list. This is all true—but they still aren't doing as much as women.

What is more, men often get to pick and choose the tasks they like to do, leaving the rest to their wives. This means that fathers often get to engage in the most pleasurable tasks—like cooking for the family or playing with the children—while mothers are left with the rest, like cleaning out the fridge or reorganizing children's closets. So even if couples think their chores are evenly split, the chores themselves can often be unequal, which leaves mothers with the lion's share of the drudgery.

I have stated evidence for this fact time and time again to the public, and I always get backlash from men. Usually, it is a man who will call in to the radio show to tell me that he shares the housework and childcare equally with his wife, and so I am wrong. Or I will get a message on one of my social media channels from a man who has had a life-changing moment after quitting his job to be a stay-at-home dad. Why am I not giving him credit?

I say the same thing that I will tell you here (in part so I can tell these dads to buy and read this book!): It is wonderful that men are stepping into more care. It is wonderful that men see the value of being a coparent to their children and copilot with their partners. It is wonderful that men are feeling the incredible joy of a deep and meaningful connection to their children. To the men of the world, I salute you—to love our families deeply is one of life's greatest gifts.

But you are either the absolute exception, or you are wrong because you don't see all that your wife is doing.

The latter is probably the truth.

I am not saying this because it is my opinion. I am saying this because we can't have that many unicorns when the data consistently shows that mothers do more. I have published countless articles using data from all around the world that all find the same conclusion.

Men, please don't put this book down! This is not an accusation. There will be no rescinding of your Good Husband and Good Dad cards; you don't even have to return your This Is What a Feminist Ally Looks Like T-shirt, if you have one. Using sociology to illuminate how women are pressured to take on an impossible load can light up everyone's life—yours too.

In part, this is because women are socialized to be helpers, trying to figure out what everyone needs before they even need it. This means women rarely have equality in their partnerships because they are often looking for what else they can do to make the family happy. This includes taking on the mental load of everything at home.

I showed this in an article that I wrote with Ana Weeks at the

University of Bath. We looked at twenty-one mental load tasks we do at home. These are mostly life organization tasks like noticing when the house needs to be tidied or keeping track of when the towels or sheets need to be changed.

What we found was that mothers were primarily responsible for 70 percent of these twenty-one mental load tasks. Fathers did some—like noticing when something needed repair or when the car needed service or researching and making financial decisions. But mothers held the rest—things like clearing out kids' clothes that no longer fit, scheduling doctors' appointments, and noticing when children's nails needed to be cut. They were researching childcare providers, tracking school supplies, and organizing after-school activities.

Mothers are doing the daily mental load churn, the stuff that happens each and every day, while fathers are holding on to the work that is, while important, rare.

The problem is that most of us think of equality through the lens of dividing and conquering specific tasks. While many of us may think we have equality because our husbands now do the dishes or mop the floors, the data doesn't show that. What we have is some sort of imbalance that is better than what our mothers or grandmothers had but far from a perfect split.

After studying these issues for decades, I have come across only one couple who has true equality—Isa and Steve, whom I will introduce you to in the next chapter. Yes, one. Is that kind of depressing? Maybe—but it's also instructive. It exposes what most of us are getting wrong: We are living with the myth that splitting the chores makes us equal and then getting frustrated when a split that seems equal still leaves us overwhelmed.

We need to take the blinders off and see our relationships for what they are—truly imperfect and probably unequal—to figure out what we want. For some of us, it may be a husband who does more of the toilet bowl cleaning, but for others, it may be sharing of the mental load around schooling. As one of my research papers showed, it may just be getting some recognition for all we are doing.

In this project, we used Swedish data on couples to see how differences in reporting on who did what at home impacted their relationships. We found that men who gave women more credit for the work they did at home had marriages that were more satisfying and stable and less likely to end in divorce. By contrast, the marriages in which men said they did more but their wives disagreed were the least satisfying for everyone—especially the wives, who spent much more time thinking about breaking up.

Sometimes we need our partners to see what we are doing, to recognize it and validate it, even if that doesn't necessarily mean they are equal sharers. In another research article, I identify this as an "economy of gratitude," based on the idea that sometimes what we're trading with our partners are a bunch of thank-yous for all the work we're doing for each other. We may not always be able to carry an equal load, but we definitely want some recognition when the scales are imbalanced, as well as a promise to take the heavier load when we need the support.

It doesn't always have to be equal—relationships ebb and flow—but it can't always be at the disadvantage of one (usually the mother). The first step is to get honest about what is going on and dispel the myth that splitting the chores is truly equal.

## WE MUST START DISPELLING THESE MYTHS

What do we do now? Well, we need to banish the pernicious myths that it's "naturally" easier for women to multitask or manage a household. We need to see that when these myths creep in, they make us less productive, happy, and engaged with life. We need to measure the impact gender myths have on draining our mental load energies. Most important, we must stop sharing them with one another and punishing mothers and fathers alike based on such nonsense.

In seeing that women—like all people—are terrible multitaskers and that men are capable of being excellent managers at work *and* at home, we can start to even the scales. We can start to see that the mental load is a complex process with seven pieces. We can start to have open conversations about how to share this work, without the underlying noise that some of us are better than others.

Using sociology as our sword and our shield, we can step into our own superpowers to create the lives we want to live by banishing expectations that we can do it all at once, or that we are the only ones who can save the day, or that we have equality when our guts tell us different.

*Chapter 4*

# Silencing Wasteful *Shoulds*, *Musts*, and *What-Ifs*

ISA AND STEVE ARE THE UNICORN COUPLE THAT I HAVE COME across in my decades of research, a model for equal sharing of all of it. Isa, my best friend and confidant, is a sociologist at a major public university. She is married to another academic, a wonderful economist named Steve. They have been married for years and have the most equal marriage I have ever seen across my decades of research. In fact, it is more equal than mine—an irony, given my area of study! In my household, tasks are allocated according to who likes to do the work, with the rest shared. But Isa and Steve are different—they split everything down the middle.

He cooks on Mondays, Wednesdays, and Fridays; she cooks on Tuesdays, Thursdays, and Saturdays. On Sundays they get takeout. The person who doesn't cook cleans up the dishes on those days. Their children, two of the most delightful humans ever born, get equal time with Mom and Dad. If Isa gets an hour or two to nap, decompress, or watch *The Real Housewives*, she then reciprocates this time for Steve to go work out, read a book, or watch his own favorite television show. They swap who is "on" with the kids on the weekends so each has some downtime to recover from work and caregiving.

It is Steve, not Isa, who tracks the household happenings to make sure everything is equal. He carries that mental load. I have asked Isa, "How did this happen?" Isa replied, "It's all Steve. He thinks anything other than equality is unfair. He keeps track of who is doing what to make sure it is fair to both of us. I know that if I married someone else, it would be much harder for me to get a fifty-fifty split. Social norms put women at a power disadvantage in most marriages, so you need a partner who is committed to seeing the work and sharing it equally to get anything close to an even split."

Steve is exactly this type of man, and just as crucially, he recognizes the mental load as work and factors it into his distribution of household tasks. He sees all the work as work and is committed to leading the conversation about keeping it equal—not equitable based on who needs what when (which can be a trap for women!) but equal. He knows that even well-meaning men can have blind spots that mean their marriages creep toward imbalance, hurt feelings, and resentment. Steve doesn't assume that if he does half the chores, he does half the work.

Rather, Steve knows each task carries its own load, and so he carries each in turn with Isa so no one feels too bogged down. Steve sees the world through the eyes of his partner and so is a critical part of the solution that I will tell you about at the end of the book.

Three cheers for Steve!

Despite her equitable arrangement, Isa deeply understands the ways in which social norms create traps for women everywhere, and having a partner like Steve means Isa can acutely see how these myths can create a serious drain on women's mental load energy.

Because Isa has this awareness, she can choose to ignore outdated norms, navigate antiquated institutions in more equitable ways, ask for help when she needs it, and resist gendered expectations that keep her further from her goals. Isa doesn't hold herself to sky-high standards, because she knows these are a trap. She doesn't hold others in her life to these expectations either, because she knows how they leave us with less—less time, less energy, less money, and less joy. A big reason that Isa can do this (and so can I!) is that we are trained sociologists.

Why is sociology such a powerful tool for this? Great question—and if you're asking it, you're way ahead of all my relatives, who are still asking, "What *is* sociology?" Well, Aunt Lisa, sociology trains us to see the ways our systems, norms, and roles create expectations about who we should be and influence the way we act. We often behave in ways intended to minimize perceived or real penalties for our actions. Many of us—men, women, kids, all of us—move through our worlds fearful of being judged for doing something wrong or imperfectly.

But when we stop and think about how we were socialized into certain roles or expectations, we can start to decide whether we agree with the expectations we're trying to meet and, even more powerfully, whether we actually care about the opinions of those who might disapprove of our getting it "wrong."

After this transformation, you can start to step around these land mines that surround us, making life feel more strategic and yourself less fearful of making a wrong step. Thinking like a sociologist means not getting bogged down in the constant internal narrative driven by socially concocted *shoulds*, *musts*, and *what-ifs* that don't align with what we truly care about or who we truly are.

Once we banish these harmful thoughts, we can move through the world with greater kindness, compassion, and grace for others when they ignore them as well. It creates a secret sisterhood that is bound by nonjudgment of others. I never feel bad when my friends forget my birthday or leave my text messages unread. I know those things aren't actually a reflection of their esteem for me, or of my value and safety as a social creature. Nor do I punish them if they fail to send me a thank-you note for a baby shower gift. I take it as a personal compliment that they know I'd rather have them spend that time lying on a couch with that baby.

This is the club that I want you to join! Our lives are too busy and beautiful to be holding ourselves to account for norms and judgments that have limited value and are a total drain. I love people unconditionally and truly understand that what may look like a slight is rarely about me. We are all doing our best with limited time and energy.

What this means in practice is that I don't think that I *should* always answer the phone when my best friend calls; if I don't have the energy to enter into that conversation with enthusiastic compassion and kindness, I'll call her back when I do. I don't worry *what if* my husband forgets the dessert when we go to a dinner party, because I know we can always solve that problem on the drive over and gain a funny story to tell the group (McDonald's sundaes, everyone!). I reject the idea that I *must* clean up the house and plan an exceptional menu before inviting friends over for dinner. Heck, I may not even change out of my pajama bunny suit when guests arrive, because it is just too comfortable. In turn, my friends know they have permission to also show up in their UGG slippers and sweatpants to enjoy the feast, without judgment. We will shine together without guilt, shame, or judgment, because those are the rules of the club.

Of course, individuals have their own personalities, preferences, strengths, and weaknesses. Some people prefer cleaner houses and more structured schedules, and some don't. This captures the wonderful variation of our being human. But more often, things we are told to care about and do are inconsistent with who we truly are as people. We do them because we are told to do them. We do them because we expect we will face a penalty if we don't. We do them to be good. This is the power of social norms: changing our choices, our lives, by holding us to standards we don't even believe in.

As a sociologist, I have learned to quiet the *shoulds*, *musts*, and *what-ifs* in my mind. How did I become so wise, patient, and wonderful (my words, of course)? I actively reject getting bogged down in the guilt and worry that anything less than perfect in my work, diet, exercise, parenting, marriage, friendships, and so on makes me a bad person. In my work, I see how *shoulds*, *musts*, and *what-ifs* make people act, behaving in ways contrary to their values because they anticipate judgments driven by cultural norms. So in my life, I make a conscious effort not to do that. I step into relationships, life, work, and greatness with less fear, anxiety, and guilt. I pause before catastrophizing, recognize what's happening, and interrupt the process of taking on a million *what-if* hypotheticals of what could go wrong. No, thanks! That delivery is not for my house. Return to sender.

Also: I am prepared for the fact that I will let other people down, sometimes, for not doing what they want me to do. And I see how women's value is so neatly tied to everything domestic, and I decide to actively reject such nonsense.

I know that perfection—especially around motherhood—is a fool's errand. As long as I am clear on why I am doing what I am doing, I can sleep well at night, because I know I can't conform to everyone's expectations and still be true to myself. I move through motherhood with little to no guilt. I am not like the typical American mother that my good friend Caitlyn Collins identifies in her research, who moves through motherhood riddled with guilt and worry. I do not believe that women putting their careers first means abandoning their families, which means that I do not feel like putting my career first means that I am putting my family second. I don't believe that I alone can pave the perfect future for my daughter. I won't move through the world feeling guilty for who I am, stressed about not being enough, and committed to burning through my mental load energy on "self-improvement" toward goals that won't sustain my soul.

I know that this type of guilt and worry leads to greater stress, more burnout, and less joy. I have seen the data; I have collected it myself. And I know there is no evidence suggesting that stressed-out, high-mental-load-bearing moms have happier or more successful children, more fulfilling careers, or happier lives. That knowledge frees us up to invest our mental loads in what we actually care about—and let go of what we don't.

I can stop shaving my legs and armpits because I hate this work (true) but still wear a lot of pink because I love the color (also true). Because I made these decisions consciously, I own them and feel good in them. They allow me to build a life that captures the imprint of my soul and to shine this light out to the world without the dimming of *shoulds*, *musts*, and *what-ifs*.

When I asked Isa how being a sociologist influenced her own marriage and family, she shared the same feelings about having her work inform her choice to reject the *shoulds*, *musts*, and *what-ifs* that get put on us through social norms.

Isa told me, "It made me pay more attention to how gender norms play out in my own life. I became more curious—it doesn't mean we always get it right, and Steve and I can act in ways that are unequal too. But we are quicker to identify this behavior as driven by social norms rather than inherent parts of our personalities. And then we can talk about them openly to brainstorm solutions that work for us both."

I witnessed this dynamic while on the phone with her. It was Steve's night to make dinner—a chicken casserole that went into an oven that started to smoke. "Hold on, Leah," Isa said to me. "You're going to get to hear us really fight now." But then, of course, there was no fighting, just a couple trying to identify solutions together.

Steve asked if he should take the chicken casserole to his mother's house to cook. Isa suggested she make burgers instead and they save the chicken casserole for another night. They were both actively trying to solve the problem rather than blaming each other for the issue. Partially, this was because neither of them "owned" the kitchen—it was equally shared. Neither felt it *should* go a certain way, so all options were on the table.

This is counter to some of my interviews, in which I heard mothers frustrated by the way their husbands cut the onions, loaded the dishwasher, or prepared the broccoli. I heard fathers frustrated by mothers' standards that pushed them out of the kitchen. These were mothers who were holding themselves to high expectations about what their dishes, broccoli, and onions *should* look like and deep guilt and worry about *what-ifs* that might reveal them as failures. They were operating under social norms that tell us there is only one way to do things (the right way!), squashing creativity. And that we *should* have perfect kitchens and perfect cooking to show that we are excelling in life.

Let me let you in on a little secret: Unless perfect kitchens and perfect onions are tied to your life's purpose, dreams, and goals, this is wasted energy.

Holding ourselves accountable to a range of *what-ifs*, *shoulds*, and *musts* keeps us in lives of less. The couples in my research who argued over how the dishwasher was loaded and the onions cut, their worry and guilt driven by *shoulds*, *musts*, and *what-ifs*, strained their relationships. None of this happened between Steve and Isa, because neither of them thought it all *should* go a certain way, and so they didn't feel this mistake made them less competent, capable, or good partners or parents.

This was a true nonissue for Isa and Steve because neither of their identities was tied to it. They just didn't buy into the gender norm that told them, *I should have a perfect casserole to show how much I love my partner and children.* Or *What if I served my family a smoky, burned casserole? Would that make me a failure?* Casserole was just casserole, so Isa quickly air-fried veggie burgers instead. Steve would clean the oven tomorrow and the chicken casserole would be saved for another meal.

## HOLDING OURSELVES TO HIGHER STANDARDS THAN EVERYONE ELSE

How do you start to think more like a sociologist to see whether you are tying too much of your identity to what happens at home? How do we use these insights to reduce some of the wasteful churn that drives guilt, worry, and pressure we might feel around our roles as mothers? Let's start with something simple. Think about your level of agreement—from strongly agree to strongly disagree—with the following statements:

1. A working mother can establish just as warm and secure a relationship with her children as a mother who does not work.

2. A preschool child is likely to suffer if his or her mother works.

These two questions are a standard way that sociologists measure gender norms, and it probably won't surprise you that most women and men report agreement to the first and some disagreement to the second. These questions have been asked for decades, and over time, people have become more egalitarian in their expectations of mothers' work and family lives, especially among younger generations. Now the answers seem like givens; *of course* mothers should be able to work, and *of course* children will be okay.

But the challenge is that we may hold *ourselves* to more traditional gender norms than we apply when we think about others. It's one thing to ask hypothetical questions, but if I were to ask you these questions about your own child, would you answer them differently?

For example, if you're a mother, do you agree with the statement that *you* can establish an equally warm and secure relationship with your child if you work? Or do you think that being home more is critical to *your child's* parental relationship? Do you hold the same things true of your partner? Or is it okay for them to work outside the home—full time and long hours—but not you?

Do you hold yourself to more stringent expectations than other women? What does this do to your mental load?

When I asked research participant Lily, a divorced mother to an eight-year-old son, these questions, she realized that she expected her family life to look more traditional than those of other women. Lily strongly agreed that women should be able to work outside the home and that children could have equally strong relationships with their mothers who worked as with those who stayed home. But she felt incredible guilt about her full-time career and often worried her child was suffering because of her absences. Yes, as a single mother they absolutely needed the income to survive. But Lily felt trapped—her work hours were set and she couldn't do them from home.

Lily also felt like she *should* be the type of mother who spent more one-on-one time with her son. She spent a lot of her time wrestling with the *what-ifs* of all the hypothetical ways her full-time job was failing her son and damaging him forever.

Lily would wake up at 5:00 a.m. to make a special lunch to show her son how much she loved him before she rushed to the office. She would stop work early to spend a few hours with him before lights-out for bedtime and then work into the night to make up the lost work time. Lily also responded instantly to her son's emotional turmoil, even during critical work meetings, created magic-making experiences during the weekend, and drove hours across town to connect her son to his school friends.

Lily spent an incredible amount of mental load energy trying to compensate for her time away. It felt as though the only person being sacrificed in this equation was Lily, and yet she constantly felt like she was to blame—she was a bad mother for working. Lily felt like she *should* be doing things differently. All of this triggered a huge amount of worry work that crowded out her mental load.

## WORRY WORK: FEELING LIKE GOOD ENOUGH IS NEVER GOOD ENOUGH

Worry work is often driven by the fact that mothers believe they are so critical to children's futures that without their detailed attention, everything will go awry and their children will be permanently scarred.

Yes, mothers should invest time in their children and enjoy the benefits that these investments bring.

But the social norms about a mother being the singular contributor to her children's lifelong success is overblown. It is a myth and an outdated social norm that our children's success rises and falls based on mothers' efforts alone. The consequence is that mothers hold themselves to sky-high standards about what is good enough and spend a tremendous amount of energy burning through their mental load energy with worry work. It riddles them with *should*s and *musts*, but it also triggers a range of *what-ifs* that undermine mothers' confidence and make the whole parenting experience much less enjoyable.

The additional fact that life is unpredictable means mothers are constantly building contingency plans that are driven by worry work. All of this compounding drain of *what-ifs* and *shoulds* and *musts* is carried by mothers alone.

It goes something like this: *We have an upcoming trip. Do we have all the things we need? Sunscreen. Check. Underwear and socks. Check. Toothpaste and toothbrush. Check. Wait, what if it rains? Should we bring an umbrella or jacket? Or do we just buy something there? Or do we just stay in the hotel and have a rainy movie day? What if one of the children gets sick? Do we have medicines for earaches, upset stomachs, or diaper rash? Or should we just buy these there too? And what if . . . ? Should we . . . ?*

Sometimes worry work can be small and in fact leads to more informed decision-making and better outcomes. Contingency plans of bringing extra clothes just in case or making sure keys have a home to be easily found can be the difference between a good day and a bad day. But other times worry work can spiral into rumination, anxiety, and feeling overwhelmed. It can become *what-ifs*, *shoulds*, and *musts* wasted on hypotheticals.

The problem is that, as my research shows, this worry work is mostly held by mothers, and it triggers a huge amount of guilt when things don't go to plan.

It feels as if it is all their responsibility.

I don't do a lot of worry work for my family. I don't think that things going wrong are my problem. I rarely worry about the judgment of others when I violate expectations of "good motherhood" or "good womanhood." Oh, and I am messy. There are books stacked everywhere, an astonishing number of shoes in the hallway, and, between me and my daughter, a sweater (or two, or six) thrown on the back of every chair in sight. The kitchen, it's a safe bet, has dishes in the sink as we speak.

Was I always this way? Absolutely not.

I used to stress-clean before guests would come, and block the doorway when an unexpected friend showed up, so they did not think they were invited in. But the more I excavated my own anxieties about being seen as messy, and the more I saw that no one benefited from my believing that having a clean house was important to my being a "good woman" and a valuable person, the more vehemently I rejected the idea. I got clear on my goals, my dreams, and what I truly value in my life. As it turned out, an immaculate house wasn't on my list.

What was: more energy working, talking, laughing, and spending time with friends and family who fill my soul. This means I don't do a panicked deep clean before people come to my house—I let them into the mess.

Do I feel bad about this? Honestly, no—if people can't see my value beyond the mess, then they aren't my people. I know the science disproves a lot of myths about mess: that visible mess is indicative of a disorganized or even mentally ill mind (false), that it's a clear sign of laziness (nope), that it's evidence the homeowner is hostile to gender norms (okay, that one might be true—I confess I haven't reviewed the literature). I have dropped all the internal narrative saying, *I* should *clean my house before guests come.* Frankly, I often have more important things that need to be done than cleaning my kitchen. I banished the internal dialogue asking, What if *they don't like me after seeing what my life* truly *looks like?* I still invite people over because I want to spend time with them. I don't think creating a perfect experience will make us better friends.

If I had to have a clean house before I could do the other stuff—writing books, laughing with friends who drop in unexpectedly, and spending my weekends out on adventures—all of these wonderful experiences would never happen. I just didn't have enough time, so something had to give, and the thing that gave was worrying about the *shoulds*, *musts*, and *what-ifs* that often never came to pass. But the residual warmth of the company of my loved ones stays with me and motivates me to do more, be more, and give more.

Sometimes this works in my favor. Let me give you a recent example from my life. I was awoken on a Tuesday morning by a neighbor who told me that my car, which was parked right in front of my house, had been broken into the night before. Well, "broken into" is a bit of a lie, because I often don't lock my car doors. The car had been opened and someone had rifled through it. As I approached the car, with its doors flung open, I started to assess the damage.

What did they take? The unopened bag of pretzels on the floor? No. The mud-covered shoes my daughter left in the car after a recent adventure? No. The spare change that was in the center console and seemed to be covered in some sort of french fry and soda combination? Not that. What about the four jackets for when it got cold, backpacks full of homework, and smattering of socks that were in the back seat? Those were also there, fully intact. And my prescription sunglasses that I thought made me look so cool? Tried on and then thrown onto the seat for me to keep.

What had the robber taken?

Absolutely nothing.

My husband was a bit ashamed: "You know, all those neighbors looked into your car and probably thought less of you for being so messy." I assured him that I was not worried about their judgment—I am doing just fine, and they are lucky to live close to me. Then I reminded him that this was a clear victory: The sheer power of my mess warded off potential theft!

Let's be real, though—it's one thing to let some balls drop when it comes to housekeeping. It's another thing entirely to let go of our sense that we can and should control as much as possible on behalf of the people we love, especially those we're responsible for. I worry about my daughter regularly. I worry about her safety and encourage her to make better decisions. I can't watch her horse-riding lessons because I am terrified that she will get thrown off (she has, multiple times, obviously, but she hops right back on). But there are other things I refuse to worry about: I don't worry about whether the fact that she has worn her Snuggie for three days straight reflects poorly on me as a mother. I want her to do her homework but if, in the end, she doesn't, that is her problem to solve. I don't think that she is a reflection of my competence.

I want to hear about her life, give her deep empathy, and provide her with my insights. But I always tell her that my opinion is one of many and that I am not always right. She should take my opinion as one among many and make decisions that make sense for her. I am limited in my vision, and she is wise. I often get things wrong because I can't see the world through a younger person's eyes—I have limitations. I encourage her to focus on building her own passions regardless of what I want her to do.

I don't think being a good mom is measured by my daughter's successes. I do not buy the idea that has been sold to us since birth that I, as a mother, am solely responsible for the happiness and success of my child or that her achievements are a reflection of my efforts as a mother and overall value as a human. I am a key player, of course, but I am not the linchpin of her life. The world is too complex for me to hold all the cards.

I won't participate in societal expectations that set me up for failure, guilt, and worry. I won't listen to this nonsense norm that mothers' love is the only love to ward against all ills, which gets packaged and repackaged to make us feel incomplete. I won't let these ruin the magical experience of being her mom.

I want my daughter to build her life in a way that showcases her unique talents, and I am there to be her cheerleader on the sidelines. I want her to create a team of adults, friends, and family who can guide her through various challenges she is facing and for her to turn to them for advice. I want her to have many ideas, solutions, and supports around her, of which my voice and my ideas are just one. I will pick her up when she falls, but her falls are life lessons, and I don't want to remove these.

I am not a bad mother if my daughter does bad things. And I am not a good mother if my daughter does good things. I don't carry guilt around my parenting decisions, nor a huge amount of worry work driven by *what-ifs*, *shoulds*, and *musts*. I am here to love, support, and celebrate. She is here to live her own life, make her own mistakes, and grow.

Using sociology as my superpower, I see that my job as a mother is one of many that I will carry across my life, and these roles are equally important to creating my best life. There is less pressure on getting this one thing—motherhood—right, because I know it won't be perfect and we are all going to be okay.

This thinking work ultimately makes our family life lighter for all of us.

This is the struggle that many mothers face—there is just too much pressure on them to get this whole mothering thing perfect and a constant drumbeat from society writ large that any missteps will scar our children for life. I am here to tell you that this message is nonsense and that linking our success to that of our children robs us of joy, health, and lightness in our roles as parents. In no other big and important area do we say one person is solely responsible for it all—every CEO has a team behind them to make sure all the work gets done. Mothers need the same, and we need to free ourselves from the expectation that we are solely responsible for it all going right.

## IDENTIFYING YOUR CARE FACTOR

For the next step in your mental load journey, we need to get clear on the power of norms that create an incredible pressure on women and men alike through the constant *what-ifs*, *shoulds*, and *musts*. Let's start asking ourselves, *Do I really care about this? Or am I just worried others will judge me? Who are these others, and do I care if they judge me? Or am I a badass, wonderful person building a career, an incredible family, great friends, and passions, no matter the stickiness of my floors?* I think for most of us, it is the last statement that is the truth, and we need to hold on to this for dear life.

Once we do this, we can see these norms for what they are: ways of thinking that don't fit the lived realities of modern women, who hold more education, earnings, employment, and power than ever before. What if we just start saying to one another and to ourselves that working doesn't make us bad mothers? Or that the cleanliness of our homes does not reflect our moral character or make us good people? Or that we have been carrying around the weight of outdated expectations about "good motherhood" derived from a time long, long gone?

What if we see that making us feel bad about our mothering is big business and this aching to be good and worthy keeps us searching for the next fix? What if we saw that this was all a Ponzi scheme to get us to do more, be more, and consume more, all at the expense of ourselves? What if we could pull apart these pressures to take the load off, drop this wasteful thinking, and save ourselves a lot of time, money, and stress? What if we freed ourselves from the constant feeling that we are somehow terrible mothers, despite spending more time, money, and energy on our children than any other generation? What if we gave some of these resources back to ourselves?

These are the kinds of *what-ifs* that I want you to embrace. Let's banish the *what-ifs* about people judging us for failing to be perfect all the time and embrace the mantra "Good enough is good enough." Despite messages to the contrary, we can't have it all—a perfect house, well-kept kids, a full-time job, and our sanity.

Sometimes the wheels fall off. Sometimes husbands do below-average jobs. Sometimes kids wash whites with darks. It is not a reflection on us as people, and we shouldn't waste our precious energy on these things. I often think, *If I were lying on my deathbed, would I care about this?* The answer is usually a forceful no. Taking this approach helps me respond to the fact that life is messy and imperfect and extend myself grace and understanding through it all.

To activate sociology as our superpower, we need to carry worry work that makes our decision-making better. We need to drop the rumination that pushes us further away from our goals. We need to use our mental load energies to create the world we want rather than using them to survive the world we have inherited. Rejecting outdated gender norms has helped me to lighten my mental load, invest in the things I truly value, and create more joy in my life.

By the end of this book, you will too.

It is in this spirit that I introduce you to the Mental Load Audit.

# Part II
# The Unload

GETTING A HANDLE ON OUR MENTAL LOADS CAN SEEM INSURmountable. It can feel difficult to figure out what to do about it, especially when many of us are operating in mental load burnout. Sure, we carry a mental load associated with ensuring that family vacations are fun, but what are we supposed to do, stop having family vacations? Yes, we carry a mental load around children's academic achievement, but what are we supposed to do, stop helping with homework?

Dropping the mental load seems like a simple solution that will throw our lives into chaos. Yet mothers are exhausted from their mental loads and desperate for a solution—and fast.

When I talk to mothers about their mental loads, I see desperation in their eyes. They need a solution that doesn't push them into the shame, guilt, or worry of not doing everything for everyone. They need a solution that releases them from these traps and allows all their greatness and glory to shine. They need a solution that allows them to *be* more without asking them to *give* more.

I promise you that I have that solution: the Mental Load Audit. In the next chapters, I'll ask you to start treating the mental load the same way we treat another precious resource—money. I'll help you get strategic with your spending.

When I say this in my talks to Fortune 500 companies, and when I share it with my lab's focus groups, a wave of recognition washes over people's faces. For many, it's the first time they have thought of their mental load energy as valuable and finite. This framing creates intentionality and care around habits and patterns we adopted, without much thought, a long time ago.

Again and again, women who conducted an audit of their mental load said the process helped them understand where all their precious mental load energy was going. It gave them clear insight into when they were allocating their mental load energy to things that weren't important. It encouraged them to stop burning through mental load energy with rumination grounded in *what-ifs*, *shoulds*, and *musts* driven by outdated social norms they had, unknowingly, internalized—to their detriment. It supported them in figuring out whether they were doubling up on mental loads with partners, grandparents, or other people in their lives, and whether this overinvestment was truly worth it.

It enabled them to realign their energy to invest strategically in ways that were enriching their lives, bringing them closer to their values and goals, and making deposits in relationships with their favorite people—including with themselves. It let them develop their own mental load wish list to guide them as they marched step by step toward their wildest and most audacious dreams. It made the spending more visible and the rewards clearer to everyone in their families—most important, to themselves.

For many people, the Mental Load Audit process was hard and confronting work. It was the first time they'd tracked where their mental load energy was being spent and realized how far investing in themselves had fallen down the list.

It showed that, in many households, mothers were doing the bulk of the mental load for the entire family. It put in black and white that mothers' dreams and passions had long been starved. It provided concrete proof that mothers had long been operating in deficit, as well as the toll this was taking on them emotionally, physically, and spiritually.

It showed fathers whole categories of the mental load where they didn't contribute, meaning that their wives were carrying these in their entirety and alone. It helped everyone see that, for a long time, they'd been draining their mental load capacity on people and things that didn't matter, distancing them further from what they truly valued.

Completing the Mental Load Audit was a catalyst moment for many mothers to have honest conversations about the urgency of setting up new patterns that allocated the mental load more equitably in the family. Despite its being difficult work, mothers told me that the Mental Load Audit was transformational. For the first time ever, they could quantify the costs of the drains on their mental load energy and start parsing superfluous spending from enriching spending. Mothers could consciously decide when to spend mental load energy and when to conserve it. They were empowered to say no strategically, because they were now clear on how mental load spending was working against them. They started to prioritize mental load spending that brought them the most meaning, excitement, and joy.

Our goal isn't to get rid of mental load spending—it's to get smart with where we're investing our resources.

Before we start in the next chapter, let me tell you a bit about my intention in creating this audit. I wanted to create a process that helped women unlock their incredible talents by reducing their mental loads. But I've conducted enough in-depth interviews to know that any solution that adds to mothers' already overtaxed mental loads is no solution at all.

As you walk through this audit, I'll provide worksheets for those of you who love an activity. But for those of you who don't, these steps can be done without lifting a pen.

This process is about raising awareness of your mental load and how you spend it—prompting you to keep your dreams alive, even when they're buried in the hustle and bustle of daily life. I'm here to help you to start building toward the life you deserve by deepening your understanding of how and when you're spending your mental load, in both profitable and unprofitable ways. I want you to start seeing the true value of being you, to remind you that you are exceptional and worth the investment.

You can audit your mental load anywhere and anytime, with or without a pen and paper. There's no right or wrong way to do the Mental Load Audit, so pick your adventure and enjoy the journey. By the end, you'll have a mental load that is lighter, purpose driven, and exciting.

As I walk you through the Mental Load Audit, I'll showcase the experiences of parents across my research projects who have already done this work. You'll see where they got stuck, how they found their way through, and where they discovered profound insights.

Like any new budgeting approach, auditing your mental load will have highs and lows. The goal is to draw on these insights so you can strategically align your energy. You'll see how others did this, but my dream for you, dear reader, is to develop a strategy that works best for *you*. Here we go!

## Chapter 5

# Identify What Is Draining Your Mental Load

THE WORD *AUDIT* CAN SOUND SCARY, CONJURING UP VISIONS OF TAX agents knocking on your door and asking for receipts for everything you've purchased over the past two decades. If they find you neglected to declare so much as a dozen eggs on some random form you didn't know existed, you'll either have to pay a hefty fine or get hauled off to jail.

However, audits don't have to be scary. Some organizations even voluntarily submit to audits, and some do this every single year. Why would they willingly subject themselves to this? *Because you can't fix what you don't know is a problem.* By conducting an audit, organizations can clearly see their income and expenses, identifying places where their money is well spent and places they may need to scale back. They can also see how well their expenses align with their mission, values, and priorities, and adjust accordingly.

The same applies to our personal finances. If we're consistently going over our annual household budget, we need to audit ourselves, sitting down and looking at our bank account to figure out where the money is coming from and going, and how well that aligns with our values and priorities. Ignoring the problem won't fix it or make it go away. In fact, it will only make it worse. In this case, ignorance is *not* bliss.

All of these concepts relate to the Mental Load Audit, a process that helps you identify how you're spending your precious mental load energy. In later chapters, I'll show you what to do with all the information you gather using the tools provided below. For now, just leverage your sociologist superpower by getting curious and collecting your data.

## MEET CHRISTIE AND ERIC

On my socials, I posted a call for couples who wanted to audit their mental loads together as part of a research project. Christie and Eric, a married couple from Norfolk, Virgina, responded and kindly agreed to participate.

They share two school-age children, a son named Riley, who is eight years old, and a daughter, Kalissa, who just celebrated her tenth birthday. Both Christie and Eric work full time, but her job has more flexibility, so she's usually home to greet the children after school. Eric's job requires more face-to-face interaction, and he saves his vacation days to spend time with their children during school breaks.

They look like many couples across my interviews. They're both hardworking, career oriented, and dedicated to prioritizing time with their children.

When we finally got together for an interview, I started with a question I ask all my interviewees: Who does more of the mental load for the family?

"Christie," they said in unison, without hesitation.

"Eric, can you estimate your contribution?" I asked him.

"Oh, I think we have a close to fifty-fifty split. I know Christie does more, but I think I do a lot too. I think our answers will be pretty close to each other," he said confidently.

I knew Eric would be wrong, but I humored him. I've spent decades studying what people do at home, and I know that our perceptions often don't reflect reality.

For instance, a research paper published in the early 2000s showed that married heterosexual men and women are both bad at estimating how much housework they do. We all think we spend more time cleaning our houses than we do. The researchers first asked participants: How many hours did you spend cleaning your house last week? Then they tracked the actual time people spent cleaning their houses. The researchers found that when you ask people about their general time, they give a much higher number. For many of us, what feels like an hour cleaning our bathrooms is only forty-five minutes. We tend to overestimate.

Additionally, these researchers discovered that men are particularly bad at estimating compared to women—men think they're doing way more housework than they're doing. Here's where things get interesting: The study found that women are better at estimating how much housework their husbands are doing—even better than husbands themselves.

What does this mean for the mental load? It means that if I wanted the most accurate answer about Eric's contribution, I probably should have asked Christie.

I've seen this in my own work too. I wrote a paper with Ana Weeks from the University of Bath, explaining that men typically do more of the mental load for only two tasks at home: tracking the family finances and ensuring that home maintenance is completed. This leaves mothers with the mental load for everything else at home.

But when we surveyed married fathers about how much of the family's total mental load they carry, they thought they carried a lot—even though, in reality, they carried a fraction of the mental load tasks. As with housework, fathers are bad at estimating their mental load contributions.

I didn't share any of this research with Eric or Christie yet, because I didn't want to influence their Mental Load Audit results. Plus, I was intrigued to see whether their split would be close to fifty-fifty.

Regardless, this would be an insightful exercise for Eric and Christie, who, for the first time in their relationship, would start to unpack their mental loads. Thinking about all the parents who came before them, I expected that completing the audit would stir up emotions.

"As you're going through this process, please be patient and kind with each other. It's not always going to be easy, but I promise it will be worth it," I told them. The last thing I wanted was for them to be blindsided if any strong feelings emerged along the way. I assured them that this is a natural response to any process where we dive deep into our spending after keeping it hidden for so long.

Christie and Eric nodded their understanding.

"Are you ready to get started?" I asked them.

They looked at each other and then back at me before excitedly saying, "Yes!"

## PHASE 1: IDENTIFY WHAT IS DRAINING YOUR MENTAL LOAD ACCOUNT

The first thing I asked Christie and Eric to do was track their mental load spending. I explained that this is like looking at bank statements and examining all the charges to the account. I wanted them to start thinking about which mental load types they were each carrying and pin down who was spending what.

Were they allocating the mental load evenly, or was Christie holding more than Eric? What about grandparents or aunties or nannies or children? Were there areas where Christie and Eric were duplicating the same tasks, resulting in categories where the family was giving more than 100 percent? And, if so, was this spending worth it or wasteful?

## Calculating Your Mental Load Spending

Below is a copy of table 1, "Calculate Your Mental Load Spending," which you can use to start tracking where your mental load energy is being spent. You can either complete this on your own or, if you have one, with your partner. (As a reminder, all of the Mental Load Audit worksheets are also in an appendix at the back of the book.)

In the far-left column, you'll see the eight mental load types listed: life organization, emotional support, relationship hygiene, magic making, dream building, individual upkeep, safety, and meta-care. To complete the activity, you'll need to first start raising your own awareness of all the mental load you do. This could be as simple as watching your thoughts over a few hours or as detailed as making a list of everything that comes into your head over a few weeks. The first step is seeing how these eight mental load types come into your mind. You will need to consider the amount of work required for each mental load type in your household.

Then you'll calculate what percentage of that work—from 0 for none to 100 for all—each person in the family does, whether it's you, your partner, or someone else, such as a grandparent, a nanny, a friend, or your children.

Note that sometimes a percentage might total more than 100, when tasks are duplicated because we give more than 100 percent to a mental load type. (For example, if you and your husband both contribute 75 percent to "safety," that totals 150 percent.) That's okay, but we need to see it to identify whether that duplication is necessary.

From hours spent in interviews, I know that mothers are typically the source of duplication. They might go back and redo work someone else just completed. Like Stacy, who'd assign her children chores but then follow them around and make sure the chores had been "done right." If they hadn't, she'd jump in and "fix" it, leaving her both exhausted and frustrated at the end of the day. Or Marla, who'd delegated daily school pickup to her husband but then, throughout the day, worried that he'd forget. On days when she was particularly concerned about this possibility—for instance, when he had an important presentation at work and was thus preoccupied—she'd debate sending him a friendly text reminder. But this would lead to more worry about disrupting his workday, as well as potentially making him think she didn't trust him. Although she'd technically delegated the task, it still weighed down her mental load because she couldn't release herself from being the "household manager" who ensured it was all done right.

Sometimes duplication is useful, because it helps ensure everything goes smoothly for the family. But other times this is wasted spending, because it drains your mental load capacity without providing a clear and tangible benefit. It also makes delegation ineffective because we still hold on to the mental load.

To figure out your mental load spending, you can turn to table 1 below, where you can start to calculate what portion of that mental load spending you are doing and what is being done by others.

This will help you figure out if you, like Marla, have delegated the work but kept its mental load.

## Table 1: Calculate Your Mental Load Spending

*Note: Sometimes these will add up to more than 100 percent. This indicates that you are duplicating the work.*

| Mental Load Type | Percentage of this mental load that I am responsible for within the family (0–100%) | If partnered: Percentage of this mental load that my partner is responsible for within the family (0–100%) | Percentage of this mental load that others (e.g., children, grandparent, nanny) are responsible for within the family (0–100%) | Is any of this mental load being duplicated? (yes, no, or maybe) |
|---|---|---|---|---|
| Life organization | | | | |
| Emotional support | | | | |
| Relationship hygiene | | | | |
| Magic making | | | | |
| Dream building | | | | |
| Individual upkeep | | | | |
| Safety | | | | |

| Mental Load Type | Percentage of this mental load that I am responsible for within the family (0–100%) | If partnered: Percentage of this mental load that my partner is responsible for within the family (0–100%) | Percentage of this mental load that others (e.g., children, grandparent, nanny) are responsible for within the family (0–100%) | Is any of this mental load being duplicated? (yes, no, or maybe) |
|---|---|---|---|---|
| Meta-care | | | | |
| **REFLECTIONS:**<br>How did you feel after doing this assessment? Did you gain any insights? Is there anything else you want to add? | | | | |

## Identifying the Frequency of Mental Load Spending

After they completed table 1, I asked Christie and Eric to fill out table 2, "Identify the Frequency of Mental Load Spending." I instructed them to complete this table independently and not share their answers with each other until they were done so they wouldn't sway each other's thinking. I anticipated that Christie's mental load was drawn down more frequently than Eric's, even for the same tasks.

Mental load tasks are conducted at different intervals. First you have the daily activities, like keeping track of who has clean underwear, a nutritious snack, and a bottle of water before leaving for school in the morning. Other things you do multiple times a week, such as laundry or grocery shopping. Some tasks, like disinfecting your children's karate mouthguards or washing all the bedding, are tackled a few times a month or once a month. Still other duties happen less frequently—like planning birthdays, holiday celebrations, or family vacations.

Of course, unanticipated mental load tasks pop up all the time: flat tires, broken-down cars, illness in your immediate family, and so forth. Although you might not be able to identify how often these things happen, if they tend to happen within the course of any given year, you can list them in the "Other" category. Or you can be like one deeply wise parent from my interviews whose "Other" category just noted "unexpected chaos."

If you want to be able to budget your mental load, it's important to be aware of how often the mental loads make withdrawals from the account. Revisiting the personal finance analogy, table 1 helps you see what percentage of your mental load budget is being allocated to different "expenses," and table 2 helps you see how often those expenses are being paid out.

And I'll give you the same advice I gave Christie and Eric: If you and a partner are both completing this table, don't share until you're finished so you don't skew each other's responses. This isn't a group activity, nor should we look over each other's shoulders to see what is the "right" answer. This is deep thinking and reflecting work that is best done alone.

If you are a single parent, you may find that you are holding all the work across all the categories. This was a main finding from the work Ana Weeks and I published, where we showed that single moms and dads held more of both the daily mental load tasks and those that happen less frequently. Single parents were doing it all. When I talked to moms who were divorced or separated, I heard something different. Some told me about holding the mental load related to children who were supposedly under the care of their dad. Yet others found that shared custody gave them something magical—a break from all the work, including the mental load.

Regardless of which camp you are in, getting an understanding of your spending and its frequency is critical. It will help you with the next exercises in this book, in which you figure out what should be reduced, delegated, or dropped altogether.

### Table 2: Identify the Frequency of Mental Load Spending

| Mental Load Type | How often does this draw on your mental load energy (e.g., daily, multiple times a week, a few times a month, monthly, yearly, never)? |
|---|---|
| Life organization | |
| Emotional support | |
| Relationship hygiene | |
| Magic making | |
| Dream building | |
| Individual upkeep | |
| Safety | |
| Meta-care | |
| Other | |

## Weighing the Costs and Credits of Mental Load Tasks

Then I gave Christie and Eric the final table, "Weigh the Costs and Credits of Mental Load Tasks," to start thinking about the costs of each category.

When you complete this table, it's critical to be completely honest about how these different tasks affect you. As I said in earlier chapters, sometimes our thoughts and feelings around a responsibility are influenced by *shoulds*, *musts*, and *what-ifs*, as well as the myths we've been told.

We can look at children's birthday parties to see how this plays out in some women's lives.

Linda has one school-age daughter, and planning her birthday party each year wears Linda down so much she feels like she needs to sleep for two days straight afterward. She tells herself she shouldn't get so bogged down—it's only one day a year, after all. But everything about the event—from trying to figure out what to put in the goodie bags to the noise of rambunctious children bouncing around her house to the cleanup afterward—exhausts her. For her, this mental load task is a cost.

In contrast is Marcie, whose three children have birthdays in September—which makes it her favorite month of the year. She loves spending time coming up with a theme for each party, then creating custom invitations to email to her kids' friends' parents. Crafting elaborate decorations and fun activities might be the best part of all. When the month is over, she wishes her kids had birthdays to celebrate every month. For her, this mental load task is a credit.

And then there's Abby, who has two young children. She could do without all the planning and postparty cleanup, but the party itself she loves—hanging out with her fellow parents, delighting in her kids having fun with their friends, eating ice cream cake to her heart's content. The children's birthday parties are a mixed bag, so for her, this mental load task is both a cost and a credit.

Not all mental load tasks are a drain—some are credits to our accounts, bringing us incredible joy, enrichment, and excitement. Completing them gives us a sense of accomplishment and replenishes us.

And, because life is often shades of gray, some mental load tasks can be both a drain and a credit, so that should be noted as well.

## Table 3: Weigh the Costs and Credits of Mental Load Tasks

| Mental Load Type | Which mental load tasks within this category are *costly*? | Which mental load tasks within this category are *crediting*? | Which mental load tasks within this category are *both* crediting and costly? |
|---|---|---|---|
| Life organization | | | |
| Emotional support | | | |
| Relationship hygiene | | | |
| Magic making | | | |
| Dream building | | | |
| Individual upkeep | | | |
| Safety | | | |
| Meta-care | | | |
| Other | | | |

## Christie and Eric's Mental Load Audit Results

Christie and Eric were excited to start tracking their spending, so I sent them off to complete this first phase of the audit and asked them to check in with me the following week.

The next time I saw Christie and Eric, their body language had shifted a bit. The excitement had waned, and their nonverbal communication signaled that the audit had sparked something.

Tracking their spending had helped them see that their mental loads weren't being spent equally and that the costs looked different for each of them. Christie was spending her mental load on a lot of small yet costly things.

"I'm the one who says yes to bringing cupcakes to the school bake sale, organizing weekly date nights, and remembering to move the laundry into the dryer," she told me. "On their own, none of these things are particularly damaging. But the more I thought about it, I realized these were often scattered across mental load types, which requires switching between them. Over time, they add up to a lot, and it makes me feel like I'm 'always on.'"

Christie further shared that because each addition felt small, she found herself saying yes to things, even though she could feel her capacity was low or near burnout.

"I just don't want to disappoint anyone, especially my family," she said, glancing at her husband. "Saying no is hard—it feels like an act of betrayal. Saying yes feels good . . . until I have to deliver on my promises. Then I get mad at myself for saying yes to everyone." I tell Christie that sometimes we get too automatic in our *yes*es, and this leads many women, like her, to feeling overwhelmed by it all. We have to get comfortable with *no*, as it is always easier to convert a *no* into a *yes* than vice versa.

This tendency resulted in Christie being the one who stayed up late at night preparing for the next day, while Eric spent this time playing with the kids, relaxing, or recharging. This dynamic made her feel overwhelmed, exhausted, and resentful.

"Christie, even though these mental load tasks are small, when they're stacked on top of each other, they create a big drain," I told her. "It's like draining your bank account slowly, through small and sustained spending: fifteen dollars a month to Netflix, ten dollars to Spotify, four dollars a day to Starbucks, fifteen dollars to daily lunches. Over time, they draw your balance down to zero—or even into the negative—even though each task feels so minor."

She was burning through her mental load capacity with a series of small and less costly tasks, but they were a mental load drain nonetheless.

I explained to Christie and Eric that another way mental load energy can be drained is by big, costly mental load tasks. This is similar to blowing all your money on a big-ticket item, a lot of spending in one go. They can be things that are clearly bad and stressful, such as a family member falling ill or losing a job. Or they can be events that are quite positive but also stressful, like moving to a new house, starting a new job, or giving birth to a baby. Big drains can come from big events, and Christie and Eric might have experienced this type of drain as well.

"We've dealt with something like this recently," Christie said.

"My dad was recently diagnosed with heart disease," Eric shared. "He and I are close, so his diagnosis has been a big drain on my mental load."

"We spend quite a bit of time with Eric's parents, and during the past few visits, I noticed that his dad seemed short of breath. I called my mother-in-law to check on him, and it was like the floodgates opened. She talked at length about how bad his health was and how concerned and frustrated she was that he wasn't doing anything about it," Christie told me.

"What did you do next?" I asked her.

"Well, I spent weeks going back and forth between my in-laws and Eric to make something happen. I finally suggested that Eric should take his dad out to dinner to encourage him to take action on his health. After that, he finally started taking the health concerns seriously," she said.

The diagnosis had drained Christie's mental load in two ways: first through a lot of little debits to make sure people took this seriously, and then through the big debit of supporting the family through the diagnosis. Despite his father's failing health being a heavy burden for Eric's family, Christie's mental load had also been significantly drained.

This was the first time the couple could see the different ways their accounts were being drawn and why.

"I also realized that my mental load isn't scattered across as many things as Christie's," Eric told me. "I spend most of my mental load on keeping the family safe and supporting their big dreams. I want to make sure the kids can go to college and graduate without a ton of debt, and I'm constantly thinking about whether my family is safe, like whether the doors are locked at night so no one breaks into the house."

Once they put their percentages into their respective tables, Christie and Eric discovered a problem: They were duplicating some of this work. Christie was also burning through her mental load energy on the exact same tasks: saving for college and locking the doors.

"Is this duplication work worth it?" I asked them.

"No, we agreed it was a waste," Christie said.

"We decided that I should keep track of these tasks. But we'll have regular check-ins to discuss big plans and family safety," Eric added.

"I still think about them on occasion," Christie admitted, "but now I'm better equipped to stop the thoughts before they take up too much energy."

It was like putting a circuit breaker in her brain, a reminder to let Eric carry this load so Christie could get more focused on other things.

Of course, Eric and Christie also found a lot of joy in their mental loads. They both cherished mental loads spent to bring the family together, whether through small weekend adventures exploring nearby towns or more extensive trips to see relatives, friends, or faraway cities.

"We both think these mental loads are well spent, because they bring so much joy to our lives. They're definitely credits to our accounts," Eric said with a smile.

"Yes, these activities are work, but they give us a boost and carry us through the difficult and stressful weeks," Christie agreed.

While some mental loads are a drain, they can still be enjoyable and expand our overall mental load capacity, thus resulting in a net gain for our accounts.

"We also identified a few tasks we're each doing, but they carried different weights. I like to wipe down the counters or clean out the fridge, but Eric finds that detail work to be tedious. He appreciates when the appliances sparkle, so he tackles getting the handprints off everything, but I don't like this work. These are small things, but they carried different weights for us. When we compared the percentages, we realized we'd each taken on some mental load tasks that we didn't enjoy doing," Christie shared.

"Yeah, we weren't sure what to do about that. Should we figure out how to reallocate them?" Eric asked.

"Absolutely, yes," I said. "Lucky for you, I have the perfect activity to help you get all of this sorted out."

## The Mental Load "Swear Jar"

After publishing my first article on the mental load in 2021, I was approached by the Better Life Lab at the think tank New America in

Washington, DC, to create an easy and accessible activity that parents could use to reallocate their mental loads. With my colleagues Liz Dean and Brendan Churchill, I created mental load "swear jars." (For those who aren't familiar, a "swear jar" is a container placed in a common area. Anytime someone swears, they're required to place a predetermined amount of money in the swear jar.)

The purpose of this simple activity is to make the mental load's costs and credits visible to everyone within the family and to reallocate mental load tasks in ways that align with each family member's preferences. Here's how you do it.

Collect a container, such as a jar or small box, and a variety of coins—enough to be equally distributed among family members. At the end of the day, convene your family to talk about your mental loads. Set the container in the middle, and give each person an identical pile of coins.

Give each person a chance to describe the weight of their unique mental load. Small, insignificant mental load tasks are captured by pennies, while large and burdensome mental load tasks are reflected through quarters or even silver dollars. Each person takes a turn to go through their mental load tasks from that day, and as they do this, they place the corresponding coin into the jar.

By the end of the activity, everyone will have different amounts because mental load tasks are more draining for some than others. This is a simple, visual way to capture the fact that we all have a finite amount of mental load capacity—represented by the pile of coins—and at the end of the day, this allows us to see who has spent to zero and who is still holding a pile of coins. We then have an opportunity to see who's bearing an undue burden of the family mental load and redistribute those tasks.

It can also help us see what kind of cost people attach to different tasks. For instance, one person might loathe emptying the dishwasher in the morning and place a quarter in the jar on the day they completed that task. But someone else might not mind emptying the dishwasher, so they drop a penny in the jar on the day they're responsible for that job. As a family, you can then discuss whether it makes more sense for the person who put the penny in the jar to be the designated "emptier of the dishwasher."

Christie and Eric tried the coin exercise for a few days, and the results were quite startling. It turned out that they both found the general household chores draining, but for Eric, remembering to clear and load the dishes was a penny, and for Christie, it was a quarter.

"I think my anxiety around this chore goes back to my childhood. There was a lot of tension around whether the kitchen was clean," she explained. "If there was even one dish left out on the counter, my mother would lose it. And I mean *lose it.* I now have an eagle eye for dirty dishes around the house. Even though I can't always keep it all clean, just seeing a used mug or plate out on the counter weighs on me. If I give this task over to Eric, it means I can now ignore the dishes—they aren't my responsibility anymore, so I don't have to be on the lookout for them."

"How did it go when you handed it over to him?" I asked her.

"Well . . . for the first few days, I found it super stressful," she confessed. "I just couldn't turn off my constant vigilance of what dish was where—it was like the dishes were taunting me! But over the week, I started to work on not letting it bother me so much—on 'seeing' the dishes less."

"Did that work?" I asked.

"On Friday, when my best friend dropped in for a visit, I simply explained to her, 'See that dirty bowl over there? That's Eric's job.' And we both laughed."

What previously would have been a huge drain for Christie now became an inside joke. Her mental load lightened a bit from this reallocation and mental reframing—it wasn't her job anymore, so she didn't need to care. It took a while to get there, but eventually Christie could lighten the pressure on herself from this task.

Another outcome of the coin exercise was that Christie and Eric found a few tasks that each of them loved and didn't want to share. She loved organizing the children's weekend events, so this didn't drain her account very much; when she reflected on the weekend memories, they actually boosted Christie's mental load energy. Eric enjoyed anything outdoors, so ensuring that the lawn was mowed and the front stoop weeded was a treat for him. These were tasks that they each held with confidence about their costs.

There were, of course, activities that drained them both equally—like picking up the house at the end of the day and stripping and making the beds—so they decided to share these and allocate more of them to the children. By bringing the kids into the discussion, they started to see the ways they could engage their children in holding some of the mental load for the family, based on the children's own preferences too.

This approach made their kids feel more grown up and helped build their confidence and independence. And it lightened Christie's and Eric's mental loads by spreading the tasks that were the most draining across more people. The coin exercise helped them develop a new way of thinking about what needed to be done around the house and brought them together through family dinner to check in on how everyone was doing.

"This exercise isn't complicated per se," Eric told me. "It just helped us better visualize the costs of the mental loads behind these tasks and then to discuss openly how to make it work for everyone."

"It helped me to see that some of the work I'd stepped into was more costly for me than Eric," Christie said. "I realized I was holding on to these tasks that I disliked and he didn't mind doing, but we'd never discussed them. So, like, here you go—now Eric is in charge of keeping the sink drains clean and scrubbing the shower!"

They felt a lot better about reallocating this work after seeing its cost. It was now strategic, and they were working together to support each other within the family.

I was so happy that Christie and Eric had such an overall positive experience identifying their mental load costs and credits. I was glad that the coin exercise helped solidify the learnings. I could feel a lightness in their dynamic that wasn't there before.

When we gain a deeper understanding of the tasks we're completing each day and discuss who does what well and who enjoys which tasks, we can start to allocate our time, energy, and mental load capacity in ways that work for everyone. It allows us to see one another's talents because we understand them as that—talents—rather than as deficits. Expecting everyone to be great at everything at home is unfair and unrealistic.

We often have an expectation of women that they should be good at everything, even when a task doesn't align with their abilities. That myth of the "mom-ager" is deep-seated. It doesn't make any more sense for a company CEO to excel at everything the people who report to her do than it does for a woman to excel at everything required to keep a household functioning. We need to get smarter about who is good at what, celebrate their gifts, remain compassionate in the face of challenges, and start to share the rest.

## Name the People Who Drain Your Mental Load Account

Before we transitioned to the second step of the Mental Load Audit, I asked Christie and Eric to complete one last activity: identify *who* drained their mental load accounts. I instructed them to complete this process the same way I'll instruct you now.

Get out a pen and paper, or open a document on your phone or computer. Then list all the people who get a piece of your mental load energy, as well as the percentage of that energy they consume. This shouldn't be stressful or difficult. Don't overthink it—just go with anyone who comes to mind.

I've done this activity with other parents in my research project. Most of the time, the women have enormous lists, and their total spend far exceeds 100 percent. I suspect that will be true for Christie too.

I gave Christie a minute to think and turned to Eric.

"Who's getting your mental load energy, and how much?" I asked him.

"Mine's simple. My mental load energy goes to four main groups of people: my boss, my colleagues, my wife, and my children," he replied. "The allocation is pretty even across these categories."

"Is there anyone else who sometimes gets your mental load energy?" I probed him a bit.

He thought for a minute and said, "I do give a bit of my mental load to my friends, and my parents and siblings. But those are small amounts, and I usually only deal with them once a month or a few times a year. I might call my parents every once in a while to check in on them."

"What about your friends?" I inquired.

"I only connect with them in person a few times a year," he said. "These aren't major mental load drains, so they don't take much energy."

I noted all of this in a table and showed it to Eric.

"Does this accurately reflect what you said?" I asked.

"Yeah—that looks about right," he agreed.

The following table shows that Eric was rarely exceeding his mental load capacity:

| Boss | Colleagues | Wife | Children | Parents, siblings, and friends |
|---|---|---|---|---|
| 23% | 20% | 25% | 30% | 2% |

Next it was Christie's turn to name all the people that got her mental load energy.

"Well, let's see here. . . . My husband and children, my parents, my close friends, my employees, the PTA group, book club members . . ." she began, and I documented her list.

"Okay—you can stop now," I told her when we hit fifteen groups of people. If she'd continued, her list would have kept expanding, but my point had been made.

"Does this visualization accurately capture your experience?" I asked, and showed her the following table:

| Husband and children | Parents | Close friends | Immediate employees | Siblings |
|---|---|---|---|---|
| 20% | 10% | 10% | 7% | 5% |
| **PTA group** | **Neighbors** | **In-laws** | **Extended family** | **Parents of children's friends** |
| 3% | 2% | 10% | 7% | 3% |
| **External friends and acquaintances** | **Church members** | **Husband's friends** | **Boss** | **Book club members** |
| 7% | 2% | 5% | 7% | 2% |

Christie was instantly taken aback. She couldn't believe how many people were on her list. She felt overwhelmed by everything that needed her attention, but seeing it all laid out showed her how long the list truly was. Here it was, staring back at her, and she started to understand why she felt so drained.

While Eric was giving a small, contained group his mental load energy, Christie was fragmented across . . . pretty much everyone. This meant that each of the groups was only getting a small percentage of her total energy. But when she let one of them down, it felt heavy.

"What does giving to so many people feel like for you?" I prompted her.

"It's weird because I can feel that I'm weighing requests from all of these people equally. If my husband or kids or parents or close friends need something, I'm weighing their request alongside those from school PTAs, tangential work colleagues, and friends who have been long lost on purpose," she reflected.

It was something I'd heard from many mothers across my interviews. Women tend to feel that any requests for their time, energy, and attention should be granted. To say no to someone—no matter how inconsequential the person is to their life—makes them a *bad person*. What is worse is that, if the request is tied to their children, they feel like they're disappointing their children.

Christie was spending her mental load across a million different pull factors, many of which were *not* aligned with her core priorities, such as her family. Did her young children care if she ran for vice president of the PTA? No.

Christie had fallen into the trap that plagues many women, who are socialized to be helpful, kind, and giving: She was dividing her attention too widely and giving everyone her energy.

Why did she care so much if she let down her book club—something that happened every month, when the assigned book lay unopened on her coffee table? Sometimes she hid the book so she wouldn't see it and feel guilty for not reading it. But did she genuinely care if she didn't read the latest novel and thus let down five people she barely knew? Why was this impacting her so much?

The answer isn't that Christie was just kind of an uptight worrywart who was too hung up on the small stuff that didn't matter. No, that is not right. It also isn't that there was something internally broken about Christie and she just needed to chill out. No, that is a lie too.

The truth is that she was giving her energy to too many people because Christie—like many women—perceived that she might be punished if she wasn't helpful to everyone. Christie was right—sometimes people do get mad at us for saying no to the PTA. And yes, others might talk behind her back about the decor of her home, which was mostly her children's drawings taped unevenly around the house.

Christie was like many women who take on more than they have capacity for because they are trying to protect themselves from the fallout. But we need to be transparent about the consequences of being everything to everyone. Loading women up with more when their tanks are on empty is bad for their health and leads to burnout. Often we are killing ourselves over things and people that, if we paused and thought about it, we don't care about.

I reminded Christie that she had power here. She could *see* what is happening—she had not failed but was being set up for failure. Knowing this means we can start to make strategic choices about what the real consequences of letting down our book clubs, casual acquaintances, neighbors, and more are and whether we care. This shift in thinking allows us to make that decision consciously rather than feel like life is happening *to* us in ways that are out of our control.

This was the first time Christie had asked herself these questions. These are the important conversations we must have with ourselves and others, as we start to pull back the curtain on our mental load spending. Most of us have been spending mindlessly for years, to our own detriment.

But no more!

The goal of phase 1 of the Mental Load Audit is to help you identify which categories of the mental load are the most draining so you can start having honest conversations about your spending. This includes taking a minute to jot down who is getting your mental load energy and how much they are getting. What does your list look like? Is it as long as Christie's, or is it more targeted, like Eric's? Are you giving more than 100 percent across all these categories? You can do this list in one sitting, or you can watch how your thoughts move to one person or another across the week. Either way, it is critical to figure out where you are burning through your mental load energy.

Imagine trying to set up a budget to work toward one of your biggest financial dreams without ever looking at the bank balance or the bank statements. Or think about signing up for a million automatic debits for services that you thought you wanted or needed but that are now a total drain on your accounts. We tend to be more careful with our money, yet we're squandering our mental load energy, which is even more valuable—unlike money, we can never get it back!—in such a reckless way.

We must audit our accounts to see what's draining them, how often, and the associated costs. This process helps us get smarter with the spending, but it requires us to be brave and *see* what has truly been happening in our mental load accounts. In the same way an overdrawn bank account won't one day magically replenish itself, an overdrawn mental load won't one day magically be refilled—not unless you take action and start making regular deposits in it by doing mental load tasks that are crediting.

Although Christie and Eric had to navigate some challenging revelations, they had successfully completed phase 1 of the Mental Load Audit and learned a lot along the way. I congratulated them and told them they'd done a phenomenal job. They were now ready for phase 2: figuring out where they wanted to go next.

## *Chapter 6*

# Clarify Your Goals and Values

I LOVE THIS PHASE OF THE AUDIT BECAUSE IT INVITES YOU TO COME up with big, lofty dreams. You can compare it to consulting with a financial planner to set your saving and investment goals. Any good financial planner will ask where you want to be in the next one, three, or five years. Then they'll help you structure your finances to meet these goals.

Over time, your goals will change, particularly as you enter and exit different seasons in life. Once you've achieved a goal, you'll be ready to relish your success and work toward the next. This part of the audit can be used as a benchmark to determine which activities you take on, the people you say yes to, and the energy you choose to give.

In this next phase of the Mental Load Audit, you get to start thinking about your goals and values. The process has three steps:

Step 1: Create a blank space to free your mind to dream.
Step 2: Set short-, medium-, and long-term goals.
Step 3: Identify your values.

## STEP 1: CREATE A BLANK SPACE TO FREE YOUR MIND TO DREAM

I asked Christie and Eric to start thinking about their lives as a blank slate, without roles, responsibilities, or dirty socks to pick up. They're unencumbered and unrestricted. Their life is their own, and they have total control over what happens next, and over their mental load bank account.

While I was explaining this step, Christie shot me a side-eye, and I knew exactly what she was thinking. For many women, the idea of creating a life with no responsibilities feels like a wild fantasy. Yet I was asking her to weigh her own future against nothing but her dreams, goals, and ambitions.

"Basically, you need to drop all the concern, planning, and worry you're carrying to ensure your children have a bright future," I told her. The expression on her face, a mixture of concern and uncertainty, conveyed that she was struggling with the concept of imagining herself completely free to do whatever she wanted.

"I have to be honest: Even thinking about it feels like a violation of my role as a mother. What if my dreams come at the expense of my children? I'd never do anything to jeopardize their well-being," Christie said.

"I completely understand how you feel, and I know that creating a blank slate may feel impossible," I said, sympathizing with her plight. "For the time being, do you think you can humor me and pretend? I promise we'll factor in the kids later."

Christie laughed, and I wondered if she thought I'd been in academia so long that I'd forgotten what life was like in the "real world."

"Okay . . . I'll do my best," she grudgingly agreed with a wry smile.

Obviously, I love Christie!

Eric resisted this less. He knew that putting himself first was a way to support his family, and he hoped that, through this exercise, Christie would start to feel the same way. He was quite excited about where this exercise would lead them.

"Well, you have your homework: Envision your life as a blank slate—no obligations, no *shoulds*, *what-ifs*, or *musts*. We'll discuss how this went when I see you in a week," I instructed them before sending them on their way.

When I saw them a week later, I asked how it went.

"I had a hard time accessing the 'sky is the limit' part of my brain," Christie admitted. "I started by remembering when I was a little girl, dreaming about where I'd go and what I'd do when I grew up. From there, I remembered my years as a university student, where I was still dreaming big about my future. My friends and I would hang out at the campus pizza joint, brainstorming all the ways our unique talents could be used to change the world. Early in my career, I still spent a lot of time dreaming about where I wanted to go next in my career and life in general."

While she described these years to me, her face lit up, and the energy in her voice was infectious. I was glad she'd been able to tap into this light and energy from her past.

"After we had kids . . ." she began, and her voice trailed off and her face lost some of its sparkle. "We had our first child, and everyone else's dreams and ambitions kind of crowded mine out. I get it—that's part of what parents do. We become more selfless. But once I started thinking about it, I realized it felt like I'd lost a large part of myself in the process."

I nodded empathetically. I'd heard similar stories from many mothers over the years.

"What about you, Eric?" I asked him.

"After we had our first kid, I had to learn to be more selfless, too, and make some sacrifices. I understand what Christie means when she's describing this feeling of loss. But I didn't experience the same loss of my dreams and ambitions," he said.

"What kinds of sacrifices did you make, then?" I inquired.

"My social circle definitely got smaller—I didn't go to the gym every week to play basketball, and I rarely went out for a dinner or drinks with my friends from high school. I wanted to spend more time with the kids and Christie, and build my career," he explained. "So I was still chasing my dreams, and I felt clearer in my purpose: to create a better life for my family. I did whatever I thought was necessary to keep moving in this direction."

Eric's description of his experience was a theme I'd seen across my interviews. Fathers had maintained their biggest and wildest dreams, and they didn't feel guilty about this. In their minds, if they did more, the family benefited. In contrast, mothers had sacrificed their dreams, giving less to themselves, because they believed that's what was necessary for their family to have more. The majority of the time, they were unaware of this gradual progression—like sandcastles that had slowly eroded into the sea. As a result, their self-worth withered, and their dreams were starved.

"I've got to admit, I didn't fully understand what Christie had given up until I just heard her describe what happened. I feel bad that she's spent years sacrificing herself and her dreams to the chaos of our daily life." Eric took Christie's hand, and they made eye contact while sitting in silence for a moment. "I love my wife deeply and want to make this right. Her dreams are just as important, so they deserve equal investment." Christie smiled gratefully at her husband's words.

No matter how long I do this work, I'm always gratified to see how going through the Mental Load Audit brings things to light for couples and deepens their understanding and appreciation of each other.

"But we don't know how to do it," Christie said. "Where do we go from here?"

"The first thing you need to do is activate sociology as your superpower," I began. "Ignore the quiet whispers or loud voices shouting, *I should* or *I must* or *What if* . . . These are jeopardizing your confidence and limiting your ambitions. Which of these are getting in your way?

"Let me give you a common scenario that I hear a lot in my interviews of parents who are in circumstances like yours," I say to them.

"Christie, I imagine your brain is going something like this: *I feel like I* should *be more present for my children and making sure they are set up to have good lives. I always try to give them a bit more—I feel like I* must *prepare them for whatever comes their way when they're adults. I keep thinking about the* what-ifs *of trying to do something and having it fail. What if I go for this big promotion at work, and I don't get it? Or if I do get it, what does this mean for the family? I'll have to be away from home more often. What if my family suffers from my ambitions? I decide I* must *be more conservative in my dreams to be responsible for my family. I* should *just settle for less to make sure they're okay.*

"Did I get that right?" I ask Christie.

She nods. Later she'll tell me I captured something she had felt for a long time but had yet to put into words.

As you see, Christie's mindset around these issues is loaded full of *shoulds*, *what-ifs*, and *musts*. I understand this tendency. Many mothers I've spoken to see this as a zero-sum game: Investments in themselves and their work are at the expense of family. However, the fathers didn't think this way—they saw their commitments to chasing their dreams and achieving their goals as opportunities to create more opportunities for their families. I decided to try a brief thought exercise to tackle one of Christie's *what-ifs*.

"Let's look at this from a different angle," I suggested. "Instead of thinking, *What if I don't get the promotion?* or *What if it has a negative effect on my family?* can you think, *What if the promotion goes well? What if it makes me more money, and I can use that money to have more meaningful time with the family?* Basically, what if the outcome is much better than you ever thought it could be? Can you consider what your life *could* be, if your wildest dreams *did* come true?"

After reflecting for a few moments, Christie said, "When you put it that way, it does help me see the possibilities better."

This step is about creating a blank space that's free from any ideas about what you *should* or *should not* be doing. It is a place to explore your *wants* without their being hijacked by *what-ifs* and *I musts*. This doesn't mean you have to execute these plans, which might not align with your current life circumstances. The purpose of this exercise is for you—and all women—to start reigniting your ability to dream *for yourself.* I want you to practice seeing your dreams as valuable, your talents as exceptional, and your gifts to the world as essential. I want you to strengthen your dreaming muscles so that with time and practice, you'll be ready to step into your biggest dreams as they emerge.

Additionally, I want you to shift your thinking around failure—instead of taking it personally, start perceiving it as one more step in your movement toward your own personal greatness. Failure creates resilience. It creates growth. It creates grit. It makes us even more prepared for our dreams when they do come around.

I've seen this play out in my own life. Focusing on my big dreams and ambitions, and building an ability to step through failures, has helped me achieve professionally.

I always liked school, and even as a teenager I loved writing research essays. It was fun for me to learn about new ideas and put together the puzzle of my findings. As a very young child, I also liked the idea of teaching. I used to "play school" a lot after my actual school was finished for the day. I'd have an imaginary classroom of students, assigning them work and—my favorite part—doling out punishments.

Fortunately, my sadistic tendencies waned as I got older, and when I arrived at college, I started to see a clear future and knew I wanted to be a university professor. In the blank slate of my life back then, being a university professor was my dream, goal, and ambition. I worked to achieve this dream, transitioning from my undergraduate studies to graduate school to a real, live job.

The way I've described this may look like a linear path or easy success. It wasn't, and I, like many of you, was plagued by a lot of *shoulds*, *what-ifs*, and *musts* on my way to achieving my dreams.

*Should* I work a job with high demands and long hours? *What if* I wanted to have a baby—*must* I then leave this career? I *must* have a job with a good retirement plan, but graduate school doesn't, so *should* I go to graduate school? I *should* spend a lot of time with my daughter, but *what if* I need to put her into full-time day care after my maternity leave ends? *What if* I'm no good at any of this? *What if* everyone figures out that I'm a fraud and an impostor? *What if* I fail?

I heard these voices while I was trying to chase my dream—and you may be hearing some of them too. Did they help me get closer to my goals? No, they were a constant drain. Did they help me feel better on my path toward greatness? No, they made me feel uneasy, anxious, and panicked. Did they make me feel better when I achieved the successes I'd worked so hard to get? No, they were confidence deteriorating.

What's the value of these perpetual *shoulds*, *what-ifs*, and *musts*?

Nothing.

They didn't lead to better decision-making, and they constantly undermined my confidence. When I ultimately achieved my longheld dreams, these voices dimmed the sparkle of the joy of success.

These voices are just assholes.

So how do we quiet these mean, self-sabotaging voices?

We can turn to sociology as a superpower to clear out this wasteful thinking from our dream boards. From a young age, we women are told—whether explicitly or implicitly—that we're responsible for taking care of others. Research tells us that women tend to ensure they have everything perfectly lined up before they jump into anything. They enter jobs with more education than their male counterparts. They wait until they have more experience and training before asking for a pay raise or promotion. They often think they're not ready for the next career leap. They want guarantees before they take risks.

Of course, life usually doesn't work this way. Part of dreaming involves stepping into uncertainty. Just as I experienced on my own journey, women can get derailed by *shoulds*, *what-ifs*, and *musts*. These undermining thoughts quell our dreams before they even get off the ground—*in spite of the fact that women are generally more prepared than men to make the leap.* And men, who often are told from birth that it's their job to dream big and take risks to support their families, are more likely to make those leaps and reap the rewards when things do go well.

This is why it's so important to use sociology as our superpower, banishing these as self-limiting beliefs that don't serve us. We need women's dreams—*your dreams*—to be raw, visceral, and inspired. You need to feel like you deserve great things, so that when the opportunities emerge, you can see them and are ready to step into them.

This involves not only identifying our big dreams but also moving past our fears. This isn't a linear process. We often need to keep pushing past fears again and again, as new *shoulds*, *what-ifs*, and *musts* pop up along the way. It is the work of shedding our old, crusty, dusty skins to let our most awesome, impressive, and authentic selves shine through. Yes, it's hard work, but it's transformative work that benefits us, our families, and society at large. And as I mentioned, it gets easier the more you do it.

When you're tackling step 1, you might find it difficult to clear your mind of all the obligation and expectation clutter that's crowding out your dreams. Like Christie, when you're pondering what your life could look like, perhaps you're thinking it feels irresponsible not to factor in your family and other commitments. If that's the case, I have a couple of tips for you.

First, you can do what Christie did: Hit that rewind button. Take your mind back to childhood, before you had any adult responsibilities. When people asked you what you wanted to be when you grew up, what did you say? What kinds of make-believe did you enjoy the most? What could you have spent hours doing and without ever getting bored? Answering these questions can often spark an idea of what lights your inner fire and set you on a path of dreaming big about your possibilities.

Second, if considering your entire life as a blank slate seems too impossible, start with just one day. Let's say a genie grants you one wish: You can spend twenty-four hours doing anything you want. How would you spend those twenty-four hours? (I'm going to go out on a limb here and guess you're not going to answer, "Genie, I'd love to spend the whole day cleaning my house" or "Genie, I want to sit in a cubicle and reply to emails all day" or "Genie, I want to spend my day glued to my phone waiting for the next demand on my time.") You can even break down the day hour by hour. After you've envisioned an entire day, think about another day, and then a week, a month, a year.

Once you get started, you'll build momentum and energy toward embracing the possibilities, which will provide the perfect foundation for step 2 in this phase.

## STEP 2: SET SHORT-, MEDIUM-, AND LONG-TERM GOALS

Once Christie was able to reclaim some space for her dreams, I asked her and Eric to start step 2, in which they'd set their short-, medium-, and long-term goals. I informed them that some of these might be big steps that moved them closer to the bigger, soul-enriching work from step 1. But these could also be smaller goals related to their personal, family, and work life, or beyond.

Some of the questions I asked them—which you can ask yourself—are as follows: What are some initial individual targets that can be achieved? How do these preliminary steps build toward longer-term goals? Where do each of you want to be in one, three, and five years, both for yourselves personally and for the family more broadly? What are you doing now to make sure your mental load is aligned with these goals?

"I want you to do this work independently at first," I instructed them. "Christie, I want you to think about your personal goals, without the noise of the family. After you've both completed your lists, come together and share your thoughts and see where your goals align and diverge."

I shared that many who have done this work started with long lists they then had to whittle down. Others had only a handful of short- and long-term goals. Either approach is okay. The purpose of this activity was to get them to start to dream, share their dreams with each other, and begin to take the intermediary steps that would bring them closer to investing their mental load strategically. Greatness starts with a clear direction and a first step.

With this in mind, I handed them a copy of table 4, "Goal-Setting Worksheet," to start jotting down their ideas.

## Table 4: Goal-Setting Worksheet

| | Goals |
|---|---|
| Short-term (1 year) | |
| Medium-term (3 years) | |
| Long-term (5 years) | |

When we met again, Christie handed me her goals worksheet.

"Can you believe that after all of that work, some of my dreams are so small and easy to achieve?" she said with a laugh. "I can't even tell you how much soul-searching I did to figure out that one of the things I want to do is start going to a spin class a few times a week, just to clear my head. I can absolutely do this—there's even a studio right down the road. Exercise always refreshes me. So why couldn't I prioritize this before we did this audit?"

"I hear the same kind of things from moms all the time. You're not alone," I assured her.

"Along with spin classes, I'd like to spend a little more time having coffee with friends who fill my emotional cup. That also feels like an easy win," she added.

Christie, similar to many of the mothers who'd completed the audit, had entirely feasible short-term goals and dreams: learning new languages, taking music lessons, or attending pottery classes. They just needed space to think about their dreams and give themselves permission to let them take center stage. Through the audit process, once the mothers saw these dreams on the worksheet, they realized they could immediately implement some of them with only a minimal commitment of time and money. Even that small unsticking was super valuable to helping them see their dreams as important and encouraging them to reach for bigger, more ambitious goals.

"After I worked through my *what-ifs*, I felt confident that working toward a promotion is a good long-term goal, so I identified a few steps that would help me get there—like building new networks within my organization and stepping into higher-stakes projects at work to raise my visibility. When Eric and I talked about this, he was totally supportive," Christie told me.

"I'd spent years doing those kinds of things at work to build toward my dream, so I understood the value of these steps," Eric chimed in. "I also gave Christie some pointers and asked how I could support her along the way."

They'd discussed what Christie's increased investment in work would look like for the family. While they weren't totally sure how this would play out, they felt they were having much more open and honest conversations about what was working and what wasn't. And they were determined not to let the *shoulds*, *what-ifs*, and *musts* torpedo their efforts. They figured that if an opportunity emerged for Christie to step into a bigger and more lucrative role, they'd make a plan together. They were working better as a team and a family, so the challenges that big changes might bring felt less daunting.

"What about you, Eric? What kinds of goals did you identify?" I asked.

"My goals are tied to spending more time with the children and family. Christie's promotion would free up more of my time. I want my work and family life to have better balance—less time spent at work and more time at home," he told me.

"What would this look like?" I asked him.

"Well, there's a team within my organization that has a good work culture that supports people's lives outside of work. I'm going to reach out to friends I have within that group to see if they know of any upcoming opportunities. If a job emerges, I'll try to switch over to this team," he said. "In the meantime, I'll start looking around to see if there are other workplaces that may value my skills and give me more flexibility to be with my family."

None of Christie and Eric's plans were immediate—they'd built these big career shifts into their five-year plans. No one needed to act now, but they were engaged in forward thinking that allowed them to determine where they wanted to go, as well as the types of investments that were required to get there. It crystallized their individual and shared goals so they could be actively seeking opportunities that would move them closer to their dreams. They could support each other during the journey because they had a clear destination in mind. Recognizing their shared dreams had the added benefit of bringing them closer to each other as a couple.

When you sit down to plot out your short-, medium-, and long-term goals, remember that nothing is off-limits. You've already done the hard work of clearing out your mental clutter. Now you get to do the fun and exciting work of letting your imagination run wild and free.

## STEP 3: IDENTIFY YOUR VALUES

The final step of this phase is to identify your values. This is critical because it will help you better understand when mental load energy is spent in ways that seem positive but are wasteful.

When I explained this to Christie and Eric, he was a bit confused.

"How are our values different from our goals? Haven't we already identified what we want through our goals?" he asked me.

"Yes, values and goals often go hand in hand. When we work toward goals that align with our values, it can feel magical," I explained. "But other times, we might act in ways that are socially desirable but are misaligned with our values, which makes us feel terrible. This can create a feeling of uneasiness too—we sometimes can't figure out why, when we're doing something that on the surface seems good, we feel bad. Let me give you an example from my own life."

I told Eric and Christie that I have three main values: (1) to show up fully and do good work; (2) to move through life with kindness and generosity; and (3) to protect, love, and support the people I love. I try to let these three values drive my behavior and to operate with honesty, integrity, and kindness.

Here's the problem: At times I do things that aren't aligned with my values, and when I do, it makes me feel awful. It took me a long time to figure out what was going wrong. Once I realized that my actions were violating my values, I knew how to shift my behavior.

For instance, at times I take on a volume of work that I can't achieve within the given time frame. Instead of saying no to the work, I say yes and then desperately hope I finish all of it by the deadlines. Sometimes I succeed, and I feel superhuman! But other times, when people come to ask me to deliver what I promised, I can't because the work isn't ready yet. Instead of telling them this—or saying no in the first place, especially when I know I already have too much on my plate—I go quiet and feel awful about my behavior.

This scenario violates two of my core values: (1) I am not showing up fully and doing good work. (2) In my silence, which leaves someone hanging, I am not moving through life with kindness.

The end result is a double drain to my mental load capacity. I'm worried about making sure I do the work I promised, and I'm thinking about letting the other person down by going quiet. These diminish my productivity, as I expend energy feeling bad when I should be using this energy to complete the work.

After following this pattern for years, I clarified my values and learned to leverage them to help me decide when I should say no and, if I can't deliver, be honest about my limitations. Rather than being silent, I step in and communicate in ways that align with my values. I say things like "Thank you for thinking of me, but I'm at capacity right now. Can you reach out later?" rather than automatically saying yes. When the work is due, I must be direct if I need extra time or, if they can't wait, let them know they can move on without me.

Yet until I clarified my values, I couldn't see why these behaviors felt so draining to my mental load.

I've heard other mothers express feeling this way in lots of different circumstances. Like Jenny, who forgot to reply to a text message from a friend who'd asked her a question. Days passed, and when Jenny remembered that she hadn't replied to the text, she was overwrought with guilt and embarrassment. Jenny values being a good friend and being proactive, and she felt her lapse had violated both of these. By the time she recalled the text message, the time frame in which her friend needed an answer had long since passed, and Jenny struggled with how to proceed. Should she just let it go? Should she text her friend and apologize, saying it had slipped her mind? Her friend didn't nudge her either. Did that mean her friend was mad at her?

You can see how even something as simple as a dropped text message reply can quickly and easily drain your mental load.

Or there was Marcia, a single mom with an amazing but demanding job at a nonprofit organization. She valued being present for all her son's school activities, but she also valued being a hardworking and dedicated employee. One year, her organization's annual fundraising gala happened to land on the same night as her son's spring program at school. Marcia felt conflicted, especially because she knew she'd have to violate one of her values and disappoint either her employer or her son.

In the weeks leading up to both events, she dodged questions from her boss about how she was planning to be involved in the work event, and she changed the subject when her son asked about her attendance at his program. Whenever this happened, Marcia felt worse and worse about herself.

In the end, Marcia realized that her higher value was being present for her son's school program. She finally told her boss that she wouldn't be able to attend the event but she'd make sure to delegate her usual responsibilities to people she knew would do a great job. That night at the dinner table, she told her son how excited she was about seeing his school program. His huge grin told her she'd made the right decision.

Once she clarified her values and was honest with herself and her boss about them, it was easier to set a boundary, say no, and do less. Her mental load was relieved, and she felt much better about herself and her future ability to make decisions that aligned with her values.

Back with Christie and Eric, I asked them to give this exercise a try.

"I want you to see where your values and goals align and figure out when you're acting in ways that violate your values, to the detriment of your mental loads. This is a chance to clarify what you want from life and who you want to be," I told them.

"Also, identifying your core values is very important but also very personal work," I continued. "I encourage you to do this work independently and, if you feel comfortable doing so, share your values with each other, but not necessarily with me. I want you to get clearer on your values as a couple without my prying eyes."

I'd done this work with my husband, Casey, and we realized we had the shared value of moving through life with kindness and generosity. This explains why we often give our money and time to others in ways that make us personally worse off. It explains why Casey made personal financial sacrifices to make sure his employees had money to eat and pay their rent during the pandemic. It underscores why I often bring home lost cats and dogs and then plead for them to stay with us forever.

These situations might create conflict in other marriages, but my husband and I cherish these behaviors in each other because they're essential to and aligned with our values. Once we both understood this, our decisions felt more like connectors than dividers. This shared value tethers us together, and we celebrate each other's generosity. It's part of what makes us wonderful for each other.

If you struggle to clarify your values, you can find many different values inventories and assessments online, which can be a great starting point. My hope is that after you've completed this exercise, you'll be able to appreciate all the ways your values show up in your life and get excited about aligning your decisions with them.

Now that you've completed this phase of the Mental Load Audit and have more clarity on your goals and values, let's move on to the next phase, where you'll have an exciting, energizing opportunity to trim away those things that are moving you further from your big, audacious dreams.

*Chapter 7*

# Align Your Mental Load Spending

THIS PHASE OF THE MENTAL LOAD AUDIT INVOLVES THINKING about which of your mental loads are pushing you further from your goals, thus making them harder to achieve.

This process starts with raising your consciousness about your mental loads. Run each item on your mental load list through a filter, asking, *Does this one get me closer to my goals or not?* Observe these thoughts and see if any patterns emerge. For instance, maybe you keep saying yes to work projects that are moving you further away from your personal goal of spending more time with your family. Or perhaps you're so caught up in your extended family's needs and demands that you don't have time to pursue meaningful self-care.

These types of mental loads may be weighing you down and holding you back from your dreams. Another critical part of this process is to start considering ways you can cull, cut, and reduce these loads and implement some of those changes.

To help with this work, you can use table 5, "Top Mental Load

Burdens." Of course, you likely have more mental load burdens, but initially focusing on the top three is more manageable and allows you to tackle the most draining items on your list.

I provided a copy of this table to Christie and Eric to help them with this phase. Also, I told them that this work can be confronting and suggested that they work slowly and support each other throughout the process.

### Table 5: Top Mental Load Burdens

| These are the top mental load burdens that are moving me further from my goals: |
|---|
| 1. |
| 2. |
| 3. |

When I spoke with Eric and Christie after they completed this worksheet, Christie was excited to share one of her findings with me. And I was excited to hear about her epiphany!

"I discovered a critical filter that will help me identify my wasted mental loads: the value of a six-year-old's Halloween costume," she triumphantly declared. Eric and I both laughed, and I was super intrigued.

"Tell me more!" I insisted.

"My daughter's elementary school had organized a Halloween costume parade that would award a best-dressed winner in each grade. Our daughter was determined to win that prize, but I'm neither crafty nor spooky," Christie said. "I tried to share the mental load with Eric, but he didn't get what the big deal was."

"I couldn't understand why we couldn't just get a boxed costume and some fake blood from the grocery store," Eric said with a shrug.

"We ended up fighting about the costume, which made me feel petty, tired, and overwhelmed. At the time, I was convinced that the work was worth it, for the magic-making memory it would create for our daughter. Our daughter and I spent evenings and weekends hunting for the perfect costume. I spent my mental load bank account into the red to make sure my child had a mermaid costume that included hand-stitched sequins—which I sewed on myself, of course."

"What was the result of all this effort?" I asked her.

"Our daughter placed second in the school parade, but a month later, the costume landed in a box, unworn and forgotten about."

For Christie, this heavy mental load investment was based on the idea that she always had to give full effort to her daughter (a *should* or a *must*), even when that extra time was unnecessary. She took on all of the life organization and magic making of this task. Then, because the situation caused a rift with Eric, she had to do some relationship hygiene work afterward to smooth things over.

"Eric and I never did quite see eye to eye on this, but now I can admit that he was right," Christie said.

Eric couldn't suppress his smile at this admission.

"Although I didn't have the language for it then, I just didn't see the point. I knew it wasn't a good investment of time or energy—it was going to drain too much from Christie's mental load account," he added.

"And the kicker is that our daughter doesn't even remember how hard I worked to help her with that costume. She only remembers her bag of candy and running around the neighborhood with the other kids," Christie said with a sigh. "Even though she's forgotten, I realized it's an important memory for me, because it's become a benchmark for wasteful mental loads I'm *currently* carrying. I've started to ask myself, *Is this worth the cost of a six-year-old's Halloween costume?* If it's not aligned with my goals and not worth more than a mermaid Halloween costume, I just won't do it."

I knew exactly what this felt like, and I shared a story with Christie and Eric about one of my own wasted mental loads—wasted on someone who wasn't worth it.

A few years ago, I was striving toward my goal of being tenured at the university, which would result in many benefits: job security, a salary increase, higher status, and access to additional resources. To achieve my goal, I needed to dedicate more time and energy to publishing my work, securing research grants, and being a superstar teacher. This meant I had to work more hours, but the work was new, exciting, and interesting. I loved investing my mental load energy in this work that would ultimately build my career.

However, I started to realize that a lot of my mental load energy was being directed at one problematic colleague. Let's call him "John." John was rude and dismissive, and he undermined me every chance he got. Ironically, he held no power over me, and if we're being honest, I had more power than he did! This meant that his words had no effect on my career in either the short or the long term.

In spite of this, when his emails landed in my inbox, I'd often ruminate on his unkind words for days afterward. It wasn't lost on me that these dynamics were likely gendered—that he resented my success as a young woman. He seemed determined to cut me down.

I was perpetually in surveillance mode, waiting for the next email to drop or the next mean comment to spew forth. I spent a lot of time replaying the most recent slight and developing a range of great comebacks to his previous comments. This, of course, was wasted energy, because I did not, in fact, own a time machine and thus could not travel back in time to blast John with these well-scripted quips.

This thinking work was self-indulgent and an absolute waste of energy. But once I realized how this mental load work was taking me *further* from my goals, I took control and made it stop.

Here's what I did, in case you want to implement some of these strategies with the "Johns" in your life, whether coworkers, parents-in-law, snarky school moms, or other nuisances.

First I set up an email rule so all his messages automatically went into a folder that I could access when I wanted, if I wanted. (I have five people in this bucket now!) Then I tuned out his comments in meetings. Finally, I muted him on all my socials, even when he commented on my posts in supportive ways.

I made a strategic decision to give John less of my mental load energy and instead to focus that energy on working toward my promotion—which I ultimately got.

Mothers often carry wasteful, unproductive mental loads that push them further from their goals. For me, "worrying about John" was my top mental load drain. For Christie, it was a six-year-old's mermaid costume. Our stories are cautionary tales: You don't want to squander your energy in this way. Identifying these drains on your mental load can provide important markers to help you know when you're being diverted.

For instance, every time my mind started to wander to John, I'd remind myself, *Promotion!*, and shift my thoughts elsewhere. This approach didn't always work, and sometimes I'd still end up in a deep "John is the worst" rumination. I'd spend hours on the phone with my best friend at work, lamenting about the latest John-based drama.

Even so, the more intentional I was about steering my thoughts away from John, the better I was able to slam the brakes on this train of thought, recognizing that it was unimportant. It was debiting my account without gaining any reward. I had to get serious about setting clear boundaries on John in real life and in my brain. I had to create strategies to stop the drain, hold myself accountable, and redirect my energy toward my goals.

Once you're aware of your own mental load drains, you can be proactive about coming up with strategies to ensure they don't continue to move you away from your goals. A lot of this work involves saying no and erecting and maintaining boundaries, particularly around relationships. It can be hard work, and you must be intentional and vigilant, but the more you do it, the easier it gets.

## CURATE YOUR "STARTING LINEUP"

After you have a better sense of your wasteful mental load spending, the next step is to think about the high-priority people, groups, or experiences—ideally up to five—to which you want to allocate your precious and limited energy. These don't have to be perfectly aligned with your goals. For example, sometimes spending more time with our children puts us further away from career goals. Rather, this process is about prioritizing people and activities as a way to cut out the things that drain your mental load but don't deserve your energy.

For Christie and Eric, this was the follow-up work from phase 1, where Christie realized that she couldn't give her energy to all fifteen groups of people she had on her list. She had to determine who deserved her energy and then cut the rest.

Eric had an easier time with this task because he was giving his energy to only a handful of people—and maybe he needed to give a bit more to others, to help lighten Christie's load. But Christie found this process nearly impossible.

"Who are the five people, groups, or experiences that are absolutely nonnegotiable for you?" I asked her.

"I don't know how to do this. So many people need my time and energy: my children, my extended family, my clients, my community, and my children's school. . . . Eliminating any of them feels like a violation of one of my core values—being there for others," she lamented.

Christie was clearly plagued by the *should*s that we often ascribe to women: *I should* be kind, and *I should* be helpful. If someone asks, *I should* give. But in saying yes to everyone, Christie was letting many of them—and herself—down. She didn't have enough energy to give to all of them without burning herself out.

"How does it feel, this belief that you have to be there for all fifteen groups of these people?" I asked Christie.

"Honestly, it's overwhelming, being everything to everyone," she conceded.

Christie needed to once again use sociology as her superpower, to see how social norms telling women they *must* always be perfect, likable, and helpful are leaving women bone-dry and setting them up for burnout.

"Let me tell you a story from my own life," I began.

One day, my fourteen-year-old daughter called me out for being what she perceived as an imperfect mother.

"You never put any effort into any holidays when I was little," she complained. "I even had to hide my own eggs!"

She'd been comparing her experiences to those of families she'd seen online, who planned elaborate, perfect Easter egg hunts every year. Her complaints didn't rattle me because I'd been strategic in my decisions. I have goals related to my work, not in creating online content showcasing my family's adventures. I'm not one of those people, and my job and interests pull my time, energy, and insights into a different world. I use my talents where they lie.

"No, I don't put a lot of effort into holiday celebrations. But we've traveled the world together," I pointed out. "I've prioritized some types of magic making over others."

My lack of Easter brilliance was an intentional choice, not a reflection of how much I loved her. Instead of feeling guilty or that I'd failed my child in some way by forgoing Easter magic-making duties, I'd been strategic in my investment, which allowed me to work toward bigger goals that ultimately benefited my family.

When my daughter's accusations flew, I genuinely felt fine about my choices. This is a child who has been to more countries than most of her peers and can navigate an international airport like a pro. We often talk wistfully about a particular family vacation when life feels overwhelming—the magic of that experience has stayed with us over time. I know that I'm not a bad mother because I don't hide Easter eggs.

Once we start to employ sociology as our superpower and get clear on our real goals, we can see these social traps for what they are and not get stuck in their quicksand of guilt, rumination, and shame.

"I understand what you're saying," Christie told me after I shared my story. "But it's hard to give less to others. It just doesn't *feel* right."

It was obvious I needed to help get Christie unstuck.

"Let's try this. I want you to create two lists: a 'now' list and a 'future' list. The 'now' list includes your top five people, and the 'future' list is for those who are important but don't urgently need your attention," I explained. "Think about this like a soccer team. You have more players on your team than you can have on the field at any time. Who's your starting lineup? And who can be substituted in from the bench? They can't all play at once, but you also haven't cut them from the team. You can sub one in and one out as needed, and sometimes people get ejected from the game, but they can come back to play another day. They are not gone forever. They are just out for now."

"Okay, this analogy feels helpful," Christie said with relief. "I'm already rethinking my relationships with others—especially my sister, who is currently sucking up my mental load but should probably be benched for a bit."

Christie revisited her list from phase 1, of all the people who get a piece of her mental load energy:

| **Husband and children** | **Parents** | **Close friends** | **Immediate employees** | **Siblings** |
|---|---|---|---|---|
| 20% | 10% | 10% | 7% | 5% |
| **PTA group** | **Neighbors** | **In-laws** | **Extended family** | **Parents of children's friends** |
| 3% | 2% | 10% | 7% | 3% |
| **External friends and acquaintances** | **Church members** | **Husband's friends** | **Boss** | **Book club members** |
| 7% | 2% | 5% | 7% | 2% |

"If you have this many people on the field of your life at the same time, it's going to be just as chaotic as it would be in a soccer game!" I said to Christie. "I want you to start narrowing down your groups to give yourself greater space to work toward your goals." I handed her a clean piece of paper to create her new and improved list.

She sat with the original list for a while, crossing out items. Then she made a new list with her top five.

When she showed it to me, I was delighted to see that she'd even added a surprise guest: herself, along with her dreams and goals.

| Husband and children | My (not his) parents | Work | Close friends | Myself (building toward my own dreams and goals) |
|---|---|---|---|---|
| 40% | 20% | 15% | 15% | 10% |

A few weeks later, I checked in with Christie to see how it was all going.

"After deciding who deserves my energy, I felt better equipped to respond to life's ups and downs," she told me. "However, I couldn't always give my energy the way I wanted. Sometimes demands from my immediate employees spiked up, which meant I had less time for my husband and children—or vice versa. But the percentages were a gentle reminder to rebalance when I could."

"Does it seem like it's getting easier to 'bench' people?" I asked her.

"Definitely! I used to feel guilty about spending limited time with extended family. For example, I have a brother, and I enjoy his company. But he didn't make my top five. Because of that, I felt like I could let go of some of the pressure I put on myself to always remember important dates in his kids' lives. If I am being honest, I also want to give him some grace when he forgets about everything happening in my kids' lives. I always had this needling feeling like we weren't close or there was something wrong with our relationship. Now I can see that we just have limited energy that was being given to our top five. There isn't something wrong with us—we just are busy. It feels like a relief to take this pressure off myself and to move into our relationship a bit lighter."

This was a boundary Christie had never been able to set before. Through the Mental Load Audit process, she now understood that she was operating at a deficit and therefore needed to focus on a smaller group of people, who would receive the bulk of her mental load energy. Having this laid out in a clear way gave Christie guideposts and helped her start saying no when demands weren't aligned with her bigger goals and the priority people at this point in her life.

Oh, and in case you're wondering, Christie did finally quit that book club!

## DITCH OUTDATED SOCIAL NORMS

When cutting back on the number of people who receive your mental load energy, you can use sociology as your superpower to explore the ways your mental loads are made heavier by outdated social norms, such as some of the myths we discussed in chapter 3:

Myth 1: Women are better multitaskers.
Myth 2: Women are better household managers.

Gloria is a high-energy mom who homeschools her four elementary school–age children. She loves coming up with fun, creative crafts and projects that correlate to her kids' lessons, as well as planning field trips to further reinforce their learning.

However, since she's home all day, her husband assumes that it's easy for her to keep up with all the housework on her own—just throw in a load of laundry in between lessons, right? The same with grocery shopping, cooking, paying the bills, and anything else related to maintaining the household.

When her husband comes home from his stressful corporate job, he's ready to kick back and relax and have fun with the kids. Yet Gloria feels like that's when her second work shift is beginning, as she scurries to get dinner on the table, clean up everything afterward, then make sure everyone does homework and is ready for bed.

At the end of the day, after everyone—including her husband—is in bed, that's when Gloria's third shift starts. She reviews the lesson plans for the next day of school, confirms she has all the ingredients she needs for tomorrow's meals, tidies up the kitchen, and so forth.

After completing the Mental Load Audit, Gloria sees that while she's a gifted teacher for her children, household management isn't her strength. The multitasking she does every day is draining her mental load bank account into a negative balance, leaving her no time for either self-care or the close friendships she values. Though she understands that her husband's corporate job is stressful and demanding in its own ways, she recognizes that there's a tremendous imbalance in the expectations around household duties—things are definitely unequal, and even though Gloria wants to be a stay-at-home mom who homeschools her children, she doesn't love doing everything that comes from this decision.

Gloria used to agonize over this contradiction. She should be happy that her husband earned enough so she could stay home. She should be grateful that she got so much time watching her children grow. She should feel like her life was a privilege. And yet having nearly all the household labor land in her lap, on top of the work of a full-time job teaching her children, was overwhelming. Gloria felt like an ungrateful failure.

Gloria wasn't a failure. Rather, she, like all of us, was a human with certain skills and preferences, including a love of Play-Doh sculptures and an utter disdain for sweeping the floors. Gloria also lived in a world where she was told that she should love all of this because that is what makes her a "good" mother. Lies! Gloria was a good mother *and* had personal preferences about what she liked and loathed doing. We all do. And so Gloria needed to offload some of the nonsense.

Gloria knew she and her husband needed to sit down and have an honest discussion about how to allocate their time and energy to better manage these tasks, and perhaps see if they could include the children in some of these activities. She needed to rebalance the scales a bit to lighten her load.

All these same issues surfaced in my conversations with Christie and Eric. When I asked them to use sociology as their superpower and start thinking about how outdated social norms made their mental loads heavier, Christie was quick to respond.

"I know I've absorbed the idea that I'm inherently better at some of the work at home," she said. "I step in when I should step back, and I'm critical when I should give praise."

"I can verify that's true," Eric agreed. "I know I'm doing much more than what my father did, but I want to be an equal sharer with Christie. I don't expect or want her to step in—I can handle it. More importantly, I *want* to do the work at home."

I told them about a research project I'd recently published, which provided some insight into what was going on in their relationship. With Brendan Churchill and Sabino Kornrich, I looked at how fathers in the United States were spending their time in housework and childcare across generations, comparing baby boomers, Gen X, and millennials. We found that with each subsequent generation, fathers have stepped into more housework and childcare: Gen X fathers are doing more than baby boomers, and millennials have increased their time contributions compared to Gen X. Eric was right that fathers in his generation are doing much more at home than previous generations did.

The problem is that mothers are still doing more than fathers across all three of these generations. Even more problematic is that mothers haven't dropped any work compared to mothers in older generations. This means that everyone is spending just as much time—and in some cases, even more time—caring for children and the home, in addition to working full time and then some, and any number of other responsibilities. We're all so damn tired from spending hours with the children, doing the dishes, replying to emails, navigating the emotionally messy family group text, transporting aging parents to their doctors' appointments, searching for the lost soccer cleat, monitoring the incoming RSVPs for the birthday party, baking the cookies for the school fundraiser, researching the safest smart devices for tweens . . . On and on it goes. No wonder everyone is so exhausted and our social and sex lives have dwindled.

For Christie, this statistic resonated deeply, as she felt like she was often doing just as much housework and childcare as her mother did, if not more. But Christie was also working a full-time job on top of it and carrying a mental load in each—for work and for home. She continued to do more and more, finding her time crowded out by a range of demands.

I asked Christie and Eric to start thinking about the ways these social norms were making their mental loads heavier (for Christie) or lighter (for Eric). I wanted them to start using these filters to understand when these myths about women were creating unhealthy and unhelpful dynamics.

"When you hear those voices in your head, you can remind yourself of the facts. And when other people spout these myths, you can correct them with the research I've shared with you," I encouraged them. "I want you to shed these outdated ideas so you can enjoy the freedom and happiness that are being repressed by all that noise. This is just another part of your mental load unload."

I then congratulated Christie and Eric on completing the first part of the Mental Load Audit, the unload.

And congratulations to you too!

At this point, you've gotten clear on your mental load spending and its associated costs. You've also started culling and cutting, evaluating and reducing the investments being made in people or groups that aren't central to your life, as well as mental loads that are pushing you further from your goals. The purpose of all this work is to create space to work toward your big, bold dreams.

In the next phase—the mental reload—you'll start to rebuild your mental load with purpose, to move you even closer to a life that's more aligned with your goals and values.

# *Part III*
# The Reload

*Chapter 8*

# Create a Mental Load with Purpose

THIS NEXT PHASE IS THE FUN PART, BECAUSE YOU GET TO START thinking about the mental loads that bring you the greatest joy: your mental load *loves*, *mores*, and *musts*. Although having a mental load is necessary and unavoidable, this process is about identifying the things that credit your account.

For example, would having a house full of loud, messy, endlessly hungry teenagers be a nightmare scenario that drained your mental load account into the red? Many people would say absolutely! Yet for me, it's life-giving.

My house is the place where the teenagers come to hang out, eat, make TikToks, and laugh. I love having the kids there, and I try to create a safe space for teenage memory making and adventure. I mostly work from home, which means that my work is often interrupted by one of these teenagers coming downstairs to share their deepest anxieties, worries, fears, dreams, and joys. I'm always hearing the latest drama and offering support—which makes me happy, because I'm good at this emotional support work.

A house overflowing with a gaggle of teenagers also means I spend part of my weekend stocking up on snacks at the grocery store, cleaning up piles of dishes and trash, and cooking heaps of spaghetti. I make runs to McDonald's, KFC, or the pizza joint to buy everyone their favorite fast food.

All of this generates a lot of life organization work and housework, and it can, at times, be disruptive. But I love it! The teens' presence and energy creates a residual warmth in the house that carries through the week, and I find it enriching. While other parents may find hosting teenagers all weekend to be draining, I never want anyone else to take a turn with the fun. When I meet a parent for the first time, I usually say, "Your kid is going to spend a lot of time at my house—and no, you don't have to reciprocate in any way."

I enjoy spending time relationship building with my teenage daughter and her friends. It's a key mental load that I covet, and it aligns with my value of shining my light onto others with generosity and kindness and connecting with those I love the most. It is aligned with the person I truly am, is a priority on my mental load list, and is an investment in the person I was born to be. Even though it can be a drain, I feel good about spending my energy on this.

So send your teens to my house!

## MENTAL LOAD LOVES

The goal of this section is to figure out what you love—not what you're told to love—and invest your mental load energy strategically. Because you're now using sociology as your superpower, you can see why sending teens my way to mess up my house and disrupt my days shouldn't create guilt in other parents. I love it, and I won't judge you for your child spending days on end at my house, creating piles of trash.

Once we've clarified our own "mental load loves," it helps us better appreciate those of other parents. We can support mothers and fathers who say they like taking children to amusement parks (my nightmare), baking elaborate desserts (I'd rather die), or doing any form of crafting (no, thank you!). We can let people enjoy their own personal mental load loves without our feeling any guilt for sticking with our own preferences.

Starting this phase with Eric and Christie, I asked them to identify the mental loads they loved doing—the things that enriched their lives.

"Oh, is this like the work we did to find out what was crediting our accounts?" Eric asked.

"Yes. You've already done some of this thinking work when you audited your mental loads. Now take that work and crystallize it by identifying the top mental loads you love and wouldn't want to give up. Refine your list. Get clear. Put it in one spot as a reminder," I instructed them.

Our mental load loves are the things we don't want to lose. Sometimes these get us closer to our goals. Sometimes they move us further from our goals—like me having a bunch of teens interrupting my workday—but we love doing them anyway. These are the mental loads that we find enriching, invigorating, and replenishing and that bring us great joy and fun.

To document their lists, I handed Eric and Christie a copy of table 6, "Top Mental Load Loves," and asked them to get to work.

## Table 6: Top Mental Load Loves

| These are the top three components of my mental load that I *love* and find the most exciting, enriching, or replenishing: |
|---|
| 1. |
| 2. |
| 3. |

Christie and Eric thought about the mental loads they loved and found it was a mixed bag.

"I enjoy tracking our children's likes, desires, and favorite things," Christie shared. "This isn't necessarily a mental load that's crediting—it can be draining at times. But I love turning those little insights into magical moments. Our son was into gummies, so I picked some up at the grocery store he hadn't seen before, to surprise him during family movie night. Every time I think about the look on his face, it makes me smile. So, yeah, tracking all of those things creates extra work in my brain, but it's definitely a mental load love I want to keep."

"How about you, Eric?" I asked him.

"I love spending my mental load researching the best spots for our next vacation or for short trips. It can take me days to plan it all, but I love finding places off the beaten path—it's a fun challenge. And the joy it brings my family makes it a valuable investment that feels worth the effort," he told me.

In completing this task, they realized that one of their shared mental load loves was thinking big strategy for their respective careers. Christie loved to think about which connection could lead to a big payoff at work, while Eric loved dreaming up new products that could be innovative in his field. These mental loads had the potential to accelerate their careers. More important, this became a point of connection between them as a couple. Now that they understood why those mental loads enriched their marriage, they started prioritizing those conversations in bed at night. It was fun for them to bounce their latest ideas off each other and offer advice.

I wanted them to hold on to these mental loads, because they are what makes our lives rich and meaningful. Putting them into a list helps keep us on track.

## Your Mental Load Loves

This is the point in the process when you start pulling together all the work you did in phases 1 and 2 of the Mental Load Audit. Especially look at your information in table 3, "Weigh the Costs and Credits of Mental Load Tasks" (page 118), where you generated lists of mental loads that are costly, crediting, and both crediting and costly.

Mental load loves are the ones you want to keep, nurture, and celebrate. These are often the creditors—the good stuff in life that gets stored up, making sizable deposits in your mental load bank account.

Yet, as Christie and Eric discovered, sometimes these loves are found in your "costly" and "crediting and costly" categories. They drain your time and energy, and they aren't necessarily aligned with your big dreams and goals. That's okay! These loves have value because *they align with your values*. They increase your capacity because they allow you to make withdrawals from your account when life is challenging or stressful. Therefore, these mental loads should be an investment priority.

## MENTAL LOAD NEEDS

Your "mental load needs" are the things you must do because they're vital to your overall success and well-being. These are the kale-eating and dentist-visiting mental loads that probably aren't as enjoyable as your loves. However, you need to do these things to stay on track toward achieving your goals.

With Christie and Eric, I asked them to think about the mental loads they needed to do in order to continue working toward their greatness. I gave them a copy of table 7, "Top Mental Load Needs," to document their findings.

### Table 7: Top Mental Load Needs

| These are the top three components of my mental load that I *need* to maintain to get closer to my goals: |
|---|
| 1. |
| 2. |
| 3. |

This task encouraged Christie to reflect on the ways she interacted with their children.

"I *need* to keep letting my children in to do the work, to prepare themselves for their daily activities—like having my daughter make her own lunch or my son cut his own oranges for his soccer game," she explained. "Even if they do it wrong, it's important for me to not step in. They need to hold this work so I don't have to."

As the children had gotten older, Christie had been asking them to take on greater responsibility for where they needed to be and what they needed to do. Even so, she often slipped back into her mom-ager role and took over these tasks when they weren't happening as quickly or as perfectly as she wanted. She had greater awareness that intervening in these tasks was often to her detriment. She was conscious that she *needed* to step away from these mental loads and let the children hold on to these tasks independently, regardless of the outcome. She needed to stop hovering and monitoring to reduce her mental load drain.

"I've started embracing the mantra of 'Good enough is good enough,' and now I realize that my son bringing fifty imperfectly cut orange wedges for his team's soccer halftime break is a parenting success, because it's moving him toward greater independence. Instead of these situations being a judgment of my parenting, they're creating cute memories of my children figuring out how to move through the adult world," Christie told me with a smile.

I could tell that her mindset shift about letting all of this go—celebrating her children's efforts and letting these experiences credit, rather than debit, her account—was lightening her load.

Similarly, Eric was trying less to be perfect at work. He realized that he needed to give his best energy to his family—not his leftover, tired, and distracted end-of-the-workday energy.

"I'm trying to be more present and focused when I'm home with Christie and the kids," he informed me. "I need to protect that top-quality energy for my family by shifting away from being constantly available at work."

Upon reflection, Eric had realized that to achieve this, he'd need to let down more people at work. Logistically, that meant prioritizing the most important pieces of his work and no longer working after these were completed. Sometimes he needed to let emails go unanswered, especially those sent after work hours. He needed to stop taking work calls at 6:00 a.m. and ignore the panicked texts he received during dinnertime. Eric needed to enforce stricter boundaries between his work and family life.

"I do feel a twinge of guilt in planning to give less to work," he admitted. "But almost all of my mental load energy has been spent supporting my colleagues, which means I have less in the tank for my family. I know I need to shift the balance and save some of my best energy for them—especially if I want to work toward my goal of being a more engaged father to my children."

## Your Mental Load Needs

When you're completing table 7 to identify your top mental load needs, you can refer back to table 3, "Weigh the Costs and Credits of Mental Load Tasks" (page 118), and table 4, "Goal-Setting Worksheet" (page 143). These two tools combined will help you see which tasks move you closer to your goals and whether these tasks are costs, credits, or both. Then you can assess which mental loads are worth the cost and which ones aren't.

For instance, Christie was carrying a mental load regarding her son's soccer team snack. But this mental load was a cost that moved her further from her goal of teaching her children to be more independent. She needed to adopt the "Good enough is good enough" mindset to drop that mental load. Then she not only freed up that mental load balance for things she loved but also experienced the joy that came with watching her son take pride in doing something on his own—and serving others in the process.

Only you can decide which of your mental loads are needs. Even if they're those less desirable kale-eating mental loads, if they align with your values and move you closer to your most important goals, then they're important enough for you to make them a priority.

## MENTAL LOAD MORES

The final stage of creating a mental load with greater purpose is to identify the top mental load components you want to give *more* energy to. These are the "mental load mores" that you currently aren't doing but that are critical to working toward your goals.

When I spoke with Christie and Eric, I brought up her desire to get a promotion at work.

"How can you give a bit *more* of your mental load to make that dream come true? How do you need to invest more strategically?" I asked her.

I could tell that Christie was hesitant.

"You look concerned," I said. "Can you tell me what's on your mind?"

"I don't know if I can find the bandwidth to do more. I already feel like I'm running at top speed, and now you're asking me to accelerate? It feels overwhelming to think about giving more when I'm already giving so much."

"I completely understand what you're saying," I reassured her. "But remember the first steps of the Mental Load Audit, which showed where you were spending too much energy? For example, you and Eric identified that you both were spending too much energy tracking the children's safety—and that you were doubling up on this work. You and Eric agreed that you would drop it."

"Yes, that's right. Not worrying about the kids' safety all the time would free up some of my bandwidth," she agreed.

"Also, remember the people and groups you decided weren't in your top five: the cousin who was calling you a lot for emotional support, the book club, your in-laws, and so forth. Now that those have been demoted to the bench, you can allocate some of those resources toward giving more to your work, which will move you closer to your goal of getting a promotion."

The more Christie used sociology as her superpower, she was better able to see that establishing boundaries in her life didn't make her a bad person. Trying to be everything to everyone was setting her up for endless cycles of disappointing others, as well as stirring up the associated negative thoughts and feelings. She was getting comfortable with saying no without guilt, and she'd lightened the pressure on herself to make everything perfect.

All of this meant that Christie was cutting through wasteful mental load spending and had a bit more capacity to invest in her dreams. The next step was to prioritize getting herself closer to the promotion that had been in the back of her mind for years, putting her dreams into action.

"If we don't start investing in your dreams now, Christie, then when?" Eric chimed in. "It's like when we decided to become parents—no time is perfect, so we just have to embrace it and try."

"Also, keep in mind that you don't have to execute on these mental load mores right now, if it feels like too much. But you do have to get clear on what more needs to be done, so when you do have the bandwidth, you already have a plan in place," I reminded her. "You can, of course, start to offset your mental load burnout with some rest. When your energy is replenished and you're ready, you can use some of your mental load surplus to start working toward your dreams."

Christie pondered this for a moment.

"Well, like Eric said, there's no harm in at least trying," she said.

I'd encountered this hesitancy across my interviews with mothers: They knew they needed to start investing in themselves but needed an extra nudge to get unstuck.

I am here to be that extra nudge, to remind you and other women that investing in yourselves isn't selfish—it's selfless and empowered.

We all want to live in worlds where women's dreams are prioritized, because women create better worlds for everyone. Research shows that women use their power and influence to create better communities, that women politicians enact policies that help improve other women's lives. I've read about women CEOs who run companies and make more stable financial decisions to ensure their companies' present and future. And over the years, I've met hundreds of women who are committed to using their talents to make the world a better place.

Embrace your dreams, because we all need them!

After sharing this impassioned rant with Christie and Eric, I gave them a copy of table 8, "Top Mental Load Mores," to help them think through where they could invest a bit of additional time and effort to move them closer to their goals.

## Table 8: Top Mental Load Mores

| These are the top three components of my mental load that I want to give *more* energy to, in order to accelerate progress toward my goals: |
|---|
| 1. |
| 2. |
| 3. |

When I met with Christie and Eric again, they told me they'd spent the past week thinking about what Christie working toward a promotion would look like in practice.

"I decided I needed to give more energy toward building my networks across my organization, which is located in multiple states," Christie began. "But we realized that if I'm serious about a promotion, we might have to move to make that happen."

"How do you feel about that, Eric?" I asked him.

"Well, an interstate move could be challenging," he admitted. "But it could also be a fun adventure that would allow the kids to make new friends and build their independence. It might not be easy, but it is feasible."

"I started to think about ways to raise my visibility across the company," Christie said. "I'd need to attend more out-of-state conferences and workshops to make connections in person. I have to talk to my boss about whether there's money in the budget for me to attend. But if not, Eric and I agreed we should draw from our own finances to help me work toward this dream."

"It will drain my mental load more, with Christie traveling for work," Eric added. "But we agreed this investment of our time, money, and mental load energy is worth it because we understand this time apart is an investment in our shared future."

"It's wonderful that you're on the same page with all of this," I congratulated them. "How about you, Eric? What mental load mores did you identify?"

"To be honest, my mental load mores seem a bit impossible," he said.

"How so?" I asked.

"I want more work-life balance, but how do I get there? It all seems a bit nebulous and hard to access," he said with a sort of helpless gesture.

"You're right: 'Work-life balance' is another myth we get sold that makes us feel like we aren't doing things right," I affirmed.

This is yet another problem caused by outdated social norms. We expect fathers to be fully engaged in their families—spending more time with children, nurturing them, and being more emotionally available than previous generations. As I've learned across my interviews with fathers, these expectations are critical to the way they are trying to parent. But we also have competing social norms that tell us being a good worker means we're unencumbered, totally committed, and never distracted at work. We're supposed to be autonomous beings who care about nothing but our jobs and never have to leave because our child barfed at school.

For parents, but especially for fathers, figuring out how to reconcile the idea that they're supposed to be totally engaged with both their children and their workplace creates a huge amount of mental load turmoil. Across my interviews, I'd hear anguish from fathers who couldn't figure out how to get it right. They knew they wanted to be different from their fathers, whom they saw as being too invested in work. They wanted to be more present for their children physically *and* emotionally. But to actually do this? To tell their employer "no" when they were investing in work to bring more money to their families? It felt impossible.

Eric felt this acutely, and he couldn't figure out how to give more than he already was, either at work or at home.

"I wish I could give you a simple answer, Eric, but I can't," I said with a sigh. "I've spent decades looking at these topics, and I think a major problem is that we don't value caregiving, even though care is essential to our humanness. At some point in our lives, all of us will be called upon to care for someone we love. Yet our workplaces and policies aren't set up for this reality. This means we can't quite figure out how to make it all work. Let me give you an example from my own life."

Eric and Christie settled in for story time.

I had my daughter when I was twenty-nine years old and working on a doctorate at the University of California at Irvine. At that point, I'd been working on my PhD for five years and was far enough along to finish—if I could find a job.

With the Great Recession of 2009 looming and my belly swelling, I was offered a job at the University of Hawaii at Hilo. The pay wasn't great, but I'd spent part of my childhood in Hawaii and knew the people there have a love for children and community that is something very special. Unlike many expectant parents, I had done research that better prepared me for the reality that transitioning into motherhood would be hard. I knew I'd need the support of my community.

I started my position as an adjunct instructor, which meant I had to teach more than a full professor—four classes a semester and, to make ends meet, a few in the summer—and was paid less to do so. Since I'd just started the job, I had almost no accrued vacation time.

Casey had recently started a job at the Hilton hotel down the road and had zero vacation time or parental leave. Our daughter's birth didn't even get him out of a single day of work. Between the two of us, I was the main earner, so we couldn't live without my full income. The childcare options in Hilo were limited, and even if we could secure a spot in a childcare center, we didn't have enough money to pay for full-time care. I was highly educated and employed full time but still couldn't afford the support I needed to balance work and family.

We had a plan, though: One day, I'd just stop showing up to teach my class, because I'd be in labor at the hospital. Then one of my colleagues would generously cover my classes for a few weeks. I would be back in the classroom with baby in tow two weeks later.

I paid students by the hour to care for my infant while I stepped into the classroom to lecture. People rallied around me to help, but it wasn't ideal to return to work so quickly.

Sadly, my experience wasn't atypical for the U.S., where one in four mothers returns to work within two weeks of giving birth. Now I had joined their ranks.

In those first months, I was sleep-deprived, hormone riddled, and exhausted. I *almost* rear-ended another car and killed a wild pig (two separate incidents, for those who are asking) because I was distracted by my shrieking infant in the back seat. I'd show up to class and my breasts would leak, heavy with the milk sent to nudge me to reconnect with my hungry child. I'd try to squeeze in research in thirty-minute intervals between nursing and my daughter's naps, but I could never build any momentum toward meaningful progress.

Quite simply, I was a mess, and I should not have been back at work. I was a safety hazard for everyone involved, including the wild pigs of the Big Island. But we needed the money, so what could I do?

Upon my becoming a new mother, my mental load was plagued with a range of ruminations: *Have I tanked my career? What will it look like to return to work? Will I ever get out of these maternity pants? Is this baby going to absorb all my energy, and I'll lose myself in the process? Will my husband still find me attractive? Am I making a million bad decisions that put me further from my goals and dreams?*

My husband fared no better with our daughter's birth and the transition to parenthood. I went into labor at 9:00 p.m., which allowed him just enough time to change out of his work clothes, guzzle a beer, and down a chicken leg to prepare for ten hours of helping me through contractions and, finally, the appearance of our baby girl.

He took the next two days off work, forgoing his future weekend to spend one day basking in the glorious Hawaiian sun with me and our new baby and the second day shopping at Costco. I was livid with him for leaving, but now that I'm older, I see this decision for what it was: an act of love to make sure we were stocked up on diapers, toilet paper, and snacks before he had to return to twelve-hour workdays at the hotel down the road.

Casey, too, was typical of new American dads, who don't fare much better than moms when they welcome a new child. Fewer than 5 percent of fathers take more than two weeks off following the birth of a child. My husband was balancing his own mental load, plagued with questions: *Will my new family have enough food and diapers to make it through the day while I'm at work? Can I take a bit more time off, or will my boss penalize me? How am I going to soothe this child without being able to nurse? Am I making a million bad decisions that put me further from connecting with my family?*

Our experiences were distinctly American. The U.S. is the only industrialized nation in the world without a national and universal paid parental leave scheme. Childcare in the U.S. is expensive, difficult to access, and of varying quality. Unlike other countries, where childcare is free, widely available, and high-quality, the U.S. demands that parents navigate caregiving alone, through the market and with a patchwork of friends and family. And as my research shows, each U.S. state offers different resources to mothers. Hawaii is one of the best, while my home state of California is one of the worst. Yet I still struggled because childcare is so localized—do you have a spot in your neighborhood? More important, can you afford it?

Affordability and access to childcare have only worsened since the pandemic, leaving many parents with few options. Parents are at the mercy of their employers, who may cover the gap in care—meaning women in high-paying jobs have employers who offer them leave and flexible work in their retention packages, and those in other jobs have access to less. Many of those women work jobs that support women in high-paying professions, as caregivers, cleaners, nannies, and in-home nurses.

None of this—and I mean *none* of it—is conducive to creating some sort of "work-life balance." Rather, we're often living in worlds of work-life chaos.

After six months, I did eventually get a spot in a good day care, but I could only afford to pay for part-time care. The balance became a juggle and we did our best to make it work.

After I shared this story, Eric looked at me with the saddest eyes I'd ever seen, which is the typical response when I describe what life was like after my daughter was born. It's just so extra.

But it's the lived experience of many mothers, especially those without the workplace benefits tied to professional careers. I think it's an important story to tell, because it shows that achieving work-life balance is often far outside of our control.

Using sociology as our superpower, we can see how the systems are setting us up to fail—and then refocus our energy on fixing those systems.

"We need more men—like you, Eric—in this fight," I told him. "We need better policies. We need more empathetic workplaces. We need men stepping into and valuing care. We need to see this as something we take on together and support each other on the way. We need more connection and less hanging women out to dry."

I concluded by saying I hoped my story provided them a deeper understanding of the challenges we all face, in addition to motivating them to use their mental loads to create a more caring world.

Eric gave me a steely-eyed response, which let me know I'd convinced him.

"Welcome to the fight!" I told him with a smile.

## Your Mental Load Mores

Maybe you're like Christie and Eric, and the thought of doing *more* fills you with anxiety and dread. That's perfectly understandable! As we've discussed, many of our systems aren't set up to support any kind of work-life balance, let alone our top goals and biggest dreams. So even if we're taking on tasks that move us closer to our goals, finding the time and energy to execute on them can seem daunting, if not impossible.

One way you can feel less burdened by this idea is to look at the goals you identified in table 4, "Goal-Setting Worksheet" (page 143), and consider your starting lineup in relation to your goals. Just like Christie, you can explore ways to transfer balances from one place to another. For instance, Christie decided to ditch the book club, focus less on her in-laws' needs, and stop paying so much attention to her needy cousin. All of that energy could then be allotted to her goal of getting a promotion at work. In this way, instead of giving more to people and groups that weren't moving her toward her goals—and may, in fact, have been moving her away from them—she'd be giving more to things that truly mattered to her.

As I mentioned to Christie, identifying a mental load more doesn't mean you have to act on it right now. Sometimes when we're doing this Mental Load Audit, it generates not only a lot of mental work but also a lot of emotional work. Some women don't realize how completely drained and overwhelmed they are until they see the evidence there on the page. At times they feel angry, betrayed, hurt, and frustrated, whether with themselves or with others.

If this is where you find yourself, give yourself permission to decompress. It's hard to take on more when you're sorting through strong feelings and doing inner work.

But I promise you that after you've gained the clarity this process brings, once you see it, you can't unsee it. It will be harder for you to be satisfied with the status quo, and you'll be motivated to do more—because your children and community need what your fulfilled dreams can offer.

When you're strategic with allocating your mental load, you're moving toward the goals and dreams that will make our world a better place for everyone.

Of course, if you're prioritizing those top loves, needs, and mores, that means other things fall down the list. But some of them, particularly your needs, still must be accomplished. What can be done?

This is where you can tap into the magic of delegating, which we'll explore in the next chapter.

## *Chapter 9*

# Delegate Some of Your Mental Load

THE LAST STEP OF THE MENTAL LOAD RELOAD IS DELEGATING, which can be difficult—especially for mothers. Mothers' brains often hold a series of steps about how something gets done. This means it can be challenging for others to see the scope of the work and learn how to do it, or mothers might struggle to teach someone else how to complete a task.

Imagine delegating something—let's say registering your children for summer camp—to a grandparent and saying, "This is how I'd do it. On Thursday at three p.m., during a weekly work meeting, I get this thought in my head that I need to remember that summer camp registration is only a week away. This thought will feel ferocious and make me sweat a little. But I ignore that. Then I subtly put my phone under the table so my boss can't see and add the camp registration deadline into my calendar, with a reminder on the day before and the day of so I don't miss it. Got all that?"

The task's invisibility means that it's completed in a series of microthoughts performed everywhere and anytime, all of which add up, creating a heavier mental load. Delegation becomes difficult because one person—usually the mother—holds all the pieces internally, in their mind. But it's important to figure out what can be delegated so mothers can lighten the load. As Eve Rodsky, the *New York Times*–bestselling author of *Fair Play*, teaches us, delegating means delegating the *entire* task, handing it off to someone else without any leftover mental load residue.

In one of my meetings with Christie and Eric, I asked them to start brainstorming ways they could potentially delegate the work of their mental loads to others. To help prompt their thinking, I told them about a current research project I'm working on, which involves pinpointing services, apps, and products that are effective in delegating the mental load. Part of this project involves the story of my friend Olivia.

## A VIRTUAL ASSISTANT EXPERIMENT

Olivia is an executive at a Fortune 500 company, and she's always looking for ways to outsource so she can spend more quality time on the things she loves. Recently, she tried a virtual executive assistant program. For one year, Olivia had someone available for a set number of hours per week to do whatever she needed, whether the task was work or family related.

As Olivia began outsourcing some of the family's needs, she found that the virtual assistant couldn't get it quite right. The summer camps she selected were too far away, too expensive, and too poorly rated. The family vacations she planned were too adult, lacking an understanding of the pain of having small children in the car for hours or at a three-course meal. Family stuff proved more challenging for the assistant because children's needs are highly personal to each child and each age.

However, the virtual assistant was excellent at helping with the work and adult stuff, such as organizing work events and business travel or flagging hot restaurants and free gallery exhibits.

Olivia's mental load at work started to lighten. Unfortunately, her mental load at home intensified, since she had to decide what to delegate, strategize with the virtual assistant to ensure she understood what was needed, and then monitor her work. Often, when the work was done, Olivia had to fix it.

In the end, the virtual assistant *duplicated* rather than reduced the family work.

While it wasn't a total loss—after all, some of her demands at work were effectively delegated—having a virtual assistant didn't solve Olivia's mental load problem.

I told Eric and Christie this story because, across this research project, I've found that outsourcing the mental load can be tricky. We often look for solutions that don't yet exist, and those that do are often a mixed bag.

Part of the reason there's no magic solution for reducing the mental load is because the mental load is complex: It's eight different types of mental loads completed in seven distinct steps, and for a range of people in our family, work, and life. For this reason, we must be realistic about what we can and can't outsource. We can't expect perfection. We need to stop and think and be strategic.

I asked Christie and Eric to start thinking about what solutions could work for them, because outsourcing is key to lightening the mental load. And I'll ask you to do the same.

Although my friend Olivia had a mixed experience with the virtual assistant, it could be something you want to trial, even if only for a month or two. Before you go down that road, you can refer to your Mental Load Audit and assess those tasks, whether at work or at home, that drain your mental load but could be outsourced.

For instance, maybe planning your company's annual fundraiser takes a lot out of you, especially rounding up items for the silent auction. Perhaps a virtual assistant could secure the donations and send the follow-up thank-you letters, including photos from the event, to each of the donors.

At home, maybe scheduling everyone's appointments consumes a lot of time, especially because you spend a lot of time on hold. You could task a virtual assistant with scheduling everyone's annual checkups, haircuts, dentist appointments, and so forth.

These are just a couple of ideas, but I hope that by the time you finish this chapter, you'll have even more ideas for ways you can outsource both personal and professional tasks.

## BURIED UNDER AN EMAIL AVALANCHE

A few weeks later, when I reconnected with Eric and Christie, they told me they'd stumbled upon one area of their life they wished they could delegate: school correspondence. They talked about the way their children's schools taxed their mental loads in ways no other institution did.

"It's this unrelenting stream of communication from schools, pinging my phone at the most inopportune times: during my morning commute and key business meetings and on evenings and weekends," Eric lamented. "One day, I received seventeen unique messages! After that, I muted all correspondence from the children's schools."

"What would happen if there was an emergency?" I asked.

"They can call me from the ambulance," he answered.

Christie huffed and interjected, "No, they'd call me."

"That doesn't surprise me," I said. "One mother I interviewed explicitly told the schools not to contact her because she often worked in a secure area without cell phone service. Despite that clear directive, the school always called her first anyway."

Christie was right—Eric could mute the school correspondence without serious consequences. And, yes, Christie probably would be the one on speed dial. Schools often assume the mother is the default parent, unencumbered with work or other demands, freely available to swoop in when things go wrong. Because children are used to Mom's primary care, she's often the first one asked for when a child spikes a fever, nits are discovered, or feelings are hurt. Mom usually is the parent automatically contacted when things aren't okay.

"I'm also the one the children come to when something is forgotten," Christie added. "I find the more menial stuff draining, like filling out the eighteen millionth school excursion form or paying the seven-dollar fee for the next school visitor. I get nothing back from it, but if it goes undone, watch out. My kids are on the phone sobbing because I forgot that today is International Book Day."

Christie kept an eye on this constant stream of information because she didn't want to risk the children suffering if something went undone. Yet Eric and Christie agreed that these kinds of tasks drained their mental loads, with little reward and no end in sight.

We didn't end up in this bind by accident. For schools, digitizing correspondence to parents through technology is a no-brainer. It reduces the risk of children forgetting to bring things home, allows teachers and administrators to tell parents about important events in one space, and provides a platform for documenting children's successes and challenges. For parents, having everything in one place also seems like a win-win for their life organization.

So why do school matters severely tax parents' mental loads?

A central theme that emerged from my interviews with parents was that school correspondence isn't corralled—anyone at the school can add anything at any time, and it instantly hits parents' inboxes. Sometimes it is flagged as "URGENT" or "FOR ACTION." But mostly it is voluminous: In one day, parents can get separate emails from every single one of their children's teachers—art, science, social studies, language arts, and so on. That's a lot of messages to keep track of. It's the very definition of information overload.

And the messages arrive all day, every day. I recently got an email from my daughter's high school telling me that school was canceled the next day because a teacher had Ebola. Another email a few hours later told me the school's network had been hacked. Both of these messages arrived between 11:00 p.m. and 1:00 a.m.

Like me, many parents find the contact excessive and at the worst possible times, thus making it difficult to track what is critical and what can be ignored.

If you want to tackle your own email avalanches, you can take matters into your own hands.

With school emails, a first step could be to reach out to the school and ask if they're willing to institute a system to minimize the volume of emails parents receive each day, or if they can create and implement policies around when teachers and other school officials can send correspondence outside of the school day.

Another approach could be to set up rules in your email to ensure that important messages from school rise to the top of the pile. You can set up the system to scan for words and phrases like *important*, *remember*, *don't forget*, and so forth.

Of course, there's no perfect way to tackle the email avalanche problem, and we'll do what we can to try not to get buried under it. But can we outsource some of this labor? This is a key question I've been asking in my lab. I've stumbled upon a particular tool that could help: technology.

## TECH TO THE RESCUE

Would solving this problem require the technology to be designed better, to allow parents to specify what gets elevated to the top of their feed? Or do we need to design technological systems that are more effective at filtering incoming information? Or should the people who send out the correspondence do more curating before hitting Send?

The answer is yes to all three. We need schools that are conscious of the ways correspondence taxes parents' mental loads and pushes them to ignore messages because their inboxes are overwhelmed. This approach benefits the school as well, because they can be sure parents are seeing the important stuff that needs attention. When emails are inevitably unread, it can create misunderstandings and hostility between parents and educators. Effective communication between these two groups is crucial for these relationships and their success.

We also need technology that is better at filtering this information to help us glean the important stuff without having to read the entire message. For instance, my Gmail tells me when I've forgotten to pay a bill or respond to an email. The technology is already embedded and reading our correspondence to tell us what we missed. Can this technology be leveraged at my child's school, reminding me when I'm about to forget Book Day or a critical assignment? It can, and a few start-ups are trying to do this.

Two people I spoke with who are trying to solve this problem are Verity Tuck, woman founder of Goldee, and Avni Patel Thompson, woman founder of Milo. Both have created apps using generative AI to keep track of all the happenings at school and day care. The idea is simple: You feed emails, photos, or voice notes for birthday invites or upcoming school events to the app, and the AI reads everything and creates calendar invites reminding you what needs to be done when. The technology does work that parents don't have time for—the sorting, sifting, reading, and reminding work.

Is this type of technology a game changer? I think so. We're living in a world that will be increasingly powered by generative AI. Why aren't we applying these to the challenges parents, especially mothers, face? Why aren't we leveraging these powerful technologies toward reducing our mental loads?

Goldee, Milo, and similar technologies may offer some relief. However, developing these types of technologies is expensive. Startups are cash starved. It requires a lot of money to change the world. Men control most of the venture capital money that's invested in new businesses. Currently, only 3 percent of venture capital money goes to women, and men make 85 percent of funding decisions. We know that most men, particularly rich and powerful men, don't carry the work at home. How can they truly see the problem's urgency, if they don't personally experience it?

While the thought of draining your mental load by researching solutions might exhaust you in and of itself, you can prioritize and strategize by looking for options that address the mental loads you find most problematic, whether it's because they're taking you further from your goals and dreams or because they're simply a burden you no longer want to carry.

And, as we've discussed, don't underestimate the power of AI. It's improving faster than we can find ways to use it, and mothers around the world are using it every day to complete tasks—taking their day's agenda and helping them create a schedule and set their priorities, helping them plan a family vacation, or tracking down a reputable car repair shop that's open late on weekdays.

The reality is that some of the solutions we need don't yet exist. Mothers have told me that having a safe, reliable ride-sharing service for children would be a godsend to transport their children from point A to B after school. Is such a thing feasible? Absolutely! In some countries, a system to have someone else shuttle children to and from school already exists.

Let me tell you the most remarkable story about one of my best friends, Maria.

## A CARE SYSTEM THAT RELIEVES THE MENTAL LOAD

Maria lives in Stockholm, Sweden, with her partner, teenage son, and daughter. After Maria's daughter was born, she and her husband took parental leave (paid and shared, of course). Then Maria's daughter was in full-time day care so she and her partner could return to work.

When I visited Maria during her pregnancy, she opened her front door and pointed to the day care center across the street.

"That's where my daughter will go," she told me.

"Is this common?" I asked her.

"Yes," she answered. "Most Swedes live close to a day care center."

During my visit, I witnessed childcare educators leading gaggles of young children in snowsuits through parks. Caregiving was an integral part of daily Swedish life.

When Maria's daughter was diagnosed with a rare developmental disability after birth, the plans changed, but only slightly. Maria's daughter still went to the childcare center across the street, but her daughter had her own assistant, who worked with her in the childcare room. Maria's daughter still got to socialize with the other children in her neighborhood and had one-on-one help to move her through her day.

When Maria's daughter was school-age, she began attending an elementary school specifically designed to support children with developmental disabilities. It's located across town, so each day, a small black taxi picks her up and drops her off at school. Maria and her partner go to work and don't have to scramble to coordinate drop-offs and pickups.

"Do you ever feel guilty about sending your child to day care and going to your job?" I asked her.

She looked at me, perplexed.

"Guilty? No," she said. "Sad to be separated? Sometimes. Overall, I'm grateful that my daughter gets to grow, learn, and connect with other children in an environment specifically designed to support her."

In Sweden, the systems are designed to support caregiving *and* employment. There are safe and reliable resources to outsource care—childcare centers that are affordable and easy to access and small black taxis to shuttle children from one location to another. This is done to make sure everyone—including Maria—can work and care in ways that are lighter and easier for parents. While these ideas are a fantasy for mothers living in other countries, they're the reality of mothers living in Sweden.

Let's adopt some of that reality to help shore up our care infrastructure and lighten some of this load. Once we do this, we'll see that the problems are easily fixed, if we invest enough money to get it right.

As women, we have more power and influence than we tend to realize. We can petition our governing bodies to enact more mother- and family-friendly policies and encourage them to provide resources like those found in other countries. (Or we can run for office ourselves, whether it's for the school board or in the government.) We can encourage our employers to do the same, reminding them that it's a win-win when employees have a more balanced life. We also can support advocacy groups that are already doing amazing work in this space. We can and should do it.

But we also need men. We need men to be advocating for the

same issues and, importantly, we need men who are in positions of power to understand the incredible strain women are under, even if they themselves don't live it. We need these men to be willing to use their reputations, finances, and companies to make work, life, and policies better for caregivers. We need everyone on board, and we need action now.

## MEAL-PLANNING SOLUTIONS

While I'm telling Christie and Eric about my work exploring ways we can use technology to lighten the load, Christie has a light bulb moment.

"One of my mental loads is organizing meal prep," she told me. "Each Sunday, I take an hour to prepare for the week and write the meals on a chalkboard. That way, if either of us comes home early, we can make dinner. It also stops my kid from repeatedly asking me what's for dinner."

This may have seemed like a small piece of her life organization, but it smoothed the after-work transition and freed up some of her time so she could think about other life goals.

"However . . ." Christie paused while considering her words. "Sometimes I'm annoyed about spending time doing this on Sundays, when I'd much rather be outside reading a book in the garden. But now I understand this as a mental load need, and it's critical to saving me from turmoil throughout the week."

Since meal planning moved her family toward other goals, Christie started to think about it less as a chore and more as a family essential. But she didn't need to hold this work alone—it could be outsourced.

"Maybe our kids could do the meal planning one week?" she wondered aloud. "It might mean we'll be eating pizza, grilled cheese, and pasta most nights, but who cares? Or maybe there's an app that can help me build out meal plans and shopping lists in ways that don't require anyone to do this work. Eric likes finding new and cool apps—maybe he could take the lead on figuring out what we'll eat for the week and, along with the children, set up the meal plan and shopping lists."

She turned to Eric and asked, "Could you see if you can find something like that for me?"

Eric looked up from his phone with a triumphant smile and said, "Already on it!"

In identifying meal prep as a key mental load that she could outsource, Christie realized the value in spending the time to offload this to others. It was critical to keep the family on track, but it was work Christie didn't have to do all by herself. Fortunately for her, it seemed that technology was already there to save the day.

I gave Eric and Christie a copy of table 9, "Mental Loads That Can Be Delegated," to fill out. I already knew that Christie was going to have meal planning as one of the mental loads on her list!

## Table 9: Mental Loads That Can Be Delegated

| These are the mental loads that could be delegated to others—done by other people or apps, or purchased—to lighten the load: |
|---|
| 1. |
| 2. |
| 3. |

You might find the same is true in your situation. If meal planning is something that's a mental load drain, you can try different solutions. If coming up with the meals is a challenge, you can either find an app or ask AI to give you a recipe based on the ingredients you have on hand and the amount of time you have before dinner must be on the table. If you have picky eaters, maybe you can ask your children to each give you a list of their top five meals. You can turn this into a menu you keep on or near the fridge, and each week, they can tell you their meal choices. (I don't know about you, but I don't have time to cook meals my child then refuses to eat.) There are apps out there where you can upload recipes, and when you create a menu for the week, the app will generate a grocery shopping list for you.

Never underestimate the potential for technology to ease your mental load. While there might be a learning curve or a small financial cost involved, those short-term losses can lead to long-term gains.

## BUILDING AN ECONOMY OF CARE

When I asked Christie and Eric to think about other ways they could outsource their care, Christie became a bit hesitant.

"I think outsourcing to other mothers in my neighborhood would be amazing," she said. "For example, they know which day cares and summer camps are good. I could just ask them instead of spending hours researching those things myself. They're also probably tracking free events at the local community center and other activities that work well for certain age groups."

These moms had all the intrinsic knowledge Christie needed in order for her to outsource her mental load. Yet something seemed to be in the way of her going down that road.

"What's standing in the way of your doing that?" I asked her.

"It just doesn't feel right," she told me. "They're all exhausted, just like me, and I don't want to weigh them down more."

"I completely understand the feeling," I said, empathizing with her. "One of our biggest impediments to lightening our mental loads is the lack of a well-developed economy of mothers to support other mothers with care."

Currently, mothers are often turning to an army of women—grandmothers, aunties, babysitters, nannies, and friends—to care for their children. In the absence of a comprehensive care system like those in some countries, families are at the whim of who currently has time, energy, and space available to care. If families don't have anyone to rely on, they must piece together solutions that are often stressful for those organizing them—typically the mothers.

Mothers turn to one another for tips, tricks, and advice, from potty training to summer camp enrollment. But it's hard to outsource any of the actual work to other mothers. We stop short of saying, "Could you make my child that beautiful lunch too?" or "Could you help decorate my house for Halloween as well?" This is because most mothers trade labor through an informal exchange network: We do work for one another for free so that later we can ask for the work for ourselves. Or we don't ask for anything because we don't want to pay back the favor later on.

When my daughter was young, I'd try not to rely on other mothers' help because I, like Christie, felt bad about asking other burned-out mothers to do more. If I did ask another mother to pick up my kid, I'd carry the mental load of remembering this until I'd evened the scale by picking up her kid.

Honestly, I didn't want a bunch of random five-year-olds at my house, because all I wanted to do was be alone, eat Doritos, and watch trashy TV. (Teenagers are another story! They entertain themselves and will join me on said couch to eat Doritos and watch *Love*

*Island.*) I often wouldn't ask for help, even if it wouldn't be a burden for the other mother, because I didn't want to create an obligation to return the favor.

What's more, a small part of me didn't want other mothers to know that I couldn't hold it together. I'd make extraordinary efforts to pick up my kid every day, even if that meant I had to cut work meetings short or sit in forty minutes of traffic. I didn't want the double penalty of being a woman who can't do it all *and* who burdens other overwhelmed mothers.

We expect mothers to be self-sufficient and solve all their problems, even at the expense of themselves.

Why do we do this? Why do we carry so much guilt and shame about not being perfect? Can't we create something new that allows us to ask for what we need?

I wish that we had an economy whereby mothers could do this work for money, so I wouldn't have to feel guilty or remember to balance the scales. I wish that we would build an economy that showcased women's incredible talents *and* paid them fairly for this work. This is an essential step toward ending the belief that women should be giving away this work for free.

In my own life, I've seen a glimpse of how this could happen.

My friend Emma is a professional baker, and her husband is a chef. This means that her children come to school with lunches that include foods like Tuscan white bean soup and homemade crusty sourdough bread. I hate cooking, so I throw a peanut butter and jelly sandwich and a whole uncut red bell pepper into a bag and hand it to my daughter.

But what if I could pay Emma to make a bit extra for my child too? What if I could drop this work I hate and instead pay a friend to do the work she loves?

One day I floated this idea by Emma, and she was excited. She'd dreamed of opening a small business feeding children hot, delicious, and nutritious lunches. What a gift this would be for us all! But then neither of us followed up, so we both ended up with less.

I think neither of us followed up because, as I mentioned, mothers are hesitant to ask other mothers to do more work. I knew that Emma was already managing a lot—two kids, a few dogs, a husband with an intense full-time job, and her own work. Who was I to come back in and say, "So have you added one more thing on top of that to solve *my* problem?"

I hoped that I'd planted a seed that would lead to a new and beautiful tree. But for many mothers, I think it's hard to harvest our ideas when we're planting them in soil that has been degraded by a million other demands.

Also, it's difficult for mothers to gain confidence to step into big, bold visions that aren't guaranteed to succeed. They're fearful of pulling money, time, and energy from the family to build for themselves, because there's often not enough margin.

We also tell mothers that stepping away from their kids to take time for themselves is selfish, which is a poisonous social norm for women's ambitions. When we do this, we lose out on the incredible dreams of mothers that would benefit everyone.

But what if we started to create this investment? What if we gave grants, loans, or start-up money to the mothers of the world to solve problems for other mothers? What if we gave them childcare support and helped them build their confidence? What would happen if we started investing seriously, heavily, and generously into mothers' ambitions, dreams, and goals? What kind of trees would grow then?

This idea isn't as far-fetched as it may seem. We have a range of services that help with "men's work," like leak fixing, gutter cleaning, and lawn mowing. We also have a range of services that connect us to people who do this kind of work: Airtasker, Taskrabbit, Craigslist, and, to some extent, Uber. So we have tech solutions for men's problems too.

Where is the similar network for tasks like party planning, summer camp finding, and cool lunch packing? Why can I pay someone to weed my lawn, but I can't find anyone to cut veggies for school lunch?

In very big cities with very rich people, some of these services exist—I can hire someone to wash my clothes or plan a birthday party—but it's often exorbitantly expensive to pay for this type of outsourcing, and it's not nearly as commonplace as hiring someone to do yard chores.

We generally still expect "women's work" to be done for free, and we judge women who do it poorly. We feel guilt and shame when we reveal we can't do it all, in part because providing a nutritious meal and a perfect birthday party is consistent with our social norms about being a "good" mother and holds more cultural weight than mowing the lawn. That expectation makes it more difficult to hand the task off to others.

This could be an opportunity to dismantle this norm and create more for women—more wealth, more time, more money, more energy—by matching this work to those who love it and paying appropriately for it.

For instance, what if I could pay Emma to bake a little extra bread for my kid? I'm not envisioning something huge and expensive—just a small network of moms trading their best skills, but not for free. I want them to be paid. It would be like an online platform of local moms who can showcase their talents. To do this, we need long-term, continued, and sustained investments in women. We need money coming into women's ideas, endeavors, and businesses. We need strategic investment into economies of mothers supporting other mothers to create worlds of more.

I wished I could have handed Christie and Eric a list of products, services, and people that could solve all of their mental load problems. Need someone to come clean dog vomit off your floor after you come home from a long day at work and still need to cook dinner? Not a problem—call this 1-800 number. Can't remember when you were supposed to make that next dentist appointment or which baby ibuprofen is okay? No need for drama—it was all saved in a list Google created by reading your emails.

These kinds of solutions don't yet exist because we're still in the research and development phase and need investment. Even so, among our own circles of mom friends, we can establish these kinds of exchanges. And who knows? Maybe one of you reading this book will be the person who invents the next amazing tool that helps mothers outsource some of their mental load!

My hope is that because of this book and my research, we can all see the true value of our mental loads and the cost of letting them continue to be overwhelmed, and that these insights will inspire great investment in solutions—human, machine, and technology—to help all of us lighten our loads.

This is my dream for the Christies and Erics of the world—as well as for myself and for *you*.

In the meantime, I want to tell you about a solution I trialed, using something that has stood the test of time to reduce some mothers' mental loads: cold, hard cash.

## Chapter 10

# Money Changes Everything

AFTER CONVERSATIONS WITH THOUSANDS OF MOTHERS, ONE THING became apparent: Mothers felt an incredible amount of guilt about using money on themselves. This aversion blocked them from lightening their mental loads, investing in their health, and creating the lives they deserved. These mothers didn't see themselves as a priority, and thus their needs dropped to the bottom of the list. They'd forgo medical care or days out with friends to save cash for some hypothetical family emergency or someone else's need or dream. They were afraid to spend money to give themselves a break because they were worried their husbands would be upset with them or they would come back to a disaster.

Yet these same mothers described how integral they were to keeping the family running. It was hard for them to recognize that their investment in themselves was an investment in their family. A critical step for mothers is for them to start seeing that strategic investments in themselves can create lives of abundance.

To lighten their mental loads, I gave a handful of mothers some cash to spend: four hundred dollars for one month. I picked mothers who were carrying some of the heaviest mental loads because they were solo parenting, were managing children with complex needs, or had partners who worked long hours. They had audited their mental loads. They had identified their goals and values. They had figured out what they could and should delegate to others. They had figured out what they could realistically outsource.

I handed over the cash with one simple instruction: "Spend this money in any way that reduces your mental load." Here are four of their stories.

## KATRINA'S STORY

Katrina had an infectious enthusiasm. She was warm, wonderful, and funny, and by the end of the interview, I felt like I'd known her forever.

Katrina lived in Naples, Florida, and was a single mother to a smart and sensitive twelve-year-old son, Brian. Katrina worked for a midsize technology company that helped organizations integrate AI into their systems. Katrina wasn't particularly sciencey, but she was good at understanding people, and people who use technology. She was highly valued at her job and working on making her next career move to a higher position.

She'd recently repartnered with a wonderful man named Aaron, who cared deeply about Katrina and her son. "I didn't know men like this existed," she gushed to me. "His company shut down during COVID, which meant he had more time at home with us. He spent that time making sure the house was clean, meals were made, and Brian was doing okay. It was such a breath of fresh air after everything that happened with my ex-husband, who wasn't very attentive. I did it all in that relationship."

Katrina felt grateful for a home life that was harmonious after living in one that was not. This meant that she could focus her mental load energy on making moves at work, which was exciting but also felt big, scary, and, at times, stressful.

Her upbringing in a working-class family in Des Moines, Iowa, was stable but didn't allow for a lot of extras. When she moved to Florida as an adult, she bought some real estate that increased significantly in value over time. "I got lucky, but I always have this little voice in my head telling me to not get too ambitious, or spend too much, or take on too much debt. I grew up in a modest family, so everything I'm doing is new—like building a high-paying career and having a house that's worth some money. Sometimes I'm so proud of myself, but other times I feel scared, like *Who do I think I am?* It feels like I'm always waiting for something bad to happen and wipe this all away. I know where this worry comes from: My parents didn't have much and drilled into us that with one wrong move, it could all be lost. But it creates a mental load in my head that's running on constant dread."

Life was hard for Katrina when her husband left and she became solely responsible for Brian's care physically, emotionally, and financially. "Thankfully I had a good job and a house. Otherwise I don't know what we would have done to get by," she told me. "But it still all falls to me, and that can be so stressful. I don't make enough money to overcome the absence of a dad in the home. I can't outsource everything, so I still do it all."

Katrina was in mental load debt. Her audit showed she was overdrawing her mental load account severely, and she, too, found the unrelenting churn of the mental load draining. Her new partner took on a lot of the family's mental load, but Katrina found being a single parent exhausting combined with a full-time job.

She said that although she was good at her job, getting to the next level was proving complicated. "I'm trying to get promoted, but it seems like I can't raise my visibility enough to break through. One of my ideas was shared with my boss, and he loved it. So now I'm trying to figure out how to tell him I'm interested in a job with more responsibility, without looking too pushy. Plus, one of my coworkers is being a total jerk, and I'm doing the dance of being firm without being labeled bitchy, so people don't turn against me. I'm thinking about this a lot—how to be a woman at work—and it's sucking up a bunch of my mental load."

When we discussed how she might spend her money, Katrina instantly tried to figure out how to spread the benefit to her son and partner. "I'll get a meal delivery service, so we won't have to cook. Then Aaron can have a little break too. Or maybe I can buy my son his Christmas gifts early, so that's off my mental load later."

"Those are great ideas, but I'd like you to pause and think about how you could spend the money on something that directly benefits *you*. You don't have to take this money and maximize the return for your family. I just want it to lighten *your* mental load. You can do that any way you want—no strings attached and no guilt," I told her.

After I said this, Katrina noted, "Well, my best friend and I take an annual trip away for the weekend. Nothing too fancy. Just a few nights in a hotel in New Orleans to laugh, eat, and sleep. We're both cautious with our money, so we share a room. We don't spend too much on ourselves when we're there. But if we had your money, it would be fun, and I could treat us a bit."

For Katrina, the weekend away still carried a mental load about not giving too much to herself, not overtaxing her bank account, not being too indulgent. She felt some guilt about being on vacation when the money could have been used or saved for the family. I pressed her a bit on this.

"If your son were on the trip, would you feel bad about spending this money for him to have a good time?" I asked.

"Nope," she responded.

"If your partner, Aaron, told you he was taking four hundred dollars for a weekend away with his friends to decompress, would you tell him it was a bad idea?" I continued.

"Nope. He works hard and deserves it."

"Why can't you give this money to yourself, when you work hard and deserve it too? Use sociology as your superpower to see how we tell women that their self-sacrifice is critical for the family's success," I encouraged her. "Is withholding four hundred dollars to make a recharge trip more enjoyable worth it?"

"Well, when you put it that way, no, not really," she conceded. "I guess all I can do is give it a try and see if spending the money on my vacation reduces my stress and my mental load."

I sent Katrina off with four hundred dollars to spend on her weekend away with her best friend and also asked her to keep track of her mental load over the subsequent month.

The first week, when Katrina was supposed to leave for her trip, was, as Katrina put it, "a perfect storm of unexpected issues." First she hurt her back and had to take a whole day off work for doctor and chiropractor appointments. Then her son's school closed for emergency repairs, which meant she brought him along to those appointments. Next her work dropped in a bunch of last-minute meetings, deadlines, and demands that made Katrina wonder if she wanted a promotion at the company or needed to look for a new job. Finally, her ex-husband dropped her son off early to go back to work, which threw off her schedule.

"I thought about rescheduling my weekend away with my friend," she told me. "But work would be there when I got back, and I needed the time away—especially after such a stressful week. So off we went to New Orleans."

Katrina and her friend had an absolute blast. With the extra money, she didn't have to worry about whether the trip would result in a higher credit card bill. She was able to splurge on a round of drinks, a decadent chocolate dessert, and matching sweatshirts. For a change, she didn't think about money during the trip.

"I was able to live in the moment rather than fixating on these additional expenses. I normally feel a lot of anxiety after buying small indulgences, but this time, I didn't. It was free money so could be spent freely. And it brought me so much joy and ease of mind," she was pleased to report.

When she returned home, her wonderful partner, Aaron, had made sure the house was cleaned, the fridge stocked, and the laundry put away. Katrina noted that her ex-husband wouldn't have been as considerate, so she would have lost some of the luster from the trip after walking into a messy home. Aaron helped her keep her mental load in holiday bliss mode.

Katrina felt excited to step back into her family life after having spent a weekend away. After some time away, she saw the work drama with new eyes. "When things get stressful, I keep reminding myself, *This is just a job*, and I'm trying to be more patient and less reactive."

When I reconnected with Katrina after her month of documenting her mental load, she described her experience in the cash pilot as a "phoenix rising." She explained to me: "I hadn't realized how much of a mental load I was carrying around work. I think I was pretty unhappy, and that bled into my family life. It all felt like too many things loaded on top of each other. Then, when I'm supposed to take time to recharge, I end up stressed out about the money. I always feel like I could be doing better with my money and giving more to my family. I rarely take money for myself, and when I do, I don't feel good spending it."

The cash I'd given her held none of the emotional attachment that her own money did. It was free. It was a gift. It had no strings attached. Katrina, for the first time in a long time, was able to spend money on herself in ways that felt truly enriching. She could quiet the little voice inside telling her she didn't deserve it. This time away was incredibly restorative for Katrina, so the money was well invested. It wasn't the same as some of the self-care solutions she'd bought before—a few yoga classes, a new app asking her to breathe every twenty minutes, or a meal tracker. Some of these were productivity apps wrapped up in the guise of self-care, which meant they added to Katrina's mental load instead of relieving it.

But a weekend away with a best friend and delicious chocolate? That was a true investment in Katrina's future.

She told me, "I've been riding this high from that weekend away. I can't believe it made such an impression on me. It showed me how important it is to prioritize my own mental health and self. When I do, it brings all these benefits beyond me and back into the family."

Katrina knew that life would continue to throw her curveballs, and she still hadn't sorted out her next steps at work. But the memories from that trip gave her a boost when things felt heavy. The residual warmth of time with her best friend, without any other worries, would uplift her through the rest of the year.

## SASHA'S STORY

Sasha lived in Portland, Oregon, with her seventeen-year-old daughter, Iria. Sasha also was a single mother. She worked at a nonprofit during the day, and at night she was building her own business to support, coach, and empower other women. She was smart, articulate, and confident—someone who could hold a room and inspire a generation.

She carried a mental load similar to other single mothers' in that she was responsible for doing it all and ensuring that everything went well. Sasha's Mental Load Audit reflected that she was in mental load overdraw, and she carried almost 100 percent of the family's mental load tasks, although she shared parts of life organization and dream building with her daughter.

Her daughter, Iria, was independent, intelligent, and outgoing, so Sasha was working on guiding Iria toward her own greatness while simultaneously giving her the space to make her own decisions. It was a balancing act that could be difficult to get right, and Sasha spent a lot of her mental load thinking about how to best support her daughter.

Sasha's ultimate goal was to build her business so she and Iria could travel the world together. For Sasha, new experiences, new countries, new foods, and new people were total credits to her mental load account. She actively sought opportunities to spend time and money on making sure this cup was filled.

Additionally, Sasha was the one her friends turned to during difficult times, because she was a good listener and provided emotional support. This work mostly credited her bank account but could sometimes be a drain, especially with friends who took but rarely gave.

Sasha also found she somehow became responsible for work outside her job description because she was good at things like fundraisers, donor events, and community outreach. While this was important work, Sasha was often given this extra work without her having raised her hand to do it, which took away from her other goals and dreams. She often felt like she was in two worlds: the one she was currently in and the one she was trying to create through hard work, grit, and determination.

"I constantly feel like I should be digging deep to give more and like my tank is running on empty at the same time," she told me.

When I sat down with Sasha to talk about where she'd spend her money, she struggled to land on something.

"I love spending time with my friends and creating new and exciting experiences. Maybe I could treat them all to a night out at a cool restaurant? Or maybe I could get a new couch that fits my new space? But I could also pay for my daughter's phone bill up front and then not think about that later on. Or maybe a pedicure? I always feel better after a pedicure," she brainstormed aloud.

"These are all perfectly legitimate options, as long as they reduce your mental load," I said, before asking her, "What is the block here? It seems like you have a lot of great ideas but are having a hard time deciding."

Sasha thought about that for a minute.

"Gail, my mother," she responded.

Sasha was raised in a family where she never saw her mother sit down and rest. Her mother worked a full-time job during the day and then came home to cook dinner, sweep the floors, and vacuum the stairs. Gail was always moving.

"My mother is a deeply religious woman, so part of it was this ideal that we should always be busy and giving. She never took time to rest. The only times I ever saw her lying down during the day were the handful of times when she was really sick," Sasha shared.

This made it difficult for Sasha to rest without feeling an incredible sense of guilt and dread. She also anticipated the equal parts shock, judgment, and anger that would come from her mother if she mentioned that she'd gotten four hundred dollars as a gift and spent it on something Gail would consider frivolous.

Women have been socialized to believe that giving to themselves and taking time to rest are selfish. Men aren't taught or held to this same standard. Both her mother's influence and the way women are socialized formed a huge block to Sasha spending the money the way she needed: unconditionally on loving herself. The image of Gail shaking her head disapprovingly was a powerful deterrent.

It took Sasha six weeks to get back to me. By then, she'd thought very consciously about how she'd spend her money and was going to make sure each cent was spent in a way that maximized relief from her mental load.

The first week was particularly difficult for her. Her daughter started a new school year, which required significant mental load energy and money to buy new shoes, clothes, and supplies. In this week, Sasha divided one hundred dollars across four items: gas for her car, groceries for the house, a dance class, and brunch with friends.

"I spent the money on a combination of *needs* and *wants.* It wasn't easy to spend the money this way, because I kept wondering if I was spending it 'responsibly,' which forced me to unpack some childhood wounds. But ultimately, I balanced out my spending on things we needed, like gas and groceries, which reduced my mental load there, a dance class, which always brings me joy, and brunch with my friends to build social connection, which I desperately needed. Ultimately, this made me feel more balanced this week," Sasha shared.

She felt pressure to "get this right," but by aligning her spending with how it credited her mental load account, she felt much better about her decisions. She wasn't being irresponsible—she was being strategic.

In the second week, Sasha's job at the nonprofit had been eliminated, and she was being laid off. She was scrambling to pay her bills and find a new job that would float her family until her coaching business took off. She used half the audit money to pay an overdue phone bill, to make sure her and Iria's phones weren't shut off. As she noted, "I had to spend the money this way so I could start applying for jobs. It stressed me out but also allowed me to solve the problem quickly and move on to bigger challenges—like finding a job."

By week three, Sasha hadn't found work yet, but she used a bit of her money to go to a book club event that served free food and wine. "I just needed something to switch off all the stress in my brain, and this gave me a little reprieve from the constant negative churn in my head. Plus, I love a free cheese board," she said with a smile.

In week four, Sasha was still looking for steady work, and the bills were piling up. She didn't know what the world would bring her next or where she'd spend the last thirty dollars from the mental load experiment. So she saved this money for a future date.

When I met with Sasha to discuss how her month went, she talked a lot about the emotions this experiment raised for her about spending her money "right." She wanted to hear about how other women spent their money and what worked well.

Sasha's spending had somewhat relieved her mental load, but she said, "I kept thinking about whether I should have spent my money on a bigger expense. I mean, getting four hundred dollars in a month is a lot of money, and I spent the money on smaller things, which I thought would help me get the most out of it to reduce my mental load. But maybe I would have felt better if I'd spent it on a big something?"

Because this experiment happened at a time when Sasha's finances were strained, it raised a lot of additional emotion for her around money. She said, "I didn't realize how much mental energy was going to weighing every financial decision I made—small and big—to see if I was doing it right. I didn't realize how much pressure I'd put on myself. Sometimes money is just money, and we have to blow it on stupid crap every now and again."

Would she spend her own money to reduce her mental load in the future? Absolutely, now that she saw how intrinsically they were linked.

Obviously, four hundred dollars wasn't enough to overcome the loss of her income, so Sasha's mental load was strained by looking for a new job. But Sasha also realized that sometimes she needed to spend a little money on frivolous purchases that filled her cup and lightened her mental load. Through this process, Sasha realized she was giving the same mental load energy to financial things big and small, whether purchasing an expensive coffee as a once-in-a-while treat or saving for her monthly rent.

Sasha decided to work on unpacking the reasons money was such a trigger that created so much rumination and drained her mental load capacity. She could now better see when her mental load energy around money was poorly spent and when she needed to use money to fill her mental load bank.

An unexpected job loss that triggers economic insecurity and sends the entire family into chaos is a problem in the U.S. This situation creates incredible stress and strain on our mental loads.

Remember my wonderful friend Maria, who lives in Stockholm, Sweden? On one of my trips to visit her, I asked about their social safety net, including what happened when they lost their jobs. The answer was that the government steps in and provides people with a small amount of money to pay their rent and bills—and you receive that money for an extended period of time. (The U.S. also provides unemployment benefits, but they vary greatly by state and often aren't enough to replace a lost salary or meet basic living expenses.) You don't lose your health care, childcare, or after-school care, because care is considered a social right, so the government provides it regardless of your employment status. You also don't have to leave university, because university is free, as the government pays for that too.

"Wow!" I said. "Your government really cares about you."

As we were discussing this, Maria's partner, Thomas, jumped in to tell me, "It's about creating a strong safety net, so we can take big risks and innovate without fear of losing our houses, our health care, and our families. This is one reason so many big companies come out of Sweden despite its relatively small population—like IKEA, Mojang, and H&M. We're told to try to do big things that may fail because the state will be there to support you. It actually promotes capitalism."

I found this interesting, because we always think of the Swedes as being so altruistic, but they have a second-order result, which is that people can continue to work when life's inevitable bumps emerge. The system is more about supporting people in times of need so they aren't a drain on others. It's about allowing people of working age to self-actualize, to be their best selves, so they can be more productive at work.

Maybe if Sasha had lived in Sweden when she lost her job, she could have built her own business to coach, support, and cheer other women toward their greatness. The U.S. loves innovation and entrepreneurship, so if we could take a little from Sweden and give it an American spin, she'd have an even greater chance of success.

When we invest in women, we invest in ourselves. As I will discuss later in this chapter, we need good safety nets to help mothers transition from surviving to thriving.

## AURORA'S STORY

Aurora lived in a suburb of Phoenix, Arizona, with her two teenage daughters. She was widowed and repartnered with a wonderful new husband, George. Life was peaceful for them, and her daughters were happy. She came from a big, boisterous, and loving immigrant family, and she loved to spend time with them, reveling in the weekend scopa matches, Saturday cookouts, and various birthday parties, christenings, and sports events for her nieces and nephews. Her daughters loved having a big family around to spend time eating, laughing, and gossiping. George, a super easygoing guy who grew up in the country, knew the value of a life spent surrounded by loved ones.

All of this brought Aurora incredible joy, but it also taxed her mental load. Aurora's family expected her to do a lot. Always.

"Sometimes I feel like I have to be everything to everyone else, and I can lose myself," she told me. "George is so wonderful and picks up the slack with the girls. Sometimes I feel guilty because he shouldn't be doing this work for them—they should be doing it. I mean, he didn't necessarily sign up for cleaning up after two teenage girls."

Aurora was the heartbeat of the family, so this meant she was the one the girls called when life went awry, friends had conflict, or any of them needed to be picked up and driven somewhere. Aurora's generosity was so immense that when we were conducting her interview, she offered to run to the store to buy me a Baked Alaska after I had told her I'd never had one.

"It will only take me ten minutes. Promise!" she swore to me.

Her kindness was infectious, and I instantly fell in love with her positivity. I could also see why people around her relied on her so much. She volunteered without any hesitation or hostility. She was a bright light who wanted to hear about your life and step in to help if she could.

All of this helping could mean that Aurora got placed last on the list of family needs. Therefore, her dreams, ambitions, and goals had been neglected for a long time.

"I didn't realize this until I did the audit. I like to help others—it comes naturally to me, and it feels good. I do enjoy it. But over time, I've slipped a little too heavily into helping others and neglecting myself. I can feel there is so much more for me in this world, and I just need to start investing in my dreams and saying no a bit more." For Aurora, that meant taking a hard look at where she was going and what she wanted to do.

Aurora didn't think she was in mental load debt before the audit—she thought she was in surplus. She felt like she had enough energy to enjoy life's moments, respond to emergencies, and plan for the future. She occasionally found her mental load exhausting, but she thought it was infrequent.

The audit was deeply emotional for her because it was the first time she'd seen where her energy was going.

Aurora felt grateful for the life she was living and the people surrounding her, and this came through initially. But when she saw where her mental load was being spent—75 percent of the emotional support, 80 percent of the magic making, 70 percent of the dream building—she was crushed to realize how debiting to her mental load account these drains were.

"I'm a high-energy person, so I think I always felt like I had enough energy for everything and everyone. But the audit made me face how little I was giving to myself. I hadn't realized," she acknowledged. "I do it all because I love my family and helping other people. I just didn't see how much this was draining me. I didn't see how imbalanced the energy flow is—it's all going out and not much is coming back to me." This was a very emotional truth Aurora had to face.

"This has to stop," she said with resolve.

When I offered her the money to reduce her mental load, not surprisingly, Aurora's first instinct was to use it to support the family. At first, she thought she'd buy a robot vacuum, because she had two dogs that left fur everywhere. In her house growing up, the floors always had to be clean. This meant no one could play in the house, for fear of tracking in dirt. Friends were welcome but only outside, to reduce the trail of mess a group of children inevitably brought.

Aurora ultimately decided their existing vacuum cleaner was doing a good enough job, and she wanted to get something that helped her and didn't necessarily benefit the family so directly.

Next she thought about taking a course in woodworking or

interior design. Aurora worked as a building designer, but her ultimate goal was to start her own business. This would be one step toward her dream of working as an interior designer who could build custom furniture for people's homes. Aurora liked this idea, which was also a way to give back to her family.

"If I invest more in myself, this will ultimately benefit us all, if I can earn a bit more money," Aurora told me. "But going back to school is still too focused on my family. I'd be doing that for them to have a better life. I'll eventually go back to school, but I want to use this money on just me."

After further thought, she finally decided what she wanted: jewelry.

How would jewelry reduce her mental load?

Aurora had already felt a shift from the audit and our conversation, and she intended to invest in herself more. Jewelry was solely for her—something she could wear each and every day to remind her of her value, worth, and purpose. She wanted her Superwoman cuffs, and as it turned out, she could buy those online.

Did jewelry actually help reduce Aurora's mental load?

In week one, she'd planned to buy herself a beautiful Vivienne Westwood necklace, but the cost would have pulled from the family's savings. "I just didn't feel like I could take that money, and it made me feel so guilty," she admitted.

That week, their chocolate lab, Bruno, got grass seeds stuck in his paws, so he had to go to the vet and have them removed, which was expensive. "I kept thinking that I have this extra money for the audit, so I *could* spend it on Bruno. But once again, I'd be giving to the collective and not to me."

For Aurora, it felt weird to spend the money on herself because she hadn't realized how deeply she'd been socialized to give to others and to feel like giving to herself was a sin. She told me that her previous husband used to ask her, "What did you spend my money on today?" when she'd return home from shopping. "I was working, so this was my money too. But I felt so much guilt for spending it," she said. Aurora had starved her spending so severely and for so long that it felt almost impossible to use the money to reduce *her* mental load.

In week two, the guilt was still there. But Aurora decided she had to start somewhere, so she bought herself a sandwich: "Not just any sandwich—from one of those fancy bakeries with thick bread and so stuffed with chicken salad that it almost doesn't fit in your mouth." The cost? Fifteen dollars.

After pushing down the guilt and quelling her hunger by eating the entire sandwich, she decided to buy a loaf of bread from the same bakery. It was so crusty and delicious on the outside and soft and chewy on the inside that you couldn't say which part was better. What did she do with said loaf of bread?

"I ate half of it in the car on the commute home from work, because I didn't want the kids to get to it. It was supposed to be just mine, and so there I was, hollowing out the soft, heavenly center while driving sixty-five miles per hour down the freeway. I knew that if I got home with this loaf of bread intact, the kids would instantly cut into it and eat the entire thing. On the drive home, I started with the inside and moved to the crust. I need to tell you that it felt liberating," she told me.

Aurora was having her *Thelma & Louise* moment. But Louise, as it turned out, was a sourdough loaf.

It wasn't until week three that Aurora's guilt about spending the money started to wane. She was on a weekend getaway with her best friends, and she popped into a local boutique to buy a cooler she'd coveted all summer.

"I wanted this retro cooler to put my makeup in, but I couldn't justify the price. But then, all of a sudden, it was like a breakthrough. I bought the cooler, a small purse, and a ceramic painting of a mother and her children, which I hung in my house. I spent all the money and, for the first time ever, didn't feel any guilt."

Her partner, George, was excited for her. He felt like she gave so much to others that she deserved to spend a bit on herself.

When I met with Aurora a few weeks later to see how it all went, she told me that she felt a seismic shift: "Doing that audit was so confronting to me. I had to step away a few times, cry, and come back to it. There were a lot of truths I didn't want to see. But once I saw them, I knew I had to change. I couldn't unsee it, and I couldn't go on this way. I had to give more to me."

In clarifying her goals, Aurora started working toward a degree, plotting out her future design business (she already has a name picked out!), and spending money in fun and soul-enriching ways.

"I was in the city the other day and saw this awesome hat that cost a hundred and fifty dollars. The old me would never have spent that kind of money on myself, but I wanted it. So I bought it without guilt. I wore it to work the next day, and it's on my nightstand, to remind me that I deserve great things. That I am worthy. That I am here to take good care of me and, as a result, my family."

As we closed the interview, Aurora told me something profound: "You know that painting I bought with the audit money, of the mother and her children? Everyone who comes to my house thinks it's Mother Mary and her children. But part of the reason I felt so connected to that painting is because I thought it was me. I'm here to take care of my children, and no matter what happens in my life, I have the strength, tenacity, and will to overcome it."

For Aurora, the painting was a constant reminder of her next steps in life, to live in less fear and more abundance. She didn't need to constantly be "on" with her mental load, and she could give to herself and her children in ways that weren't always perfect. Aurora started to lighten her mental load and invest a bit more in herself, because she knew it would all be okay in the end.

## FREYA'S STORY

Freya was in her mid-forties, with curly brown hair and a beautiful smile. She had two elementary school–age children, a boy, Henry, and a girl, Lilah. Freya and her husband, Jim, met at university, where they happened to be in the same Introduction to Psychology class. They dated for years and one day married in a small ceremony in upstate New Hampshire.

When they were first married, Freya and Jim both worked full time and enjoyed sharing the ups and downs of their days each night.

"We had these independent lives, but then we'd come together and laugh about the recent workplace nonsense or get angry on each other's behalf, if someone was treating us poorly," Freya told me. "It felt like we would come together on equal footing, and we were a real team."

A few years into their marriage, Freya got pregnant with their first child, Henry. "We were both so excited to be parents, but then it was like, *Oh, who is going to do this work?* We sat down together, and I said, 'I'll take a step back from my career to care for our children,' so it all fell to me."

Freya went part time at work and spent the rest of her time caring for the children.

When I interviewed Freya, now that her children were both in elementary school, she was starting to think about how to rebuild her career. She felt overwhelmed by her current situation. Jim worked long hours, which limited his family time. This left Freya with the children for what she termed the "witching hour," that unrelenting period between dinner and bedtime.

"Our children have food allergies and strong preferences, so dinner is complicated. I have to weigh what's nutritious versus what's easy versus what may have an allergen and what may not be eaten.

It takes a lot of my mental load energy because we can't just wing it. I'm often cooking three different meals to please everyone."

On top of the meal prep, Henry needed extra support on his homework, and Lilah was having a hard time connecting with her friends at school. This meant that once the children came home after school, Freya was "on" until bedtime, making sure everyone's needs were being met.

"Have you spoken with Jim about how difficult this all is for you?" I asked.

"Yes," she responded. "But he feels so overwhelmed with work that he doesn't know what he can do. He once said to me, 'This is what we agreed to.' I thought that was a temporary solution, and eventually I'd return to my career. I didn't think that me stepping back years ago would be the long-term solution. Yet he did, so we clearly miscommunicated here."

Freya understood her husband's perspective. They lived in an incredibly expensive city, and his salary paid for the bulk of their living expenses. And Jim's job was demanding—he had to bring in new clients to meet his sales targets, so the pressure was intense.

On weekends, he tried to pitch in more by doing the things he loved, like cooking meals for the family. However, as Freya noted, these beautiful and elaborate meals produced a mound of dishes that she then had to deal with, and oftentimes the children wouldn't eat parts of the meals, meaning that Freya had to instantly supplement with something simpler.

She was reluctant to raise this with him because she knew he was trying, but it made her weekends less relaxing. In addition, at any point on a Saturday or Sunday, Jim would close the door to his home office and catch up on a few hours of work.

"We aren't necessarily doing anything during that time, just hanging out," she noted. "But it feels kind of sad for him to close the door to work. I enjoy us all being together in the same room. He misses out on this shared time by prioritizing his work."

When Freya conducted the Mental Load Audit, it showed that her mental load account was majorly overdrawn, and she was carrying the bulk of the mental loads across all the categories at home. Her drains were severe, and although she enjoyed spending time with her children and connecting with her husband, the list of demands overwhelmed the list of credits. Freya found that pretty much everything about the children's school was debiting, as she had to be constantly vigilant to ensure Henry was being supported in the classroom and Lilah wasn't being bullied on the playground.

Freya confided to me that she felt social pressure to say she should give the bulk of her mental load to her husband, children, and parents, but if she were being honest and were totally unencumbered, she'd put most of her mental load into building her career and taking care of herself. That radical shift would move her closer to her goals of (1) finishing the master's degree she'd put on hold after having her babies and (2) getting her dream job as a curator at a museum. She'd spend more time working on ambitious projects and less time taking her children to speech pathologists, eye doctors, and orthodontists.

Through her audit, she identified a few solutions to lighten her mental load: hire a cleaner, pay for a meal delivery service, and have her husband take on more.

"Jim is only home for about an hour after work before the kids go to bed, so I want him to spend that time with them and not do more dishes or whatever," she told me. He wasn't a solution for lightening the housework. However, the meal delivery service and cleaner were feasible and within their budget.

"Why haven't you used one of these in the past?" I asked.

"I couldn't ever justify spending the money on these things when the kids needed so much—like braces now and university degrees later. We also don't own a house yet, so we're saving for that. It always feels like there are more important things to spend money on."

"Would your husband be opposed to you spending money on a cleaner or meal delivery service?"

"No. He thinks these would be a good idea, so I could take a bit off my plate and be less stressed."

Her biggest obstacle seemed to be herself. She couldn't justify putting herself first on the list when everyone else needed so much. She was supporting *their* dreams, focused on making *their* lives easier. She had lost herself, and any solution that put Freya first felt elusive.

This was where I stepped in to give Freya money to lighten her mental load. She opted to spend her money on a meal delivery service to help during dinnertime at home, which was a great source of stress. Freya took my hundred dollars per week and added some of her own money to cover it all. This felt more rewarding to her than a one-off purchase and would make her day-to-day easier.

Each week for one month, I asked Freya to document how this experiment was going.

In week one, Freya noted that her mental load was lower than the week before. She wrote, "Knowing that I had mostly precooked meals at home meant I could spend less time thinking about dinner and doing the shopping. That little voice asking, *What should we have for dinner tonight? Do I have all the ingredients at home? Do I need to go to the store?* and then figuring out whether I had time to go shop between work and picking up the kids was *gone*!" This freed up more time for Freya to spend at work, for as she said, "I no longer feel like I'm shirking my job by leaving forty-five minutes early to get to the store. I get this time back and can keep working, which makes me feel less guilty." Having the food prep done also made Freya feel happier, more energized, and calmer.

In week two, Freya's work volume picked up, and her son had a few meltdowns that required her to increase her energy expenditures.

"I still had the benefit of not having to think about the meals, and this 'freed up' extra mental space," she reported. "It means I don't feel like I'm constantly spinning out of control with the constant to-do lists and ruminating thoughts. But it's not that my mental load goes to zero. Somehow, something else takes its place—and this week, it's work and kid meltdowns."

By week three, Freya started to revert to old patterns of thinking, such as *Oh no! What will we have for dinner?* Then she'd feel a sense of relief when she remembered the meal delivery sitting in her freezer.

She started to reflect on *why* she felt so much angst over her family's meals. She went fully into sociology-as-a-superpower mode and googled images associated with the words *children* and *nutrition*. She almost exclusively found pictures of *mothers* feeding children healthy meals and realized she'd been socialized to be the family food gatekeeper: It all started and ended with her, which meant her husband was off the hook.

Freya realized she hadn't ended up in this role by accident. She'd spent a lifetime being told her family's nutrition was her responsibility. And Freya was suffering as a result.

By week four, Freya's mental load had spiked. This had nothing to do with the meal delivery service and everything to do with the children's schools. That week, her son Henry had to take a standardized test that started at school at 7:50 a.m., compete in a public speaking event, finish his science project, and attend an awards ceremony. It was a lot for one week, and Freya was responsible for ensuring he was ready for all of it.

"I wondered, *How am I supposed to prepare a ten-year-old for a public speaking contest?* He doesn't even like to talk to adults when we have friends over, yet somehow I'm supposed to build his confidence to talk in front of the entire school? How is this my responsibility?"

Freya also had to run a booth at the school carnival and train another parent to run the snack bar at the weekend soccer event. Freya's mental load had stacked up in a way that no meal delivery service could solve. The service helped, but her mental load was completely overflowing and her capacity drained.

At the end of week four, this experiment made Freya think more critically about gender norms. She commented at great length about the societal pressure on mothers to make a range of small and big decisions to ensure their children are set up for life: "I just keep thinking, if I can give them a bit more—healthy food, time preparing for school, public speaking lessons, emotional support—maybe they *will* go to Harvard, have a great career, and be set for life. The thinking is illogical, but it's there being constantly fed by a culture telling us that anything less than exceptional is a failure. I feel like I'm the person solely responsible for their entire life's success, so I try to give a bit more at the expense of myself."

Society tells mothers they're the linchpin to children's successful futures and they alone are responsible for mitigating any hardship. But how can one mother, like Freya, solve all the world's problems to pave a successful path for her child? How can she overcome both rising economic inequality and global inflation and prepare her son for the debate team, all while holding a job, rebuilding her career, and trying to make sure no one ingests lactose?

Cumulatively, these tasks require more than any one person can give. We need to stop telling mothers they can do the impossible.

By the end of the month when I met with Freya, she said the money was a great gift, but it also made her realize that the meals weren't the problem—it was her mental load overload, and rectifying that wasn't a quick fix. Sociology can once again be a superpower when mothers recognize that shortcuts can't solve structural problems.

"I thought the meals would make me feel so much better. Once that was removed, and my mental load still felt heavy, I realized it was a deeper issue in my marriage," she said.

"I know that's a hard thing to recognize and acknowledge," I consoled her. "Are you feeling okay?"

"Yes. This was a good exercise for me. It showed me that my husband and I aren't communicating well, and I'm taking on too much. We'll start therapy to get to the bottom of this."

It seemed that Freya's marriage was on the line, and she had to figure out how to save it.

## SOME TAKEAWAYS

This experiment provided a lot of insight, and it proved my hypothesis: After spending the money, Katrina's, Sasha's, Aurora's, and Freya's mental load stress lessened. Did it solve all their problems? Of course not! But it did lighten their loads a bit, and, more important, they each experienced a valuable mindset shift.

While they each had different mental load needs, which meant they spent the money differently, there were several common experiences among all the women.

It was clear from the outset that all the mothers experienced weeks that were unexpectedly chaotic—dogs needing vets, jobs lost, schools closed—and this weighed heavily on their mental loads. They also wanted to be told how to spend the money. They felt there was a "right" way to spend it, and their goal was to maximize it for the benefit of all.

We know that women tend to spend their money for the good of the collective, but I wanted them to start to break this knee-jerk compulsion to give everything to others. I wanted them to begin focusing on spending it on themselves.

I could sense that the women felt they needed permission to use the money on something they thought was frivolous, whether a pedicure or a necklace or a vacation with friends. They often saw spending the cash on themselves as a sign they were a bad mom or a selfish person for not putting the family first. This created a sense of guilt among all of them, as they often couldn't justify spending the money on self-care or personal needs. In one woman's final audit, she remarked that she'd be "the weak link in the family" if she used the money on herself. She'd perceive herself as "the member of the family that's not working to make it better. I have to make it better. Because that's my job."

They'd happily spend the money to help their child or husband to reduce their load and improve their life. Yet these women weren't so kind and generous to themselves. As Freya noted, "I feel like the idea is that I'm 'supposed' to be able to cope, and if I'm not coping, then I'm doing something wrong, and I don't deserve to use money to lessen my mental load. I should be able to do it on my own, and that's the marker of me being a good mom."

The irony is that these moms were stressed out, and spending the money did lighten their loads. It didn't eliminate their loads—far from it. But it did provide some relief from all the other stressors in their lives. It became a touchstone from which to draw strength to keep going, allowing them to operate more from a place of abundance instead of scarcity.

Whether we realize it or not, our upbringing often informs our thoughts and feelings around money. For instance, if you grew up in a family of limited means or one that focused on frugality even if the means were there, it can be hard for you to "justify" spending money on things you feel are nonessential—even if you know it would be a good investment, whether for your financial or mental and emotional well-being. You might operate from a scarcity mindset, even when that doesn't fully reflect the reality of your financial situation.

It's important for you to examine your thoughts and feelings attached to money, to unpack them and see if they're influencing your spending in a detrimental way. You also live in a culture that constantly tells you that you are imperfect, but that, lucky for you, there is a solution, and it only costs $9.99! But, ultimately, you have to do the work to figure out which charge to your mental load energy is actually worth the money, even if the charges seem small.

This takes slowing down, reflecting, and getting clear on your goals and needs. The Mental Load Audit is one tool to help you do that work. There is no one-size-fits-all solution, and what you need tomorrow may not be what you needed yesterday. But knowing you are worth the investment is the first step.

Money is not the only solution, and I'm not asking you to solve the complex mental load problem with your bank account alone. Many high-powered and wealthy women leave their jobs because it's all too much. But if we're going to tackle the mental load, we need all the tools at our disposal. Money is an important and powerful tool, so we need to start thinking about how it can be part of the equation. We also need to identify ways to unlock money for women to spend on their own mental loads.

Companies often give workers money for services, like gym memberships, to support their mental health. Why can't they give them cash to relieve their mental loads? Governments often invest strategically to encourage their citizens' health in ways that improve life for us all. Why can't these payments be focused on lightening parents' mental loads? Doctors often prescribe medicine to help decrease our stress. Why can't we be thinking about ways to lighten the mental load there too?

At the end of the experiment, I asked Katrina, Sasha, Aurora, and Freya one simple question: Would you feel any guilt if this money to reduce your mental load were provided to you by your workplace or through a government grant? They unanimously answered, "No!" If the money came for free, they'd use it to create a life of more for themselves and their families. It was the feeling of taking from the family that plagued these women, even though they were one of the most important parts of the family.

While money alone can't solve all our mental load problems, it's a start and a resource that can be leveraged today. It's also an effective way to break down gender norms that tell women they aren't worthy, that they should be constantly giving and don't deserve anything. Even small amounts of money—for sourdough loaves, wine-and-cheese book clubs, and chocolates with friends—had a powerful impact on the mothers' mental loads when mindfully spent. It helped them start to see themselves as people who deserved investment. It built confidence and made them reach toward bigger dreams.

Women sometimes put their dreams on hold because they're worried about being perceived as overly ambitious and selfish—a heavy mental load of trying to navigate the workplace as a woman. They might dim their sparkle for this reason, which can prevent others from seeing them as the shining stars they are. However, as I've well established by now, the world needs women's dreams and ambitions to become reality to make everyone's lives better.

This isn't about spending mindlessly on anything that comes along: It's about consciously using money to lighten your mental load. You can start with just a few dollars, to be mindful of what that spending is doing, how it's impacting your mental load, and when and where you might want to spend more.

Throughout this book, I've encouraged you to be more mindful about the ways you're spending your mental load. Now I'm asking you to stop spending your money without considering your mental load.

Women of the world, spending money on yourself is neither shameful nor selfish! Rather, as these four mothers illustrate, it's a meaningful and impactful act of self-love when spent in ways that strategically reduce mental loads.

## *Chapter 11*

# How to Talk with Our Spouses and Get Results

AFTER WRAPPING UP THE CASH PILOT PART OF MY RESEARCH PROJect, I couldn't stop thinking about Freya. I wondered about her marriage to Jim. Did they get to therapy? Was it helpful, strengthening their relationship? Or did they ultimately separate?

Had all the stress lessened for Freya, or was it all worse, with little hope in sight?

The Mental Load Audit and cash pilot experiment had shaken up her marriage, but I had no idea what ultimately had happened.

You can imagine my surprise when, on an unusually warm spring day, I received an email from Freya asking if we could get together so she could update me on how her mental load journey had gone over the past year, because, as she told me, "A LOT has changed!" (Caps and exclamation point included in original email.)

I was thrilled to hear from her and immediately set up a time to talk the following week.

When we met, Freya told me that participating in the audit had saved her marriage and changed her life. She was like many mothers who participated in my research project: They were near burnout and needed a solution fast. She'd thought the meal delivery service would be that solution. It helped, but it didn't solve the real problem at home.

That real problem, according to Freya, was that she'd given up a lot of her life to support her family. She felt she'd lost a lot of herself in the process. When Freya tried to share this discovery with Jim in the months following the audit, it didn't go well.

"It felt like my concerns weren't being heard, and we had huge conflicts. Jim felt like I kept asking him to do more at home, and he didn't have more in the tank. Jim said he was already on the verge of burnout from the demands of being the sole breadwinner for the family. He was with the children on weekends and evenings. He took them on adventures. He cooked them special dinners. He was doing the dishes at night. He told me he didn't have any more to give. What's more, Jim said that if he was being honest, he resented that I kept asking for more. Why couldn't I understand that he was just as exhausted from trying to hold it all together?"

Freya understood Jim was caring for the children at home. That wasn't up for dispute. Still, she felt Jim wasn't taking on the mental load that was necessary to support the children. Freya was carrying this work alone, doing the added emotional layer that sat on top of everything in the family. Even though they had a lot of time together, Freya often felt very alone.

She spent months trying to explain this distinction to Jim. It felt like he couldn't understand it. Or if he did, it felt like he couldn't take on more. Freya couldn't figure out which was true, and either answer felt like an awful reflection on their marriage.

For Jim, these conversations felt like a violation of their contract: They'd agreed that she'd be in charge of the family and he'd be in charge of making money. They'd chosen for her to use her mental load on the family so his could be free for work. Why was Freya trying to change the rules now? It didn't feel fair, and Jim felt overwhelmed by the ask.

It went back and forth like this for months. As Freya told me, she was scared that her marriage was over. They still loved each other. They still wanted to be together. They were committed to each other. They just couldn't seem to get past themselves to better understand each other.

"It was scary for me," she confided. "It took me a long time to figure out what the problem was. After finally seeing the problem for what it was, I had to be brave and ask him for the solution: taking on more of the emotional mental load. But what if he couldn't do it? What if in asking for what I needed, he was going to leave me?"

These distressing and disorienting thoughts plagued her mental load for months. Freya didn't want her marriage to end, but she also knew it couldn't go on like this anymore. Once she saw the problem, she couldn't look away.

"I think it's hard for women to identify what exactly they need, because they have spent so much time masking their needs for the good of the family," I said, before looking at her pointedly to ask, "Was this your experience?"

Freya nodded emphatically.

"Part of the reason things got this bad was because it took a lot of processing work to identify the real problem: that I felt I held the emotional work of the family. Initially, I thought it was about getting Jim to do more. But even when he did more, I still didn't feel lighter. Then I thought it was because the kids were so demanding, but as they got older and more self-sufficient and their demands lightened, the problems in my marriage remained."

After Freya realized that a meal delivery service wasn't the true fix, she had to do the hard work of figuring out what was going wrong: Freya needed a partner who could notice the moods of the family and offer help when things got tough.

"Once you realized this, did you tell Jim explicitly?" I asked.

"For a long time, no," she responded. "I felt like it was often easier to do things alone, even if that made me angry in the moment, than to tell him exactly what was wrong."

Freya picked up more of the work of the family, got increasingly efficient in delegating physical tasks to Jim, and figured that doing motherhood "right" meant suffering in silence—all the while complaining about her husband to anyone who'd listen. It didn't improve Freya's experience at home and often left her feeling like an outsider in her own marriage.

For Jim, all this additional work made his home life feel a lot like his work life. He'd come home to someone who had a list of things for him to do, and he felt pressured to get it all right. It felt like his marriage was on the line, but he couldn't exactly figure out why. He frequently disconnected from Freya because of this pressure—she felt more like a boss than a wife and a partner. Even their conversations developed a boss-employee dynamic, and Jim needed a break from office politics at home.

He often retreated into his room to be by himself, which made him feel further isolated. He needed the escape, but it also made him feel worse. He, too, couldn't articulate why until they pulled apart this puzzle.

The pressure and loneliness were the reasons he wanted his time with the children to be light, fun, and playful. He needed a release from the pressure, so the children became a mechanism for this. Yet, as Freya noted, this continued to strain their relationship, because she was left doing the hard stuff. Jim was the fun dad, and Freya became the mean mommy. They couldn't seem to shift away from these roles, which made their partnership worse.

## THE TRAP OF SOCIALIZED GENDER ROLES

This dynamic was a clear pattern that emerged from my interviews with heterosexual parents. Moms and dads had stepped into socialized gender roles that made doing all the work of parenting, while concurrently keeping their marriage strong, very difficult. These roles pushed the marriages to the brink because they created incredible pressures based on different expectations of what constituted a good job. These couples were doing gender in ways that had a negative effect on their lives.

This pattern didn't emerge with the LGBTIQ+ parents I interviewed. They didn't unconsciously step into roles based on gender. Rather, they strategically decided who was going to do what, when, and how. LGBTIQ+ parents identified who was good at each task, yet they didn't necessarily hold these tasks forever. If one got bored with doing the work of a certain task—like doing all the dishes or making the doctors' appointments—they'd hand this off to the other parent. Allocations of mental loads weren't life sentences but rather constantly negotiated based on the preferences and demands at the time. Unsurprisingly, this created less conflict among LGBTIQ+ parents than among their heterosexual counterparts.

LGBTIQ+ couples didn't necessarily have more equal arrangements than their heterosexual counterparts—often one partner was doing more than the other. Rather, they had a deeper understanding of what each partner was going through because they lived in the same social world. No one had to spend time explaining to the other what their experiences in the world felt like. They understood each other when they said they were feeling social pressures and penalties tied to being a mom or dad. They were understanding of what that felt like, because the other partner felt that pressure too.

Therefore, conversations about the mental load, parenthood, gender identities, and sexuality weren't met with as much resistance and included greater mutual understanding. Problems were understood quickly and without pushback. The partners felt heard and understood. As a consequence, solutions emerged with less hurt, anger, and frustration.

LGBTIQ+ parents had figured out the secret to a meaningful connection without conflict: They entered these conversations with greater empathy, because they had a shared understanding that facilitated their relationships and deepened their connections. This was counter to the heterosexual parents I interviewed who, like Freya and Jim, often felt that expressed frustrations sounded like attacks and shut the door on building deeper understanding of each other's worlds.

A transgender parent in my interviews described this reality perfectly. He shared an experience where he, presenting as a dad, forgot to bring a white T-shirt to the school's Tie-Dye Day. Frantically, he ran to the car to find an often-used and very off-white kitchen towel that could be sacrificed. When he returned to the classroom with said towel in hand, the teachers rejoiced, exclaiming, "Yay, Dad!" He walked out feeling like a hero.

In my interviews he reflected, "I would have had a totally different experience as a mom and would not have been celebrated for my subpar solution to my forgetfulness. It was so stark to me, the different ways I was being treated now that I was moving through the parenting world as a dad, compared to when I was presenting as a mom. I mean, like, wow!"

This father could clearly see the traps left for mothers and the secret parenting supports that are provided to dads.

No wonder Jim was having such a hard time understanding Freya. His experiences were completely alien to hers.

It took months for Jim to understand that Freya wanted him to participate in work he perceived as frivolous, because doing so took the weight off her shoulders and showed that he cared. Much time passed before he understood that the consequences of the mental load were serious for Freya, and she was carrying a different load than he was. He had to listen deeply, ask questions, and refrain from defensiveness.

As I've previously mentioned—and as I've told couples who have completed the Mental Load Audit with me, like Eric and Christie—going through this process can be emotional and raise issues in your marriage that you either were unaware of or may have been choosing to ignore. As many of those who've gone through this process have told me, once you've seen it, you can't unsee it.

Therefore, as you're trying to address what's draining your mental load capacity, it's critical to keep an open mind and open lines of communication. Continually remind yourself, and each other, that at the end of the day, everything you're trying to accomplish will produce greater strength—for both of you individually, for your partnership, and for your family. Not only that, but it will bond all of you together as you choose to support one another and your family in new and different ways.

It also can be helpful to discuss the issues within the context of the specific gender roles you're feeling hemmed in by, using this formula: "Because I'm a woman, I feel like X." For instance, if housework is overwhelming you, it can be clear and transformative to say to your partner, "Because I'm a woman, I feel like I'm expected to have an immaculate house" or "Because I'm a woman, I feel like I'm expected to be super nurturing and maternal all the time." Truly, your partner might not even realize you feel this way. For all you know, he might think your house *is* immaculate! (Remember, men do see the mess! Yet women's standards aren't always the same as theirs.) And he might be able to share ways that you *are* nurturing and maternal, even if you don't recognize these actions yourself.

The challenge here is to get clear on the ask and communicate it directly. For many women, who have spent decades burying their feelings and hiding their needs (because of socialization!), this can be a very difficult process. But I promise you that the minute you start to see what you truly need and why you need it, you will also get clearer on how to let others step in to help. Once you do, you will see that many people have been waiting for their marching orders because they love and cherish *you*. You just have to call them in.

## FATHERS STRUGGLE IN THIS SYSTEM TOO

Freya had to see some of Jim's points as well. She needed to understand that Jim was having a hard time grasping what she was saying—not because he didn't care but because he didn't share her lived experience.

Freya also had to understand that when Jim said he needed to work because he was worried there'd be consequences at work if he didn't, those fears were real too. Jim was scared he'd fail his role in the family—being the financial provider—if he didn't give work his all. Jim was worried that he might get passed up for a promotion if he didn't seem completely committed to work.

When Freya and I spoke, I shared a research study I'd participated in, which showed that fathers who took an extended leave to care for their children were less likely to be hired for a job than mothers who had the exact same qualifications and took the exact same leave. Fathers who stepped into caregiving were seen as unhireable, despite having degrees from top universities and experience working for renowned companies. Even though they want to be more engaged with their children, fathers intuitively know that many workplaces haven't yet evolved, and they'll be punished for prioritizing family over work.

Freya told me that all these discussions helped her express greater appreciation for everything Jim was doing, because he genuinely was trying.

All of this required Freya and Jim to be brave and step into conversation after conversation about their feelings, in hopes that the other would truly get it.

Maybe your partner is like Jim and feels tremendous pressure to be "on" all the time regarding his work. He, too, can use the gender roles formula. If he expressed the way socialized gender norms are constricting him, he might say, "Because I'm a man, I feel like I'd be a failure as a husband and father if I didn't give a hundred percent at work and keep climbing the corporate ladder." Like Freya, you might not realize your partner is carrying this load. You can offer to help him be more accountable about having firmer boundaries around his work, in addition to praising his value and contributions as a husband and father, regardless of how hard he works, how much money he makes, or what his job title is. Gender roles stifle men's ability to be who they want to be too. They, too, have to see the traps and step around them, and we can all be there to support them as they do.

## CHANGE IS HARD BUT WORTH IT

So what happened? Did Freya and Jim ultimately split?

Thankfully, they didn't.

Instead, they built a deeper understanding of each other and a stronger marriage.

"What did this shift look like?" I asked her.

"For starters, we both had to turn toward each other with greater compassion. For Jim, this meant getting clear on his priority—more time with the family—and breaking some of his habits around putting work first. This meant no working on the weekends and no closing the door to do a few more hours at night."

It wasn't easy for Jim—he'd spent so much time being the model employee that shutting off work was difficult. Freya described an invisible string that would periodically pull Jim back to his work. Now they had a better understanding of why this constant tug was a problem for both of them, so Freya could flag it earlier and with more empathy. Jim was more receptive to her feedback, understanding that it came from a place of connection rather than judgment. They entered into these conversations with less anger driven by animosity from long-buried feelings.

Freya told me, "I used to feel like I was a ticking time bomb, just sucking up one more problem I had to solve: people leaving wet towels on the floor, having to help with homework last minute, or picking up potato chip bags strewn around the house. It wouldn't take much—just one of these things—and then there'd be this moment of explosion where I couldn't do it anymore, and everyone would feel my wrath. I now have to get clearer on what I'm feeling and exactly what I need sooner. It helps me express it more calmly."

She gave me the example of dirty dishes left out after dinner. She used to huff around the house, picking up the dishes and slamming them into the dishwasher because she wanted everyone to know she was exhausted and angry while doing them. Did this help? Not really—it just made people flee her company and leave her to do it all alone. It created more isolation when Freya needed connection.

She spent her days operating on a slow simmer, with any small annoyance increasing her to a boil. This pattern didn't work for anyone. Not Freya, not Jim, and not the children.

Freya now saw that this wasn't a productive way to get her needs met. She had to shift her behavior too. Solving this problem required them all to step in a bit differently. The result was that the dance had completely changed, and Freya liked its new rhythm.

These were the stories I heard from many mothers, who found it difficult to articulate why getting their needs met was so hard.

One mother told me she never felt like she could ask for more from her husband because he earned more. It was a weight she carried without even realizing it and caused her to step into caregiving when she shouldn't. When she told her husband what she'd observed, he agreed money had made their relationship imbalanced. Did they want to continue this way? Both agreed they didn't and tried to take active steps to work toward togetherness, which included their teenage daughters turning to their dad for relationship advice with their school crushes (hello—he understood the teenage boy mind better than anyone else in the family!) and him sitting down to watch the latest teen drama as a way to bond.

For this mother, it wasn't until she figured out why she kept stepping in even when she shouldn't that she could finally stop being perpetually "on" for her family, especially when they didn't ask, they didn't need it, or her response made things worse. That helped everyone make sure the work was more equally shared. This mother told me, "In getting out of the way, I also let my husband step in, and this strengthened the connection between my children and their father too." This was a way to create more connection for all.

As you can see from these examples, clear, honest communication is essential to tackling the complex issue of mental load drain. Sometimes you might need to step outside of your comfort zone too—like the dad talking about boys and watching teen dramas with his daughters.

Even the healthiest, most balanced marriages require work, and when you and your partner start unpacking some of the issues involved with your mental loads, you might realize that you want or need outside support, such as from a therapist. Sometimes an impartial third party can help you feel less defensive and frustrated along the way, act as a sounding board for your concerns and fears, aid you in shifting your perspective to see things from your partner's point of view, and assist in finding mutually agreeable solutions to problems. Marriage is hard, and we need all of the tools to keep it humming.

## A FATHER FORCED TO FLY SOLO

"Was anything else critical to the rebalance in your home?" I asked Freya.

"Yes—I got sick and had to have surgery. I was immobilized and in bed for a few weeks. I couldn't do anything, so Jim had to step in and do it all," she said.

This created an opportunity for Jim to be the primary caregiver and see the scope of work that entailed. It meant he had to do both the physical and the emotional work of caring for the children, without Freya's assistance. Unlike what she'd done in the past, Freya didn't create a detailed calendar of what needed to be completed when. Rather, she let Jim and the kids figure it out on their own, to build their own rhythm without her interference.

As the primary caregiver now, Jim was the one whom the children came to when their playtime ended in tears. It was Jim who was responsible for helping with the homework, including on days when the kids were unfocused. It was Jim who was cooking the meals the children didn't like. It was Jim who had to cut his workdays short to meet the children after school. It was Jim who was feeling the pressure of doing it all in less time. It was Jim who was carrying the full weight of the mental load.

After a few days in the throes of primary parenthood, Jim came to Freya, who was propped up in bed.

"All of this is just so hard," he told her. "I didn't realize that our children could be such monsters, especially right before dinner, or that they were always hangry when they walk in the door after school."

This was the emotional mental load work Freya had been carrying for years—invisible work that needed to be made visible. This was where Freya had wanted Jim to help carry the load and to understand why it was so hard to carry it alone.

For the first time, Jim not only had seen it but also was doing it. This was different for him, and he felt empathy for Freya's experience as a result.

It's often due to a major life event that men are thrust into primary care of their children, in ways that build better understanding of the children's demands and their connection to their mothers. Across my interviews, I heard about fathers who had lost jobs, gotten divorced, or had a wife with a serious illness and thus were forced to be the primary carer. They described new insight into work that mothers had long carried and felt its weight on their shoulders. They also learned the incredible joy of one-on-one time with their children, which built a deeper connection.

In other countries, fathers taking a turn at primary care of children is the norm, and a catastrophic life event isn't required for them to gain this experience. Sweden, for example, requires fathers to take a portion of the family's paid parental leave. They call them "latte papas" because so many fathers are at the park with coffees in hand, pushing strollers and tending to children. Sweden is strategic in investing in fathers' time in childcare to help women reenter employment after having a baby. It also encourages fathers to be more engaged in childcare at the start of life, which brings a host of benefits to the entire family over time.

Children who spend more time with their Swedish dads have better social skills, language development, and overall well-being. They're then also equally likely to go to Mom or Dad when hurt or requiring help. Fathers do more housework after babies are born and as they grow, which reduces marital conflict. There's nothing like seeing firsthand the incredible chaos young children bring to prevent someone from arriving home from work and asking, "What did you do all day, and why is this place such a mess?" Giving dads the opportunity to be the primary caregivers for children is an effective policy decision—one that changes families forever.

But in countries where fathers aren't supported in this care by their governments, men are on their own to learn these lessons. As I said, it usually comes about because of an unfortunate incident. Yet these experiences are equally transformative. When I ask dads who lost their jobs and became the primary caregivers of their children if they'd do it all over again, they all agree: absolutely. They cherished that time and connection with their kids, even if the circumstances that led them there were less than ideal. It was a magical time, and they grew as people. Many wished that all dads could be so lucky as to have their experience. They hoped more men could be the caregivers, even though they knew there were social penalties.

This was the experience Jim had with his children. He got to see them in all their wonderful wonderfulness and awful awfulness, and this brought everyone closer together.

Instead of waiting for some adverse event to force fathers into the primary caregiver role, consider what it might look like for you to create that situation. Would it involve you going away for a couple of days or longer? Quite often, if one parent goes through an entire week of caregiving—dealing with whatever's required for each day of the week—they get a much better sense of what the other parent is wrestling with.

This length of separation isn't realistic or desirable for every couple or family. But even if there's a part of the day that's a pain point—such as the morning or bedtime routine, or meals—consider tasking the other partner with that responsibility so they can gain a better understanding of what you're facing in those times.

Of course, the ultimate goal is to have a society where governments and workplaces offer families the kind of support they receive in places like Sweden. While we can move the needle in our individual homes, enacting those kinds of changes will require collective effort. Until then, we have to create opportunities for all of us to step into the care.

As I got off the call with Freya, I thanked her for being so open, honest, and vulnerable with me in sharing her story. I know that women are carrying so much, yet they often don't want to reveal the hard stuff. It's difficult to dig it up and bring it into the light without fear of judgment. But hearing one another's struggles and triumphs is key to creating a new and realistic expectation of motherhood—it's messy, difficult, joyful, and enriching all at the same time.

I also thanked Freya for sharing the deepest, darkest, and hardest parts of her marriage with me.

Freya thanked me for asking her to participate in the audit. She told me that she'd spent a long time convincing herself that motherhood was supposed to feel hard and isolating—that when she felt miserable, that meant she was doing it right. But after the audit, she began to understand this was a myth that was holding her back, and she felt like she deserved so much more: "I just couldn't keep living like I didn't matter, and the audit made me realize that I deserved a great life. I had to be the one to get clear on what I needed and where I wanted to go. Then I had to ask for it."

And ask she did.

Well done, Freya!

I was deeply proud of Freya, and I'm honored I get to share her story with you.

## *Conclusion*

# What We Owe Our Daughters

WHEN I FOUND OUT I WAS PREGNANT WITH A DAUGHTER, I WAS ECstatic. I understood the world of women and knew I could guide her in a way that would make her empowered, brave, generous, and caring.

Ava, my fifteen-year-old daughter, has exceeded all my expectations. She is smart, funny, and kind. But most important, she is brave. When someone is being treated poorly or something isn't right, Ava intervenes. When a classmate living with autism was being picked on by an older classmate, Ava stepped in. She went, alone, to talk to the school administration about a class bully, even though the vitriol of this student would subsequently turn on her.

I never could have done any of that at her age. I was too determined to be what I thought the world expected of me—good, obedient, and perfect. Then people would like me, and I'd be shielded from life's big challenges.

Boy, was I wrong.

We can't hide from the biggest, scariest things in life—they find us anyway.

It was only when I started stepping outside of the boxes I was shoved into—whether by myself or by others—that I unlocked a life that was so much bigger than I could have ever anticipated. It took activating sociology as my superpower and stepping into my superhero suit.

I think we too often extinguish our power in ways that give us all less. My daughter is a fierce, competent, and wonderful human. This is how she entered the world. I've worked hard to keep these qualities intact and help her bypass social norms that chip away at women's self-confidence, self-competence, and self-expression. I want her to retain all of her wonderfulness and continue to shine on the world.

This is also my wish for you, dear reader, and all your daughters.

I want us to live brave lives and chase our wildest dreams.

But we can do that only if we create worlds that support us all.

I live in one of those worlds. Though I was born in the U.S., I currently live in Australia, a country with a robust public health care system in which all citizens are covered and the costs are affordable even if you aren't covered.

When we'd lived in Australia for a few years, my daughter broke her arm when she slammed her bike into a brick wall on her first playdate at a new friend's house. (Can you even imagine this poor mother's mental load that day?) We didn't yet have citizenship and thus weren't covered by the public health care system.

In the chaos of getting into the ambulance to the hospital, I left my wallet at home. I kept telling everyone, "I don't have my insurance card! I don't have my insurance card!" And they kept looking at me peculiarly. It turned out it didn't matter here like it does in the U.S.—they'd treat my daughter regardless.

I wouldn't receive any surprise bills for an ER visit or from a doctor who happened to be out of network (even if the hospital was in network). In fact, when I finally went to pay for the ambulance and hospital stay, they were completely covered. When my daughter went back to have an X-ray a few weeks later, I paid eighty dollars. That was our grand total for a broken arm, with no public health insurance.

I had a similar experience in Sweden when a kidney stone sent me to an ER in Stockholm. I spent ten hours in an ER bed, was given care and medicine, and left without a fuss. I wasn't denied care. I didn't go bankrupt. I was supported by a health care system that was a public good.

In other countries, health care is a public investment, like paying for sidewalks or roads. We all pay a little so that everyone can be cared for. These systems are more humane, more kind, and less punitive. These are not fantasies but the lived realities of families residing in other parts of the world. Their whole systems aren't dependent on free labor from mothers to keep everyone's worlds spinning.

What if mothers had enough mental load capacity to push back on being everyone's safety net and created workplaces, governments, and policies that could support women—and by extension children and men? What kind of a world would that be? How could we all benefit from mothers' greater energy and investment in creating worlds they're passionate about?

Across my decades of research and conversations with thousands and thousands of women, one thing is crystal clear: Mothers are running in mental load deficit, and it impacts the world we live in.

Mothers vote differently, lead differently, and step into the world differently. When they're in leadership positions, they create policies that support other mothers, their children, and their families. But when a large segment of our population—mothers, who are shown to hold more empathy, compassion, and kindness than most—is bearing the brunt of heavy mental loads, totally burned out, and running on autopilot, it's a loss for us all. It means mothers can't be fully engaged in politics, community, and leadership in the ways men can. It puts women further behind in the race to an equitable society and places hurdles to their catching up.

We live in this world of less because we've created a society where mothers are penalized for forgetting the birthday streamers. Where mothers are judged for a pile of dirty dishes by the sink and a basket of unfolded laundry. Where mothers are run ragged trying to juggle it all. Our world becomes a worse place when mothers are too exhausted to create sustained social change in political areas that are important to all of us: health, safety, and the well-being of ourselves, our children, our families, our workplaces, and our communities.

Our real problems—increasing inequality, rising sea levels, eroding democracies, gun violence, shortened life expectancies for our children, pandemics, war, and famine—are so much bigger than these outdated social constructs. These are big problems that require big solutions, and we need everyone at their maximum capacity to tackle them. To achieve this, we first must balance people's mental loads so we all can move toward having mental load accounts in surplus. This requires us to use the tools in this book to break wasteful mental load spending, and to align our mental loads with bigger problems, broader goals, and bold solutions.

In 2010, I published a study tracking the relationship between a country's gender equality in government and its average division of housework between men and women. Pairing the 2004 United Nations' Gender Empowerment Measure (GEM) with data from nearly twenty thousand participants in the 2004 European Social Survey, I found that women's representation in parliament is positively associated with men's housework hours: The more work men did at home, the more women were in national leadership.

Women's labor market status—including the percentage of women in professional positions and how much women earn relative to men—is negatively associated with women's housework hours and proportions. In other words, the less housework women do, the more successful they are at work. However, combining this with my later mental load research makes it clear: There is also a cost for *refusing* the mental load and active work of domestic labor. And as the Jennifer-and-John mess study shows, we feel it even if we aren't consciously aware of it.

But there's also a huge cost to taking on more of the load. Let's say a woman is agonizing over whether to clean her teen's room or make sure the teen learns how to clean as a life skill. She debates whether it's worse to let the place be a pigsty or worse to coddle a child who should be old enough to clean up after themselves. She frets over what it says about her parenting and the child's preparedness for life that the child would prefer to live in the squalor of stinky gym socks and discarded half-eaten pizza rolls. It's little wonder she has neither the time nor the energy to think about her presentation at work or how she might prepare a campaign to run for office on issues that matter to her and to families. We need women's mental load capacities open so they, too, can step into their wildest dreams.

When I asked my interviewees what they wanted their mental loads to achieve, the responses were simple: They wanted thriving children and happy partnerships. They wanted to do less at work. They wanted more time with children. They wanted to slow down a bit and enjoy life. They wanted to rush less. They wanted deeper connections to community. They wanted more time to walk the dog. They wanted time to lie in the sunshine. They wanted more of the good stuff and less of the constant churn of *shoulds*, *musts*, and *what-ifs*.

Parents also wanted to drop the mental loads of weighing whether their boss would be mad at them for taking a day off to care for their sick child or whether their aging parents would have enough money to get the health care and services they needed. They wanted to drop mental loads about their children being shot at school. They wanted fewer babies starving and dying around the world. They wanted people of color, including their own children, to feel safe out in the world. They wanted neurodiverse children, including their own, to enter the world with ease. They wanted the strains of the world to lessen and to feel like they sat less squarely on their shoulders alone. Mothers want to solve the problems of pandemics, inflation, global warming, and violence together, rather than feeling like they're isolated and solely responsible for keeping everyone safe.

Here, again, is where sociology becomes a superpower: It helps us understand how our laws have become outdated, where our workplaces haven't evolved, and why our families are stuck in an old model that no longer works. It shows the potential of our mental loads to take small steps toward our dreams, which often means making the world a better place for ourselves *and* our families and friends.

I want women to start working toward their dreams of putting their hands up to run for political office or of leading their companies or of guiding their families toward greatness.

How can we start to implement solutions to these major problems?

Step one is to lighten mothers' mental loads so they can be the ones driving the change. One mother argued, "Start over and put women in charge in so many places. Even when I just think about the mental load of health care, I know women wouldn't have created a system like ours, where children are denied cancer treatment and families go bankrupt from emergency room visits."

In countries like Sweden and Norway, where more women are in charge, they do have different policies. Women politicians are more focused on laws that support women and the family. In both the U.S. Congress and U.S. state legislatures, women politicians have been shown to advance legislative agendas by introducing bills that reflect their priorities on women's rights, welfare, and child-related issues. Other countries, including Australia, have political parties that have established gender quotas requiring that women hold a portion of their elected seats. These women also pass bills that support women and children; lead to better health, employment, and educational outcomes for women; and have less corruption in spending.

These aren't hypothetical worlds—they're real worlds that other women are living in. The men in these countries also greatly benefit from policies that support families and children and encourage collective support and community. These aren't communist countries, and they have capitalist economies. They are very much like the U.S., with a few exceptions: They prioritize care; they value women's contributions to education, employment, and politics; and they have concrete policies to make greater gender equity a reality.

I wrote this book with urgency, because women are suffering. They're working through all kinds of stress and trauma, whether because of personal situations, professional pressures, or political and economic turmoil. Burnout is at an all-time high. Many don't want to go back to old ways that didn't—and still don't—work.

This book provides a concrete tool kit to enact now, in order to parse through the pressures of daily life and create a plan to invest in dreams of the future. It shows the value of using sociology as a superpower to dispel old and outdated norms about men and women that hold us all back.

In this final chapter, I ask you, the reader: *What kind of world would you work to create if you were running in constant mental load surplus?*

Could mothers having a mental load surplus result in greater health, well-being, and safety for our families, friends, loved ones, and communities? More kindness and compassion when someone we love inevitably becomes sick? More focus on protecting our natural environment so we can give our children and grandchildren a secure future? More inclusion of a diverse range of people who don't look, live, learn, or love like us? Would mothers' mental load surplus lead to less destruction, conflict, poverty, suffering, and death?

What would it look like if more fathers could step into the lives they want with their families? What would it be like if fathers could take more time away from work and spend more time present with their children? Would this create a model for both girls and boys to replicate to develop their care skills? Would some mothers be able to truly hand over the entirety of work at home to fathers?

What kind of world could we create if we accounted for the costs of all the demands on our mental loads?

This is a world we all need, and it's one I want to live in.

It is a world that we can create together, by lightening our mental loads.

Let's leave our daughters *and* our sons a better world.

*Appendix*

# The Mental Load Audit Worksheets

WELCOME TO THE MENTAL LOAD AUDIT! BELOW ARE ALL OF THE worksheets that were shared throughout the book, provided for you in one location. You can use this workbook to identify whether you're in mental load burnout, track your spending, set your goals, and figure out where you are duplicating and when you can delegate. The objective is to create mental loads that are leaner, more purposeful, and aligned with your goals and values. Good luck, and you've got this!

## THE MENTAL LOAD BURNOUT SCALE

The first step is to figure out whether your mental load account is running in surplus or being overdrawn. If you're overdrawn, then you're in mental load burnout.

Total the number of *yes*es to identify where you currently are on the mental load burnout scale. More *yes*es indicates mental load burnout. More *no*s indicates mental load surplus.

| | YES/NO and why? |
|---|---|
| 1. Do you end many days feeling like you have spent more mental load energy than you started with (i.e., spending more than saving)? | |
| 2. Do you often feel exhausted by your mental load (e.g., quick-tempered, overwhelmed, loss of focus, anxious, difficulty sleeping)? | |
| 3. Do you often find it difficult to enjoy life's moments because of the constant thinking about what needs to be done next? | |
| 4. Do you lack sufficient mental load energy to respond to an *opportunity* in your work, family, or other areas of your life? | |
| 5. Do you lack sufficient mental load energy to respond to an *emergency* in your work, family, or other areas of your life? | |
| 6. Do you find it difficult to find enough mental load energy to plan for the future? | |
| **Total number of YES responses** | |

# THE UNLOAD

Next, calculate your mental load spending. This will help you identify how much of your total mental load energy is going to each category and whether you're duplicating spending with others.

## Calculate Your Mental Load Spending

*Note: Sometimes these will add up to more than 100 percent. This indicates that you are duplicating the work.*

| Mental Load Type | Percentage of this mental load that I am responsible for within the family (0–100%) | If partnered: Percentage of this mental load that my partner is responsible for within the family (0–100%) | Percentage of this mental load that others (e.g., children, grandparent, nanny) are responsible for within the family (0–100%) | Is any of this mental load being duplicated? (yes, no, or maybe) |
|---|---|---|---|---|
| Life organization | | | | |
| Emotional support | | | | |
| Relationship hygiene | | | | |
| Magic making | | | | |
| Dream building | | | | |
| Individual upkeep | | | | |
| Safety | | | | |
| Meta-care | | | | |
| **REFLECTIONS:**<br>How did you feel after doing this assessment? Did you gain any insights? Is there anything else you want to add? | | | | |

Next you'll need to identify the frequency of mental load spending in each category. Some will have daily spending and others may have no spending. This helps you figure out if you are making daily withdrawals or less frequent charges in each category.

## Identify the Frequency of Mental Load Spending

| Mental Load Type | How often does this draw on your mental load energy (e.g., daily, multiple times a week, a few times a month, monthly, yearly, never)? |
|---|---|
| Life organization | |
| Emotional support | |
| Relationship hygiene | |
| Magic making | |
| Dream building | |
| Individual upkeep | |
| Safety | |
| Meta-care | |
| Other | |

Great job! You now can see where your energy is going and how often. The next phase is to figure out whether the spending is costly or not.

Think about this like asking yourself, *Is this like a four-dollar-daily-coffee debit or more like big, giant, saving-for-a-home-down-*

*payment debit?* Or is this something you are doing that actually brings you more mental load energy—a credit into your account? Sometimes activities in each category can do both.

The table below helps you identify whether your mental load spending in each category is a cost, a credit, or both.

## Weigh the Costs and Credits of Mental Load Tasks

| Mental Load Type | Which mental load tasks within this category are *costly*? | Which mental load tasks within this category are *crediting*? | Which mental load tasks within this category are *both* crediting and costly? |
|---|---|---|---|
| Life organization | | | |
| Emotional support | | | |
| Relationship hygiene | | | |
| Magic making | | | |
| Dream building | | | |
| Individual upkeep | | | |
| Safety | | | |
| Meta-care | | | |
| Other | | | |

Okay, now that we have the what, how often, and at what cost, the next phase is to figure out the who of your mental load and what percentage they are getting. Use the following worksheet to identify who is on the receiving end of your glorious mental load energy and how much each person or group is getting.

Don't think too much about this: You can be giving to a lot of people, and your total investment may be well in excess of 100 percent of your total energy. It is okay!

The most important thing in this step is to see, maybe for the first time ever, how thin your mental load energy may be spread. You can add more boxes here to account for all your people. Or, if you prefer, you can put these into list form. There is no right way to do this—the most important thing is that you start tracking.

## Counting Who Is Getting My Mental Load Energy

| **Person/ Thing** | | | | | |
|---|---|---|---|---|---|
| Percentage | | | | | |

Now let's get clear on your goals! If you are going to align your mental load spending, you need to be clear where you are heading. Clear your vision. Tap into your blue-sky thinking. The sky is the limit!

If you were totally unencumbered, where would you want to be in the next one, three, and five years? Put these big, bold, and ambitious goals in the next table. Let your goals be as BIG as you want, because these are tied to your dreams. You can also throw in some small tangible wins, too, across the years. There's no right way to do this phase of the work, and your goals can change over time. This is the time to exercise your dream muscles and point yourself in the right direction.

## Goal-Setting Worksheet

| | Goals |
|---|---|
| Short-term (1 year) | |
| Medium-term (3 years) | |
| Long-term (5 years) | |

Okay, now that you see where you want to go, the next step is to firm up how you move through the world by exploring your values. Have a think about what you value. If you are having a hard time getting started, you can google *core values* to get an overview of what types of values guide people's lives.

If you feel comfortable, you can share your values with other people in your life. But if you don't, you can keep these values tucked away for your eyes only. Again, there is no right or wrong answer here; rather, you need to get clear on what you value to help you move through the world. The table below includes your top three, but you can expand your list to include more values.

## What Are Your Core Values and Why?

| | Values and reasons why they are important |
|---|---|
| Value 1 | |
| Value 2 | |
| Value 3 | |

Now that you are clear on your goals and values, the next step is to figure out which mental loads need to be reduced or cut altogether. Take a minute to think about the top mental load burdens that are moving you further from your goals. They may take a while to identify, but observe where your mental load thinking is working against your goals. Once you identify these, it is time to set some boundaries. Reduce these burdens' impact on your thinking, limit their drain, and, if you can, cut them altogether.

## Top Mental Load Burdens

| These are the top mental load burdens that are moving me further from my goals: |
|---|
| 1. |
| 2. |
| 3. |

Now that we have identified what mental loads are moving you further from your goals, the next step is to identify your core people, your starting lineup. If you have a long list of people you love, that is okay.

Make two lists: One is starting lineup, and the other is the people you will substitute in when life permits. You can have only five in your core—no more. Once you have identified your core, you need to allocate a percentage to each. This is not set in stone but a target for how much of your energy can go to each. Some weeks, life will intervene and your energy will blow out to some categories but not others. Other times, when life goes nuclear, everyone will absorb too much of your energy. This is okay. Just use this as a target to help keep you focused. Of course, these categories can change over time. You can come back to this list as life ebbs and flows.

## Starting Lineup: Your Top Five People Who Deserve Your Energy

| **Person** | | | | | |
|---|---|---|---|---|---|
| Percentage | | | | | |

### Second String: People Who Will Get Your Energy Later

| Person | | | | | |
|---|---|---|---|---|---|
| Percentage | | | | | |

Congratulations! You just completed the Mental Load Unload! You have just identified where your mental load is going, what is crediting and debiting, who is getting too much of your energy, where you are pushing yourself further from your goals, and how to understand where your energy should go for your dreams and core people. Everyone can't be on the field at the same time so you must get clear on who is the first string and who is on the bench (for now).

## THE RELOAD

This is the fun part. Now you are going to get crystal clear on what you want to give your mental load to in ways that are strategic. This is where you will crystallize all the work you did in the previous sections to clarify where you need to allocate your mental load energy: the loves, needs, and musts.

Let's get started!

Use the next table to identify the mental loads you love even if they are debits to your mental load account. These are the mental load loves that you need to maintain regardless of their cost.

## Top Mental Load Loves

| These are the top three components of my mental load that I *love* and find the most exciting, enriching, or replenishing: |
|---|
| 1. |
| 2. |
| 3. |

Next, figure out which mental loads you need to keep in order to get you closer to your goals. These are all the essentials that you need to maintain in order to achieve whatever it is you set out to achieve. Again, regardless of the cost, these are mental loads that you need to continue doing because they are helping you get closer to your goals.

## Top Mental Load Needs

| These are the top three components of my mental load that I *need* to maintain to get closer to my goals: |
|---|
| 1. |
| 2. |
| 3. |

Now on to the mental load mores. These are the mental loads that you need to give more energy to in order to achieve what you have set out to accomplish. Worried that you don't have any additional energy to accelerate? Don't stress—I've got you.

At this point, you should have some mental loads that you have cut, giving you a bit more space. That should free up a bit of bandwidth. Also, these are mental load mores that are tied to goals—one year, three years, or even five years from now. You don't have to execute these tomorrow. You just need to sort out what needs your energy and be ready to step in when the opportunities open up.

## Top Mental Load Mores

| These are the top three components of my mental load that I want to give more energy to, in order to accelerate progress toward my goals: |
|---|
| 1. |
| 2. |
| 3. |

Here is the last part of the Mental Load Audit: getting clear on what can be delegated. Some mental loads are too heavy or important to delegate to others. Those we may need to keep ourselves to make sure they are done right. Others are less important, more easily outsourced, or just so crushing to your spirit that they need to be delegated.

Let's clarify those. Have a think. Explore the world. Ask others in your life what works for them. Start to think about how you can delegate the mental load to someone or something else.

### Mental Loads That Can Be Delegated

| These are the mental loads that could be delegated to others—done by other people or apps, or purchased—to lighten the load: |
|---|
| 1. |
| 2. |
| 3. |

Congratulations! You have completed the Mental Load Audit! You should have a mental load that is clearer, more focused, and more closely aligned with your goals, values, and favorite people. This work is valuable and may need to be done again and again and again as life throws you all that it has in store. As you move through the world, start to think about when you are teetering into burnout or when you need a little tune-up. Even better, as you smash your goals, come back and set new ones.

My dream for you is to soar and, through careful spending of your mental load, to create an incredible, meaningful, and valuable life. I LOVE YOU! AND I WISH YOU ALL THE GREATNESS YOU DESERVE!

# Acknowledgments

A BOOK IS NEVER A SOLO ENDEAVOR. IT IS THE WORK OF MANY PEOple. This book is no exception. This book and its journey capture both the experience of bringing something new to light and the gift of others making this happen. I didn't start out writing a book on the mental load. Rather, I pitched a book on gender myths, which, I would soon learn from my wonderful soon-to-be agents Jenna Land Free and Dara Kaye, had already been written many times before. But one chapter stood out to them—the chapter on the mental load. From there, this book took its shape through countless conversations, questions, and stories about this invisible thing called *the mental load*. I had never written a book like this before, and yet these two women never gave up on me. They saw my potential and invested in me. They revised paragraphs that were too clunky and academic. They shared stories and asked questions that became the backbone of this book. They stepped in when they didn't have to. And, without them, this book would never have been given life. So, I thank them with the deepest gratitude for all their hard work.

It was after this book got sold that I was introduced to another group of incredible women who helped shape it into its current form. With the help of Marisa Vigilante, I got the first words on the page. It was Lucia Watson's keen editorial eye that saw the shape of this book and its potential to do so much more. And it was Amanda Bauch who helped me with the final push (in record time, of course!) and introduced me to the best smoked brisket in Nashville. Finally, I was lucky enough to get Hilary Roberts, a longtime, dollhouse-giving friend, to edit this book to perfection.

I couldn't have written this book without the capable support of a team, especially Sophie Squires and Kate Dangar. I thank the interview participants, survey takers, and my wonderful academic friends who have contributed to this research across decades. I also couldn't have sustained book writing without the daily calls to my dear, wonderful friend Brendan Churchill, who is always so convinced that I can do anything, including finally writing those six ISSP papers. To my hilarious friend Rita, who taught me that a cutlery drawer could actually be cleaned. To my friends Greg and Narel, who kept the house full of laughs during this crazy book-writing process. To my bestie Tiff, who has held half my heart since the day she barged into my house with a Ziploc full of home-baked cookies. To the incredible Kelsy, who is brave, courageous, and honest and always ready for a five-hour talk, even if it requires a nap after. To the silly and smart Alex and Anthony, who are exceeding in their generosity, kindness, sense of humor, and (for Ants) thick skin. To my mother and father, who showed me how to charm presidents and truly believe that I will someday end up on *Oprah*. And to my loves—Casey and Ava—who are constant sources of support, hilarity, and generosity. It is a gift to know you and to be loved by you.

Without all of this support, love, and friendship, I couldn't have stepped into the world so bravely. I love and appreciate you all. Now, let's celebrate!!!

# Works Cited


Bauer, Lauren, Sarah Estep, and Winnie Yee. 2021. "Time Waited for No Mom in 2020." Brookings Institution. https://www.brookings.edu/articles/time-waited-for-no-mom-in-2020/.

Churchill, Brendan, Sabino Kornrich, and Leah Ruppanner. 2023. "Children of the Revolution: The Continued Unevenness of the Gender Revolution in Housework, Childcare and Work Time Across Birth Cohorts." *Social Science Research* 111. https://doi.org/10.1016/j.ssresearch.2023.102868.

Collins, Caitlyn, Leah Ruppanner, Liana Christin Landivar, and William J. Scarborough. 2021. "The Gendered Consequences of a Weak Infrastructure of Care: School Reopening Plans and Parents' Employment During the COVID-19 Pandemic." *Gender and Society* 35 (2): 180–93. https://doi.org/10.1177/08912432211001300.

Collins, Caitlyn, Liana Christin Landivar, Leah Ruppanner, and William J. Scarborough. 2020. "COVID-19 and the Gender Gap in Work Hours." *Gender, Work & Organization* 28 (S1): 101–12. https://doi.org/10.1111/gwao.12506.

Collins, Caitlyn. 2019. *Making Motherhood Work: How Women Manage Careers and Caregiving.* Princeton University Press.

Coontz, Stephanie. 2016. *The Way We Never Were: American Families and the Nostalgia Trap.* Hachette UK.

Dean, Liz, Brendan Churchill, and Leah Ruppanner. 2022. "The Mental Load: Building a Deeper Theoretical Understanding of How Cognitive and Emotional Labor Overload Women and Mothers." *Community, Work & Family* 25 (1): 13–29. https://www.tandfonline.com/doi/full/10.1080/13668803.2021.2002813.

Gawlik, Kate, and Bernadette Mazurek Melnyk. 2022. *Pandemic Parenting: Examining the Epidemic of Working Parental Burnout and Strategies to Help.* The Ohio State University. https://wellness.osu.edu/sites/default/files/documents/2022/05/OCWO_ParentalBurnout_3674200_Report_FINAL.pdf.

Geist, Claudia, and Leah Ruppanner. 2018. "Mission Impossible? New Housework Theories for Changing Families." *Journal of Family Theory & Review* 10 (1): 242–62. https://onlinelibrary.wiley.com/doi/abs/10.1111/jftr.12245.

Hayes, Jeffrey, C. Nicole Mason, Heidi Hartmann, and Erin Weber. 2020. *Wide Spread Decline in Household Income During COVID-19 Pandemic Contributes to Food Insufficiency Among Families.* Institute for Women's Policy Research. https://iwpr.org/wp-content/uploads/2020/08/COVID-Food-Insecurity-Policy-Brief-FINAL.pdf.

Lamott, Anne. 2006. *Plan B: Further Thoughts on Faith*. Penguin.

Landivar, Liana Christin, Leah Ruppanner, Lloyd Rouse, William J. Scarborough, and Caitlyn Collins. 2022. "Research Note: School Reopenings During the COVID-19 Pandemic and Implications for Gender and Racial Equity." *Demography* 59 (1): 1–12. https://read.dukeupress.edu/demography/article/59/1/1/286878/Research-Note-School-Reopenings-During-the-COVID.

Landivar, Liana Christin, William J. Scarborough, Caitlyn Collins, and Leah Ruppanner. 2022. "Do High Childcare Costs and Low Access to Head Start and Childcare Subsidies Limit Mothers' Employment? A State-Level Analysis." *Social Science Research* 102. https://www.sciencedirect.com/science/article/abs/pii/S0049089X21001046.

Landivar, Liana Christin, Leah Ruppanner, William J. Scarborough, and Caitlyn Collins. 2020. "Early Signs Indicate COVID-19 Is Exacerbating Gender Inequality in the Labor Force." *Socius* 6. https://doi.org/10.1177/2378023120947997.

Peck, Emily. 2021. "Exclusive: Pandemic Could Cost Typical American Woman Nearly $600,000 in Lifetime Income." *Newsweek*. https://www.newsweek.com/2021/06/11/exclusive-pandemic-could-cost-typical-american-woman-nearly-600000-lifetime-income-1594655.html.

Rodsky, Eve. 2019. *Fair Play: Share the Mental Load, Rebalance Your Relationship and Transform Your Life*. Hachette UK.

Ruppanner, Leah. 2010. "Cross-National Reports of Housework: An Investigation of the Gender Egalitarianism Measure." *Social Science Research* 39 (6): 963–75. https://www.sciencedirect.com/science/article/abs/pii/S0049089X10000736?via%3Dihub.

Ruppanner, Leah. 2019. "Women Aren't Better Multitaskers Than Men—They're Just Doing More Work." *The Conversation*. https://theconversation.com/women-arent-better-multitaskers-than-men-theyre-just-doing-more-work-121620.

Ruppanner, Leah. 2020. *Motherlands: How States Push Mothers Out of Employment*. Temple University Press.

Ruppanner, Leah, Maria Brandén, and Jani Turunen. 2018. "Does Unequal Housework Lead to Divorce? Evidence from Sweden." *Sociology* 52 (1): 75–94. https://doi.org/10.1177/0038038516674664.

Ruppanner, Leah, Caitlyn Collins, Liana Christin Landivar, and William J. Scarborough. 2022. "How Do Gender Norms and Childcare Costs Affect Maternal Employment Across U.S. States?" *Gender and Society* 35 (6): 910–39. https://journals.sagepub.com/doi/abs/10.1177/08912432211046988.

Ruppanner, Leah, Ben Maltby, Belinda Hewitt, and David Maume. 2021. "Parents' Sleep Across Weekdays and Weekends: The Influence of Work, Housework, and Childcare Time." *Journal of Family Issues*. https://espace.library.uq.edu.au/view/UQ:cffc7c9.

Ruppanner, Leah, and Matt L. Huffman. 2014. "Blurred Boundaries: Gender and Work-Family Interference in Cross-National Context." *Work and Occupations* 41 (2): 210–36. https://journals.sagepub.com/doi/full/10.1177/0730888413500679.

Ruppanner, Leah, Xiao Tan, William J. Scarborough, Liana Christin Landivar, and Caitlyn Collins. 2021. "Shifting Inequalities? Parents' Sleep, Anxiety and Calm during the COVID-19 Pandemic in Australia and the United States." *Men and Masculinities* 24 (1): 181–88. https://journals.sagepub.com/doi/full/10.1177/1097184X21990737.

Scarborough, William J., Caitlyn Collins, Leah Ruppanner, and Liana Christin Landivar. 2020. "Head Start and Families' Recoveries from Economic Recession: Policy Recommendations for COVID-19." *Family Relations* 70 (1): 26–42. https://doi.org/10.1111/fare.12519.

Scarborough, William J., Caitlyn Collins, Liana Christin Landivar, Leah Ruppanner, and Matt L. Huffman. 2023. "COVID-19 and the Role of Gender, Earnings, and Telecommuting in Parents' Employment." *Journal of Marriage and Family* 85 (5): 1007–27. https://onlinelibrary.wiley.com/doi/abs/10.1111/jomf.12926.

Thébaud, Sarah, Sabino Kornrich, and Leah Ruppanner. 2019. "Good Housekeeping, Great Expectations: Gender and Housework Norms." *Sociological Methods and Research* 50 (3): 1186–214. https://journals.sagepub.com/doi/10.1177/0049124119852395.

Weeks, Ana Catalano, and Leah Ruppanner. 2024. "A Typology of US Parents' Mental Loads: Core and Episodic Cognitive Labor." *Journal of Marriage and Family* 87 (3): 966–89. https://onlinelibrary.wiley.com/doi/10.1111/jomf.13057.

# Index

activation of sociology, 99, 254
AI, 195–97
ambitions, sociology as superpower and, 137

birth rates, 14
burnout, 63, 73, 119, 238
  all-time high levels of, 20, 259
  guilt and, 88
  mental load burnout, 14, 103, 178
  mental load burnout scale, 30–35, 261–70
  mothers living with, 32
  parental, 18
  social norms setting up women for, 157
  urgency of dealing with, 259
  women set up for, 157

care factor, identification of, 98–99
cash pilot, 207–35
  Mental Load Audit and, 237
childcare
  access to, 184
  challenges of, 15
  fathers' sharing of, 76
  hypothetical questions about, 10, 204
  limited options for, 182
  partners' conflict over, 10
  research findings on, 18, 163
  in Sweden, 197–98, 218, 249
  in U.S., expense of, 184
children. *See also* daughters, what we owe to
  in audited family, 108
  Aurora's story, 219–24
  with complex needs, 208
  day care and, 198
  dream building for, 46
  emotional support as work done for, 38
  fathers as primary caregivers of, 76–77, 248–51
  Freya's story, 225–31, 238
  life organization and, 36
  mental loads of, 12
  neurodiverse, 54, 258
  parents's relationship building with, 170

children (*cont.*)
  shared custody of, 115
  women holding mental loads for, 16
Christie and Eric, audit of mental loads of. *See* mental load, identifying what is draining
Churchill, Brendan, 28, 123, 163
cognitive work, 27, 29
Collins, Caitlyn, 17, 87
core values, 267, 268
  identifying of, 148, 268
  violation of, 146, 157
COVID-19 pandemic, 17–22, 58–59
  drop of mothers' employment during, 18
  external pressures, 20
  need for policy changes, 20
  research findings, 18
  slowdown caused by, 58–59, 208
  unlearning of myths during, 19

daughters, what we owe to, 253–60
  burnout, urgency of dealing with, 259
  dropping mental loads, 257–58
  and fathers, ideal world for, 260
  gender equity, 259
  health care, as public investment, 255
  implementing solutions, 259–60
  mental load surplus, 259–60
  real problems affecting, 256
  safety nets, mothers as, 255
  *shoulds*, *musts*, and *what-ifs*, 257
  sociology as superpower, 254, 258, 259
  study findings, 256
  women's labor market status, 256–57
Dean, Liz, 28, 123
decision-making, mental load and, 61, 64
delegating, mental load and, 61, 62, 65, 112, 189–206
dieting and mental load, 49–50
divorce, 10, 91
  marriages less likely to end in, 80
  marriages more likely to end in, 6
  rate, 6
  risk of, 15
  shared custody and, 115
domestic labor
  cost for refusing mental load of, 257
  gender gap, 6
  standards for dads, 12
dream boards, 134–35, 140
dream building, 16, 35, 46–47, 214
  for children, 46
  mental load spending (calculation of) and, 111, 113, 221, 263
  mental load spending (frequency of) and, 116, 264
  mental load tasks (costs and credits of) and, 118, 265

economy of care, building of, 201–6
email overwhelm, 192–94
emotional support, 16, 37–40, 169, 178
  description of, 38
  fathers not investing in, 40
  friends seeking, 214
  mental load spending (calculation of) and, 111, 113, 221, 263
  mental load spending (frequency of) and, 116, 264
  mental load tasks (costs and credits of) and, 118, 265
  problems and, 72
  as work done for others, 38
  at work, 39
emotional-thinking work
  capacity for, 21
  mental load as, 11–12, 27–30
  women's additional, 20
energy. *See* mental load energy
experiments
  cash pilot, 207–35
  insight provided by, 231–35
  virtual assistant, 190–92

*Fair Play* (Rodsky), 190
family meals, 45, 199–201, 226, 229, 248
fathers
  breadth of wives' invisible work seen by, 23

categories of mental load not contributed by, 105
divorced (as primary carer), 249
dreams maintained by, 136
frustrations of, 89
guilt not felt by, 136
ideal world for, 260
impacts of leave on, 244
inequality of mental load tasks between mothers and, 79
investment of mental load energy by, 56
lack of emotional support from, 40
mental loads of, 12–13
millennial, 12
new American (typical), 184
pressure on, 240
as primary caregivers, 76–77, 248–51
struggles of, 244–45
Swedish, 249
tasks engaged in by, 77
value of parenting by, 76–77, 249
finances, mental load experiment and, 207–35. *See also* money

Gender Empowerment Measure (United Nations), 256
gender equality in government, 256, 259
gender inequality in household chores study, 5–10
gender myths, 17, 161, 251
mental load energies and, 81
outdated social norms and, 67
gender norms, 88
money and, 234
gender quotas (political parties), 259
gender roles
formula for discussion within context of, 243
men stifled by, 245
socialized (trap of), 241–44
generative AI, 195–97
goals and values, clarification of, 133–49
blank space, creation of, 134–41
core values, 146, 148
dreams, 134–35, 140
forward thinking, 145
goal-setting worksheet, 143
identifying values, 145–49
setting goals, 141–45
*shoulds*, *what-ifs*, and *musts*, 135, 139, 144
sociology as superpower for, 137, 140
steps for setting, 133
wasteful thinking, 98, 140
Goldee, 195, 196
guilt
burnout and, 88
drivers of, 89, 90
extended family and, 160
friends', 147
mothers', 19
conversations with daughters and, 38
expectations and, 220
full-time career and, 13, 91
individual upkeep and, 48
money spent and, 207, 210, 222–23, 232
rejection of, 87, 96
saying no without, 178
social traps and, 158
triggering of, 93
gun violence, 50–52

harmful thoughts. *See shoulds*, *musts*, and *what-ifs*, silencing of
health care, as public investment, 255
household managers, women as (myth of), 74–77
housework, quantifying of, 5–6

identifying problems, mental load and, 61, 64
individual upkeep, 16, 35, 47–50
description of, 47
dieting example, 49–50
mental load spending (calculation of) and, 111, 113, 263
mental load spending (frequency of) and, 116, 264

individual upkeep (*cont.*)
mental load tasks (costs and credits of) and, 118, 265
recommended purpose of, 50
as trickiest mental load type, 48
Institute for Women's Policy Research, 18
invisible work. *See also* mental load
fathers seeing breadth of wives', 23
life organization as, 36
mothers', 75
need for visibility of, 21, 249

Kornrich, Sabino, 5, 163

labor. *See also* invisible work
conversations around, 14
domestic
cost for refusing mental load of, 257
gender gap, 6
standards for dads, 12
housework
dealing with nearly all of, 162
quantifying of, 5–6
invisible, 10
of magic making, 43
market, women's status in, 256
mental load, 38
mothers burdened with bulk of, 67
mothers' informal trade of, 202
myths, 17
outsourcing of, 194
unpaid, 3, 255
Lamott, Anne, 50
Landivar, Liana, 17
LGBTIQ+ parents, 241–42
life organization, 16, 35, 153, 170, 214
children and, 36
description of, 36–37
meal planning and, 199
mental load spending (calculation of) and, 111, 113, 263
mental load spending (frequency of) and, 116, 264
mental load tasks (costs and credits of) and, 118, 265
"mom-ager" trap, 37
tasks of, 79
"treadmill tasks," 36

magic making, 16, 22, 35, 43–46
description of, 44
mental load spending (calculation of) and, 111, 113, 221, 263
mental load spending (frequency of) and, 116, 264
mental load tasks (costs and credits of) and, 118, 265
pressure felt to re-create childhood magic, 45
prioritized types of, 158
relationship hygiene and, 44–45
required effort of, 45
shunning the labor of, 43
tasks requiring, 153
marriage
at-risk, 231, 239
equal, 83
imbalanced work in, 37
Mental Load Audit's effect on, 237, 243
mental loads enriching, 173
parenthood and, 225
relationship hygiene and, 41
saved, 237, 245
meal-planning solutions, 199–201
mental load, 57–81
burnout, 14, 30–35, 103, 178
complexity of, 191
and COVID-19 pandemic, 17–22
decision-making and, 61, 64
definition of, 14
dispelling of myths of, 80–81
as emotional-thinking work, 11, 27–30
executing, 61, 65
experiment, finances and, 207–35
of fathers, 12–13
identifying problems, 61, 64
learning to see, 56
mental load process, 60–66
monitoring, 61, 62
overload of, 231

potential of, 258
scanning work, 72
schools exacerbating, 193–94
seven stages of, 61–65
shared custody as break from, 115
sleep and, 73
social media descriptions of, 28
sociology as superpower, 11, 60, 75
strategizing, 61, 62, 64
surplus, 178, 259–60, 261
task switching, 69
and unpredictability of life, 63
wasted, 154
well-laid plans, problem with, 59
well-spent, 13
mental load, delegation of, 61, 62, 65, 189–206
childcare, 197–99
economy of care, building of, 201–6
email overwhelm, 192–94
meal-planning solutions, 199–201
nonexistent solutions, 206
problem-solving for other mothers, 205
school correspondence, 192–94
task invisibility, 189
technology, problem-solving with, 195–97
virtual assistant experiment, 190–92
"women's work," 205
worksheet, 200
mental load, identifying what is draining, 107–32
Christie and Eric case study, 108–10
deep thinking, 115
Mental Load Audit results, 119–22
mental load spending
calculation of, 111–14
frequency of, 114–16
mental load tasks, costs and credits of, 116–18
naming of people who drain mental load account, 126–32, 159, 266
shift in thinking, 130
"swear jar," 122–26
mental load, myths contributing to mental overload, 66–80
"equality of relationship," 77–80
"women as better household managers," 74–77
"women as better multitaskers," 68–74
Mental Load Audit, 40, 43, 47, 106, 261–73
birth of, 22–24
cash pilot experiment and, 207–35
completed, 162, 273
concepts relating to, 108
difficulty of, 104–5
emotional work of doing, 186
first steps of, 177
goals and values, 133
issues in marriage raised while going through, 243
overdrawn mental load account shown by, 227
purpose of process of, 106
results of, 110, 119–22
single mother's story, 213–14
as solution, 104
transformational effect of, 105
worksheets, 111, 261–73
core values, 267, 268
goal-setting worksheet, 267
mental load burdens, 268
mental load burnout scale, 261–70
mental load energy, who is getting my, 266–67
mental load loves, 271
mental load mores, 272
mental load needs, 271
mental load spending, calculation of, 111–14, 263
mental load spending, frequency of, 114–16, 264–65
mental loads that can be delegated, 273
mental load tasks, costs and credits of, 265–66
reload, 270–73
second string, 270
starting lineup, 156–61, 269

mental load energy
agreed investment of, 180
boosting of, 125
burnout and, 32
dream building and, 46
emotional support work and, 39
fathers' investment of, 56
as finite, 22, 104
holding boundaries around, 43
insufficient, 31, 34
life organization work and, 36
myths creating serious drain on, 84
operation of, 29
school and, 192–94, 216
strategic investment in, 170
surveillance mode and, 154
tasks draining, 120
value of, 20, 21, 104
wasted, 49, 55, 145
who is getting my, 127, 131, 266–67
worry work and, 92
mental load with purpose, creation of, 169–87
"mental load loves," 169, 170–73
"mental load mores," 169, 177–87
"mental load needs," 169, 174–77
parenthood, transition to, 183–84
relationship building, 170
sociology as superpower, 178, 185
mental load spending
alignment of, 151–65, 266
outdated social norms, ditching of, 161–65
sociology as superpower, 157, 158
starting lineup, 156–61
surveillance mode, 154
top mental load burdens, 152
wasted mental loads, 154
calculation of, 111–14, 263
frequency of, 114–16, 264–65
mothers taking charge of, 23
prioritizing of, 105
tracking of, 110–11
wasteful, 30, 156, 178, 256
mental load work, eight types of, 16, 35–55
dream building, 16, 35, 46–47, 214
mental load spending (calculation of) and, 111, 113, 221, 263
mental load spending (frequency of) and, 116, 264
mental load tasks (costs and credits of) and, 118, 265
emotional support, 16, 37–40, 169, 178
description of, 38
fathers not investing in, 40
friends seeking, 214
mental load spending (calculation of) and, 111, 113, 221, 263
mental load spending (frequency of) and, 116, 264
mental load tasks (costs and credits of) and, 118, 265
problems and, 72
at work, 39
individual upkeep, 16, 35, 47–50
description of, 47
mental load spending (calculation of) and, 111, 113, 263
mental load spending (frequency of) and, 116, 264
mental load tasks (costs and credits of) and, 118, 265
recommended purpose of, 50
as trickiest mental load type, 48
life organization, 16, 35, 153, 170, 214
description of, 36–37
meal planning and, 199
mental load spending (calculation of) and, 111, 113, 263
mental load spending (frequency of) and, 116, 264
mental load tasks (costs and credits of) and, 118, 265
"mom-ager" trap, 37
tasks of, 79
"treadmill tasks," 36
magic making, 16, 22, 35, 43–46
description of, 44
mental load spending (calculation of) and, 111, 113, 221, 263

mental load spending (frequency of) and, 116, 264
mental load tasks (costs and credits of) and, 118, 265
pressure felt to re-create childhood magic, 45
prioritized types of, 158
relationship hygiene and, 44–45
required effort of, 45
shunning the labor of, 43
tasks requiring, 153
meta-care, 16, 35, 52–55
depleting effect of, 55
description of, 53
mental load spending (calculation of) and, 111, 114, 263
mental load spending (frequency of) and, 116, 264
mental load tasks (costs and credits of) and, 118, 265
parenting choices as, 54
relationship hygiene, 16, 35, 40–43
boundaries, 43
description of, 41
draining work of, 42
magic making and, 44–45
mental load spending (calculation of) and, 111, 113, 263
mental load spending (frequency of) and, 116, 264
mental load tasks (costs and credits of) and, 118, 265
post-rift work of, 153
pruning work, 42
safety, 16, 35, 50–52
gun violence and, 50–52
heavier loads for certain groups of parents, 52
mental load spending (calculation of) and, 111, 113, 263
mental load spending (frequency of) and, 116, 264
mental load tasks (costs and credits of) and, 118, 265
mental overload, myths contributing to, 66–80
"equality of relationship," 77–80
"women as better household managers," 74–77
"women as better multitaskers," 68–74
meta-care, 16, 35, 52–55
depleting effect of, 55
description of, 53
mental load spending (calculation of) and, 111, 114, 263
mental load spending (frequency of) and, 116, 264
mental load tasks (costs and credits of) and, 118, 265
parenting choices, 54
Milo, 195, 196
"mom-ager" trap, 37
money, 207–35
Aurora's story, 219–24
emotional attachment to, 212
Freya's story, 225–31
gender norms and, 234
investing in self, 222
Katrina's story, 208–13
mental load audit, 220, 227
mothers' guilt about, 207–8
overdrawn mental load account, 227
Sasha's story, 213–19
self as obstacle, 228
sociology as superpower, 211, 229
social safety nets, 218–19
takeaways, 231–35
monitoring, mental load and, 61, 62
mothers
desperation of, 103
difficulty in articulating needs of, 247
difficulty of delegation for, 189
drop of employment levels during COVID-19 pandemic, 18
as everyone's safety nets, 255
family's mental load done by, 105
frustration of, 89
guilt felt by, 19
conversations with daughters, 38
expectations and, 220
full-time career and, 13, 91
individual upkeep and, 48

mothers (*cont.*)
money spent and, 207, 210, 222–23, 232
ideal world for, 259–60
inequality of mental load tasks between fathers and, 79
invisible work of, 75
levels of burnout of, 32
mental loads of, 13
as one role of many, 97
other mothers, problem-solving for, 204
perfection of, 87
pressure felt to re-create childhood magic, 45
religious, 215
single
income needed by, 91
mental load of, 213
stories of, 208–13, 213–19
traded labor of, 202
working, 13, 17, 90
zero-sum game seen by, 137
myths
of children's success, 92
as contributors to mental overload, 66–80
"equality in relationship," 77–80
"women as better household managers," 74–77
"women as better multitaskers," 68–74
dispelling of, 80–81
draining of mental load energy created by, 84
gender
mental load energies and, 81
outdated social norms and, 67
labor, 17
of "mom-ager," 126
post-audit understanding of, 251
unlearning of, 19
of visible mess, 94
work-life balance, 180–81

neurodiverse children, 54, 258

*Oprah*, 47–48
outdated social norms
ditching of, 161–65
energy drained by, 22
myths and, 67, 92
problems with, 76, 181

parenthood
conversations about, 241–42
meta-care and, 53
primary, example of husband in throes of, 248
transition to, 183–84, 225
ups and downs of, 74
value of fathers in, 76
parents
burnout of, 18
dropping mental loads, 257–58
heavier safety mental loads carried by certain groups, 52
LGBTIQ+, 241–42
transgender, 242
personal finances, 71, 107–8, 207–35
*Plan B: Further Thoughts on Faith* (Lamott), 50
pruning work, 42

relationship hygiene, 16, 35, 40–43
boundaries, 43
description of, 41
draining work of, 42
magic making and, 44–45
mental load spending (calculation of) and, 111, 113, 263
mental load spending (frequency of) and, 116, 264
mental load tasks (costs and credits of) and, 118, 265
post-rift work of, 153
pruning work, 42
remembering, mental load and, 61, 62
Rodsky, Eve, 190
role models, 11

safety (mental load work of), 16, 35, 50–52
gun violence and, 50–52
heavier loads for certain groups of parents, 52
mental load spending (calculation of) and, 111, 113, 263
mental load spending (frequency of) and, 116, 264
mental load tasks (costs and credits of) and, 118, 265
safety nets
mothers as everyone's, 255
need for, 219
overloading of, 72
pushing back on being, 255
social (Sweden), 218–19
Scarborough, William, 17
school correspondence, 192–94
self-indulgent thinking work, 155
self-sacrifice, 211
*shoulds*, *musts*, and *what-ifs*, silencing of, 83–99, 104
care factor, identification of, 98–99
gender norms, 88
guilt, 88
higher standards, holding ourselves to, 90–91
perfection, 87
social norms, 84
sociology, 85
transformation, 85
unicorn couples, 83
wasted energy, 89
worry work, 92–97
sleep, 15, 18, 31, 78
social norms
burnout and, 157
bypassing of, 254
opportunity to dismantle, 205
outdated
ditching of, 161–65
energy drained by, 22
myths of, 67, 92
problems with, 76, 181
power of, 87
*shoulds* put on us through, 88, 89, 104
traps for women created by, 84
use of sociology to view, 157
sociology
description of, 85
as tool for studying behavior, 7
sociology as superpower, 10, 23
activation of sociology, 99, 254
ambitions and, 137
banishing of expectations, 81
clearing out of wasteful thinking, 98, 140
emotional thinking, 12
establishing boundaries, 178
family meals and, 229
fixing systems that set us up to fail, 185
gender myths and, 67
identification of outdated lies, 75
importance of, 140
leveraging of superpower, 108, 137
mental load, 11
mental load loves and, 170
mental load overload and, 231
mental load work (categories of), 16
money and, 211, 229
mother's role as one of many, 97
outdated laws shown by, 258
role models, 11
socialization of women from birth, 60
social norms and, 157–58, 161–65
unlocking of, 10–17
birth rates, 14
emotional thinking, 11, 12
expectations, 15
mental loads, 11, 13
value of using, 259
women's self-sacrifice and, 211
spouse, how to talk to, 237–51
change (hard but worthwhile), 245–48
empathy, 246
father as primary caregiver, 248–51
fathers' struggles, 244–45
gender roles, 243, 245
LGBTIQ+ parents, 241–42

spouse, how to talk to (*cont.*)
mothers, needs of, 247
real problem, identifying of, 239
socialized gender roles, trap of, 241–44
standards
external pressures, 9
women's self-imposed, 7
strategizing, mental load and, 61, 62, 64
superpower, sociology as. *See* sociology as superpower
surveillance mode, 63, 154
"swear jar," 122–26
Sweden, childcare in, 197–98, 218, 249

technology, problem-solving with, 195–97
Thébaud, Sarah, 5
thinking
big-picture (meta-care), 53
catastrophic, 30
emotional, 11, 12
illogical, 230
lies invading, 75
mental load energy and, 46
myths infesting, 17
old patterns of, 229
strategic, 19
wasteful, 98, 140
thinking work
auditing of mental loads and, 171
deep, 56
emotional
acknowledgment of, 38
capacity for, 21
mental load as, 11–12, 27–30
women's additional, 20
family life and, 97
self-indulgent, 155
Thompson, Avni Patel, 195
"treadmill tasks," 36
Tuck, Verity, 195
Tuohy, Wendy, 43

unicorn couples, 78, 83
United Nations Gender Empowerment Measure (GEM), 256

values, core, 267, 268
identifying of, 148, 268
violation of, 146, 157
values, goals and, 133–49
blank space, creation of, 134–41
dreams, 134–35, 140
forward thinking, 145
goal-setting worksheet, 143
identifying values, 145–49
setting goals, 141–45
shift in thinking, 138
*shoulds*, *what-ifs*, and *musts*, 135, 139, 144
sociology as superpower, 137, 140
steps for setting, 133
wasteful thinking, 140
virtual assistant experiment, 190–92

wasteful thinking, 98, 140
Weeks, Ana, 78, 109, 115
Winfrey, Oprah, 47–48
work-life balance, 180–81, 185
worry work, 92–97, 99

zero-sum game, 137